Slides from *North East Passing*, photographed at Goddard College, Plainfield, Vermont, November 1968

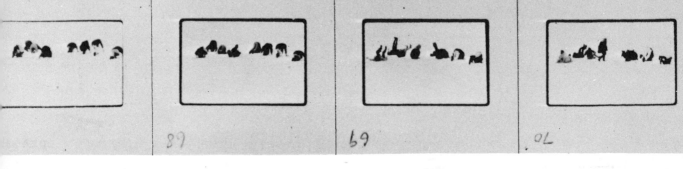

Work 1961-73

The Nova Scotia Series —
Source Materials of the Contemporary Arts
Editor: Kasper Koenig

Bernhard Leitner
The Architecture of Ludwig Wittgenstein
A Documentation

Claes Oldenburg
Raw Notes
Documents and scripts of the performances:
Stars, Moveyhouse, Massage, The Typewriter
with annotations by the author

Simone Forti
Handbook in Motion
An account of an ongoing personal discourse
and its manifestations in dance

Steve Reich
Writings about Music

Yvonne Rainer

Work 1961-73

The Press of the Nova Scotia College of Art and Design, Halifax
New York University Press, New York

Dedication: for Jani

Published by the Press of the Nova Scotia College of Art and Design,
6152 Coburg Road, Halifax, N.S., Canada
Co-published by New York University Press
21 West 4th Street, New York, N.Y. 10012

Distributed in Canada by
artscanada (The Society for Art Publications)
3 Church Street, Toronto M5E 1M2, Ontario
Distributed in U.S.A. by
New York University Press

Contents

Introduction

When I first started dancing in performances, someone said "But she walks as though she's in the street." If it could only be said "She writes about her work as though she's performing it," I would be happy indeed. That such a thing were possible. It goes without saying that a dance is a dance and a book about dance is a book. Though they may meet at the intersection of Art and Good Intentions, I find myself greedy. I have a longstanding infatuation with language, a not-easily assailed conviction that it, above all else, offers a key to clarity. Not that it can replace experience, but rather holds a mirror to our experience, gives us distance when we need it.

So here I am, in a sense, trying to 'replace' my performances with a book, greedily pushing language to clarify what already was clear in other terms. But, alas, gone. This has seemed one good reason to compile a book 'out of' the remains of my performances, letting the language fall where it may. Let it be said simply "She usually makes performances and has also made a book." There can be no comparison, therefore no need for apology.

In the course of putting it all together, Kasper Koenig and I were cast in the role of amateur archeologists. Not only did we have to deal with shards (the actual objects with which my work abounds), papyrii (program notes, published texts, and literary material used in the work), and hieroglyphics (the notebooks, which, in their fastidious verbal renderings of movement, so seductively create the *illusion* of documentation), but with those mysterious and inscrutable petroglyphs left by the visual historian of our age, the photographer. To make some kind of sense out of all this seemed at times impossible.

From the beginning Kasper kept before us a standard for a *modus operendi*: We would try to avoid making a collage-like collection of memorabilia, or 'scrapbook', by making connections wherever possible between photos, quoted texts, notebook excerpts, and texts written specifically for this book to present a comprehensive 'overview'. This has been done through placement and cross-references. In most cases photos that could not be so connected have been eliminated, even if they were 'good' photos. Similarly, 'not-so-good' photos have been included if they contained more information or illustrated a point in the text. (With all due apologies to my 'petroglyphers'!) As we worked on the layout, I realized that the limitation of the photos lay not only in the eye of the photographer. My own selection of prints in some cases took place as long as ten years ago from contact sheets that are no longer available to me. If I had the opportunity today, I suspect that I would make many different choices.

Printed programs and announcements — usually of first performances — have been reproduced in facsimile where they contain a large amount of essential information not covered in the overview — such as dates, performers' names, sequence of events, and program notes — thus serving as a table of contents to the individual works themselves. Where there is a discrepancy between printed program and photo — e.g., in place or date of performance — then additional information is contained in the photo caption. Numerals in 8-point type-face in the right margin refer to photos corresponding to the text. Reviews have been included which either shed some light on a controversy or 'problem' generated by a particular work (e.g., *Rose Fractions*), or reveal a point of view considered important but not conveyed elsewhere. The same with correspondence. It is hoped that most redundancies have been weeded out.

It was also deemed important to distinguish the different kinds of texts from each other by the use of different type-faces and spacing. The overviews, quoted texts, and scripts all appear in 11-point medium type-face. The notebooks — transcribed but not edited — are typewritten. Where it was necessary to add information within a notebook entry, such information appears in typewritten italics. The spacing of previously published texts, and of texts used as speech during performance, is more compressed vertically, and indented from the left-hand margin. The few exceptions to these general rules are noted where they occur.

It should be kept in mind that the literary element of my performance-work — as it is presented in this book — may give a somewhat distorted impression of what that work was about. Being so much more synonymous with the format of a book than the physical elements of the work, these texts are more true to the spirit of their original presentation than anything else in the book and, consequently, more lively. But, as I said before, let the language fall where it may.

The polemical conclusions of the previously published essays on *Parts of Some Sextets* and *Trio A* have been neither changed nor commented on directly. I would like to allow the tone of my more recent writing — in both script and overview — to demonstrate howsoever my uneven development from intransigent artist-as-an-outraged-young-woman. This struggle-to-change sometimes took the form of an ironic dialogue between diametrically opposed positions within a single piece (e.g., the conflict over music in *Performance Demonstration*). I would hope that for the most part, however, my process has become progressively less burdened with dogma and counter-dogma determined by others' positions, and more of an inner dialogue between my own work and needs. Enuf said.

A note of gratitude: I have been exceedingly fortunate in attracting high-quality performers. Trained and untrained alike have brought the best of their skills and intelligence to the realization of my work. Without benefit of their gifts and good humor, my way would have been considerably harder.

Y.R.
Halifax
August, 1973

An imperfect reminiscence of my studies and the beginning of a career and contingent events

Born 1934 in San Francisco. Mama sent me to tap and acrobatic schools from the age of 5. At age 8 I was mercifully allowed to stop. Then took piano lessons with piano teacher who lived downstairs. After six months of tantrums upstairs and down during which time (she used to claim) half Mama's hair fell out, I stopped that also.

I have one brother, Ivan, four years older than I. He was studying the violin around the same time, which also contributed to my mother's hair problem. He used to stomp on the violin everytime he made a mistake. At age 11 I took up lessons on the Hawaiian steel guitar (an outcome of the blandishments of a door-to-door salesman). Two years later discontinued lessons when I realized that I was never going to play stuff like *Ave Maria* very convincingly on the damn thing. Attended Laguna Honda grade school. Because I had a bad lisp, I took special speech classes; remember sitting with six other kids saying "oo-ee.ah-aw" interminably. The lisp stayed. Played very hard in the streets after school. Roller-skating, kick-the-can, hide-and-seek, capture-the-flag, heat, one-foot-off-the-gutter, jump-rope, handball. The games would sometimes range dangerously over a five-block area. When it got dark Mama would bellow out the window for us to come in. When I entered Lowell High School I very reluctantly hung up my roller skates, really resented having to grow up. Continued to lisp. Played softball with the Girls Athletic League. Took Latin for three years because Ivan had. Three hours homework every night translating 30 lines of the Aeneid. Miss Whitaker, the Latin teacher, was very disappointed that I didn't continue for a fourth year. Joined the Writers' Club. Wrote a long prudish short story about a boy who read too many comic books and ended up a juvenile delinquent. The teacher urged me to write about subjects more in keeping with my own experience. I was very pre-occupied with being 'good' in a special sort of way: getting straight A's, not taking any social risks. I had no contact with boys until I was out of high school. My two best friends were Martha Krauss — 4 foot 8, 85 pounds, with a mouth full of clamps and rubber bands and screws from which she spent a great deal of time picking her lunch every day — and Betty Helmsdoerfer — 6 feet, 180 pounds, already experienced with men, getting picked up by sailors in Market Street bars. When I last saw Martha — maybe around 1952 — she was trying to gain 20 pounds so that she could join the WACS so she could leave home. I sometimes wonder how Betty fared.

In my last year at Lowell, when I was 16, I met some people who belonged to Hashomer Hatziir, a Zionist socialist youth group. Being half Jewish (though in name only, as my funny Mama had just about forgotten everything she ever knew; she couldn't even make chicken soup.), I was accepted into their milieu. These were the first 'bohemian' odd-balls I had met, intelligent, politically radical (relative to the time), and — most important — accepting of me. Though I went to their meetings and folk-danced with them, I resisted becoming totally 'assimilated' — for instance, I refused to trade my own surname for a Hebrew one, as they had all done. The high point of this association was a two-week trip to the San Bernadino mountains during a Christmas vacation. Here the parent organization was sponsoring a seminar, with daily Stalinist indoctrination sessions and arts and crafts classes. I modeled a head out of clay, then forgot to pack it when I left. The greatest thing was hitchiking around L.A. afterwards with my friends. We went to museums and Oliveros Street and Pershing Square, where we listened to soapbox orators and were rounded up by the police and told to leave because of the 'perverts'. My father would later say that this trip was the cause of all the trouble he and I began to have. Actually, I had already begun to put up a resistance to his inability to let go of his "little Cookie".

Got out of high school (refused to go to the graduation; told them I didn't like 'ceremonies'; had also refused to go to my grade school graduation) and enrolled in S.F. City College. (That summer had lost my virginity thru the ministrations of a forty-year-old friend of my brother's who was later to make the pious pronouncement "Better me than someone else!") Did very well at City College; studied all the time. One year later was accpeted at U. of Calif. and moved into a so-called two-room apartment in Berkeley just large enuf to turn around in. First time away from home; it was heaven. After one week of classes at Cal. I panicked. I couldn't understand a word of the textbooks and the place was too big. Dropped out, moved back to S.F. (to an apartment on Clay St., my parents paying the rent). Spent my time reading, going to my shrink, and looking for work. Found several temporary jobs: running a machine that stuffed coupons into envelopes, drying prints in a photo lab. Then ran into a thirty-year-old, alcoholic, pill-popping drifter from Chicago and ran off with him in a Model-A Ford. We headed south in March of 1952; I still remember the furrowed landscape around Fresno at dawn. The car had only one window intact; we began to get into snow as we climbed Route 66 toward Flagstaff, Arizona. There the car completely froze in a blizzard. Wired home for money and took the Greyhound to Chicago. Supported my drifter for the next six months working as an order filler for Hibbard, Spencer, and Bartlett, one of the biggest wholesalers of hardware and sporting goods in the country. It occupied five blocks. The order fillers had a quota to fill per hour, and to work faster we wore roller skates. After taxes I brought home $45 a week. $15 went for our housekeeping room on the near north side, $15 went for food, and

$15 went for my drifter's booze. He ended up in a VA mental hospital (after a close brush with the law which involved me and pornographic photos) and I flew back to S.F. newly confident in my hard-won independence. For the next couple of years I worked as typist and figure clerk.

Sometime in 1955 a friend of mine, Sally Grieg, invited me to accompany her while she inquired about the possibility of designing costumes for a little theater group that occupied the old Theater Arts Colony on Washington St. (where I had seen my first live show with my father and brother when I was 12 — Maxwell Anderson's *Winterset* — and where Sally's husband, Mel, had produced something called *The Poet's Follies* the year before, in which a local stripper read from her favorite poet, Edna St. Vincent Millay). They didn't need a costume designer, but the guy behind the desk (It's funny, but I don't remember a single name connected with that outfit, not even the name of the outfit!) asked me if I had ever acted. Then he gave me this come-on about his drama school and I decided to join up. What the hell. The place was run by two guys on-the-run from New York who did a lot of talking about 'epic' theater. And — luckily for me — there was this speech teacher. Remember, I was still lisping; my tongue shot halfway out of my mouth with every sibilant. One night he said to me, he said "What other kind of 's' can you make? I showed him. He said "What's wrong with that? I said "It sounds funny to me." And he said "There's nothing wrong with it; you just have to get in the habit of doing it." So for the next two weeks I slowed my speech by half — no matter whom I talked to: boss, parents, friends, pets — and spoke with no other 's' but that new 's'. And by the end of two weeks I had it licked (sic!). Twenty-one years old and my first triumph! I was intoxicated with success. The other good thing that happened there was that they let me be on the stage. They were doing *All the King's Men* and I remember I had two parts: a member of an incited mob and — better still — the mother of the judge. In the latter role the lights came up on me sitting on a raised platform in a filmy peignoir screeeaming at the top of my lungs "You killed him, you killed him, you killed him!" I loved it. There was no doubt about it; I had become stage-struck.

Then I met a painter named Al Held, who was also on-the-run from New York, but wanted to go back. When he did, I went with him. This was August 1956. Enrolled at the Herbert Berghof School of Acting. My teacher was Lee Grant. I remember doing some scenes from Ibsen (maybe *A Doll's House*) and Sartre. I don't remember that anyone thought I was very good, although they may have remarked on my remarkable 'concentration'. When later I attended Paul Mann's Actor's Workshop I was criticized for being too 'cerebral'. They didn't believe me, they said. I couldn't generate the proper illusion. The spectacle of someone *trying* to create an illusion was not, of course, interesting to anyone, not even me. I was frustrated and confused.

Meanwhile the honeyed heavy success-and-ambition-and-fantasy-laden atmosphere of the NY art and theater worlds was everything I might have envisioned had I dared to do so in San Francisco. The 10th St. gallery scene was approaching its zenith, lots of loft bashes, and I saw lots of plays — on and off Broadway — O'Neil, Saroyan, Schiller, Shakespeare (Beckett and Ionesco were to come a little later, although I had already read *Waiting for Godot*). I took on a series of part-time jobs, usually typing, later it would be modeling for artists and art schools. We had a smallish loft on 21st St. off Fifth Ave. Then in the spring of 1957 I took a step that — all unbeknownst to me — was to be a turning point in my life. I took my first dance class. Actually I'm lying. While I was with the theater group in S.F. I had taken a modern dance class which had been so strenuous that I thought I would split my crotch if I went back, so I never did. But here in NY an aspiring composer friend, Doris Casella, persuaded me to give it a try. She was going for the exercise, but actors need the discipline, etc. It was a class given by Edith Stephen when she had a studio on 6th Ave. above 8th St. Afterwards I asked for an evaluation. She said I was very strong, but not very 'turned out'. I started to go regularly twice a week. Edith's studio happened to be where Merce Cunningham's company was rehearsing for awhile, and sometimes I would watch him through the curtains gliding around in there. Edith's classes were great; what they lacked in discipline they made up for in eclecticism. I am sure she was the only person in town using improvisation as a teaching technique at that time. In my ignorance and total lack of sophistication I was using what I learned just as fast as I learned it. After two months Edith invited me into her 'company'. (I never got used to dance groups being called 'companies' like the A&P or something.) I think I did several shows with her in Kosher summer camps.

Then there followed a succession of events of which the exact sequence eludes my memory: I saw Erick Hawkins' *Here and Now with Watchers* and decided to become a dancer; I dropped the acting classes; I became restless with Edith and started studying elsewhere (Afro-Cuban with Emile Faustin and Sevilla Fort and private lessons with Allen Wayne, paid for by my mother, my father having died in 1957); I started going to a psychiatrist again; I split up with Al Held and moved into a small apartment on E. 25th St.; I became friendly with Nancy Meehan, the first 'professional' dancer I had known; I got myself knocked up from a 'one-night stand'; I decided I was 'fucking around' in more ways that one, that I was getting too old to be a dancer, that I had better buckle down; I wrote to my mother and asked her for $5,000 so I could study full-time without having to work, not telling her that it was also for an abortion. Five days later she sent me a check for $2,500; the rest came a month later, and in the following two years she must have sent me $10,000 in monthly instalments. I could breathe easy for awhile and go about my business. I had a little slack and knew I had to make the most of it, for I was living on her savings. (Later I would support myself through teaching and foundation grants.) In 1959 I started studying in earnest. Three classes a day — two at the Graham school, one ballet.

Perhaps it was early spring of the following year when, through Nancy, I met Simone Forti. Simone's descriptions of the work of Ann Halprin, with whom she had worked on the west coast, led me back to San Francisco for Ann's summer session of 1960. Three weeks of extraordinarily lively activity. I met Trisha Brown, Lamonte Young, A.A. Leath, and John Graham. And the formidable, dynamo-like energy of Ann herself. On returning to NY I continued with ballet and Cunningham and got involved with Robert Dunn's workshop. There were very few of us at the beginning: Steve Paxton, Marni Mahaffney, Paul Berenson, Simone, and me. Bob spent a lot of time showing us and explaining the chance scores used by John Cage for his *Fontana Mix* and other pieces and analyzing the time structure of Satie's *Trois Gymnopedies*. The idea was that we might be interested in combining them in some way. In the studio on Great Jones Street I shared with Simone and Bob Morris I worked on the movement phrases I would use in *Three Satie Spoons*, my particular resolution of Dunn's 'problem'. Also rehearsed with Simone and Bob Morris on her *See Saw*, which she was about to show at the Reuben Gallery. Around this time I saw Simone do an improvisation in our studio that affected me deeply. She scattered bits and pieces of rags and wood around the floor, landscape-like. Then she simply sat in one place for a-while, occasionally changed her position or moved to another place. I don't know what her intent was, but for me what she did brought the god-like image of the 'dancer' down to human scale more effectively than anything I had seen. It was a beautiful alternative to the heroic posture which I felt continued to dominate my dance training. (At the Graham School they had told me that I should become more 'regal' and less athletic!)

By this time I was committed to the idea of being a choreographer, not just because of desire, but because I suspected that I would never be 'good enough' to dance in an official company. Although I was becoming more proficient in conventional technical matters, the chunky construction of my body and my lack of a natural litheness did not fit the popular image of the female dancer. Then I saw the work of James Waring and Aileen Passloff. Actually, I saw a kind of demonstration by Jimmy's group at one of those Friday night melanges at Cooper Union and was not too impressed — the balleticism bothered me. It was a solo of Aileen's — performed at the Living Theater — that really knocked me out. It was called *Tea at the Palaz of Hoon*. She wore a red dress with a bustle; sat in a throne-like chair; outlined her own features, breasts and nipples with a pencil; kind of 'bumped' around the chair; and did other things that I don't remember. It was very female, funny, robust, and stylish. She also stuck the pencil in her mouth and chattered her teeth. I knew she worked with a group and figured that if I wanted to work with her I had better hang around where she hung around, which was Jimmy Waring's classes. So I started to study with Jimmy — it must have been spring of 1961 — and a short time later, much to my surprise, *he* asked me to start rehearsing in his *Dromenon*, which was scheduled to appear on a festival in Montreal that summer. Jimmy had an amazing gift which — because I was put off by the mixture of camp and balleticism in his work — I didn't appreciate until much later. His company was always full of misfits — they were too short or too fat or too uncoordinated or too mannered or too inexperienced by any other standards. He had this gift of choosing people who 'couldn't do too much' in conventional technical terms but who — under his subtle directorial manipulations — revealed spectacular stage personalities. He could pull the silk purse out of the sow's ear. At its worst, dancing with Jimmy could feel like a sow imitating a swan, but I got a lot out of it. He used what I had and demanded more than I thought I had, and his instincts were usually right. In some ways he fathomed my potential more accurately than *I* could at the time. Although I have often disagreed with him on matters of taste and style, I can't dispute that he is something of a genius.

And from the beginning he was supportive of my own work. He invited me to do two solos on a program he was organizing for the Living Theater in July of '61. I remember the phone conversation; his gesture was totally unexpected; I don't think he had even seen anything I had done; he may have heard about the *Satie Spoons* from Bob Dunn. (I had performed the piece in the Cunningham studio, where Bob's class met each week.) And when Jimmy suggested that I might have another piece — in addition to the *Spoons* — for his program, my day was complete. My total oeuvre, two solos, would be 'premiered' within a few weeks! I was exhilarated beyond belief, and scared shitless. I have described that performing experience so many times that I can't be bothered re-creating it again here; so I'll just quote from a recent interview in *Avalanche*:*

(Question: "What does performing mean to you now?") "It means less and less to me; I don't need performance to survive, and at one point I did. My first intense feeling of being alive was in performance....As the date drew close, I really had the distinct sensation of butterflies in my stomach. I stood waiting for the curtain to go up — no, it didn't go up, it parted, and I had the sense of uh....it was like an epiphany of beauty and power that I have rarely experienced since. I mean, I knew I *had* them — the audience. Partly it was adrenalin, I'm sure, but also a cathartic kind of love, an intense feeling of being in the moment. It was the first time I had experienced myself as a whole person. There was no part of my consciousness that was anywhere else....in 1961 [performing] was the most urgent thing I could do".

The Performer as a Persona: an Interview with Yvonne Rainer, Liza Bear and Willoughby Sharp ed., Avalanche Magazine, New York, Summer, 1972.

For the record, the other works on that same evening were by James Waring, Fred Herko, Aileen Passloff, and John Herbert McDowell. In the early part of 1961 more people showed up at Bob Dunn's workshop: Ruth Emerson, Ruth Allphon, maybe Judy Dunn came occasionally. Ruth Allphon, Simone, and I collaborated on a piece; its title – *Stove Pack Opus* – was the result of a quick free-association by each one of us. Simone contributed stove, Ruth pack, and I opus. In a recent nostalgic conversation with Simone she reminded me that the title had proved to be prophetic: Simone became a housewife (temporarily), Ruth packed up and moved away, and I went on to make an opus (*Terrain*). Before her 'retirement' Simone did complete her own 'opus'. It was *An Evening of Dance Constructions* at Yoko Ono's loft on Chambers Street (May 1961) and proved to be way ahead of its time. I sometimes wonder if more feedback would have prevented her retirement. As things then stood, it was as though a vacuum sealed that event. Nothing was written about it and dancers went on dancing and painters and ex-painters went on making painterly happenings and theater pieces. It would be another two and a half years before the idea of a 'construction' to generate movement or situation would take hold.

In the fall of 1961 I started sharing a new studio with Jimmy and Aileen, and Bob Dunn's workshop started up again with a lot more people. There was so much going on that year that it is hard to sort it all out. I won't even try. There was a huge amount of work done, much investigation into chance procedures – I remember Elaine Summer's numbered styrofoam blocks, Steve Paxton's diagrammed ball which he spun and stopped with his index finger, Trisha Brown's dice, Steve's preoccupation with eating. The emphasis on aleatory composition reached ridiculous proportions sometimes. The element of chance didn't ensure that a work was good or interesting, yet I felt that the tenor of the discussions often supported this notion. I don't think this was at all an issue for Bob, who was happy to see so much activity loosed by whatever means. He seemed as interested in how something was presented as by what method it was made. And, of course, the Cagean idea that chance offered an alternative to the masterpiece was operating very strongly. In retrospect this must have secretly galled me, as I continue (secretly) to aspire to making 'masterpieces'. I completed *Satie for Two*, the last time I would use a formal chance score (again an adaptation of *Fontana Mix*). In March of '62 I shared a program with the late Fred Herko at the Maidman Playhouse. (I am reminded of other dancers' deaths: Ruth Sabotka, with whom I had danced in *Dromenon*, and Ruth Ravon, who had improvised with Simone and me in our Great Jones St. studio and was killed in an auto accident in Europe.) By the late spring the workshop knew it had more than enough work for a concert. I had been to the Judson Poet's Theater when it was presenting things upstairs in the loft of the church. (I remember seeing *The Great American Desert* by Joel Oppenheimer.) So I suggested that we look into the possibility of a concert in the sanctuary. Steve made the contact with Al Carmines, one of the ministers, and set up a date for an 'audition'. We actually did a mini-concert for him: I did *Satie Spoons*, and Ruth Emerson and Steve each did something, I can't remember what. Steve may have done his *Transit*. (Steve, did you do *Transit*? A distinct pall is settling over my role of historian.) Al was delighted, and we agreed on July 6th as the date for our *Concert of Dance*. (From here on, one should consult *Ballet Review* Vol.1 No.6, for a more complete perspective of what came to be known as the Judson Dance Theater. Without consulting it myself, I shall continue my meanderings.)

That first concert of dance turned out to be a three-hour marathon for a capacity audience of about 300 sitting from beginning to end in the un-airconditioned 90° heat. The selection of the program had been hammered out at numerous gab sessions, with Bob Dunn as the cool-headed prow of a sometimes over-heated ship. He was responsible for the organization of the program. It began with a sequence from *The Bank Dick* as the audience was coming in. Judy Dunn stage-managed and also performed in my *Dance for 3 People and 6 Arms* with me and Bill Davis. I remember David Gordon's macabre *Mannequin Dance* (either from the Cunningham studio or a rehearsal at the church); I remember Fred Herko on roller skates; I remember John Herbert McDowell with a red sock and mirror; I remember Deborah Hay hobbling around with something around her knees; I remember doing my own *Ordinary Dance*; I remember being in Steve's *Proxy* with Jennifer Tipton. We were all wildly ecstatic afterwards, and with good reason. Aside from the enthusiasm of the audience, the church seemed a positive alternative to the once-a-year hire-a-hall mode of operating that had plagued the struggling modern dancer before. Here we could present things more frequently, more informally, and more cheaply, and — most important of all — more cooperatively. If I thought that much of what went on in the workshop was a bunch of nonsense, I also had a dread of isolation, which made me place great value on being part of a group. But I am anticipating. Bob decided not to continue the workshop that fall. I missed the weekly sessions. Although it had been quite a while since I had relied on Bob for direction, I missed the contact and the discussions. One day before a dance class at Cunningham's I suggested to Steve that we start another workshop. He said "I'll make a sign to put on the bulletin board. Where can we have it?" I offered my studio. Later the Monday night sessions were transferred to the gym of Judson Church. Out of them came the Judson Dance Theater and more Concerts of Dance. As I look back, what stands out for me — along with the inevitable undercurrents of petty jealousies and competitiveness — is the spirit of that time: a dare-devil willingness to 'try anything', the arrogance of our certainty that we were breaking new ground, the exhilaration produced by the response of the incredibly partisan audiences, the feverish anticipation of each new review in the Village Voice by Jill Johnston and the resultant discord (from the beginning

8

she was mentioning 'this one' more, or more favorably, than 'that one'). Whatever she wrote, her columns were the greatest single source of PR since Clement Greenberg plugged Jackson Pollock.

By early 1964 various changes had taken place. Some of us began to drop out of the workshop following some 'splinter' concerts: A friend of Deborah and Alex Hay brought some of us to New Paltz Teacher's College; Steve produced a series called Surplus Dance Theater at Stage 73; 'some of us' were invited — as the Judson Dance Theater — to the Once Festival in Ann Arbor. All of this was a natural outgrowth of particular aesthetic and social alignments that were both complicated and schism-making. And there was another factor: Robert Rauschenberg, whose involvement as a designer with Cunningham made him no stranger to our concerns (he had also designed the lights for my *Terrain* in 1963), began presenting work on our programs. The plot thickens. From the beginning 'non-dancers' had been active in the group as both performers and 'choreographers': the composers Philip Corner, John Herbert McDowell, Malcolm Goldstein, and the artists Carolee Schneemann, Alex Hay, and Robert Morris. (With regard to my private life, Bob Morris and I started to live together early in '64. The plot thickens again.) But there had always been a sense that we were all in it together, that whatever the inequities, they came out of our common cause, a shared present-time. Upon Rauschenberg's entry — through no error in his behaviour but simply due to his stature in the art world — the balance was tipped, and those of us who appeared with him became the tail of his comet. Or so I felt. It was not something that I ever heard openly discussed, although I was aware of his sensitivity to the *possibility* that this might be occurring. The situation manifested itself in the change in the audiences (the power-oriented critics and dealers and glamour-oriented art-stars and collectors came *en masse*), his diligent 'stroking' — both publicly and privately — of each of us, and my not-quite-playful chiding of him for being a 'Sunday dancer'. The truth of the matter was that we were simply not in his league as far as previous accomplishment went, and there was nothing anyone could do to make audiences look at our work the same way they looked at his (and vice versa). If Bob raised his thumb it was something very special because *he* was doing it; if I raised my thumb, it was dancing. The situation was every bit as trying to him as it was to us. His association with us (or, perhaps more accurately, mine with him) was not an unmixed blessing. We got a lot of mileage out of it, both notoriety-wise and gig-wise. And the glitter-aspects of being part of his entourage were totally seductive. Beyond all that, I owe a lot to the inspiration of his daring and humor. The year I came to NY, immersed as I was in the abstract-expressionist ethos, Rauschenberg's *Monogram* opened a window on the future of my own funny-bone. I all but rolled on the floor in a convulsion of laughter when I saw it. I didn't know who he was, but I knew I was witnessing a presence at once elemental and authentic.

Bob Morris was another 'problem', in this case much closer to home. Our professional association went back to 1961 when we performed together in Simone's *See Saw*. Later he appeared on Judson programs in separate collaborations with Bob Huot and Judy Dunn and in his own solo *Arizona*. One of his most arresting pieces was *Site* for Carolee Schneemann (lying still and nude throughout a la Manet's *Olympia*) and himself (in a life-mask of his own face and manipulating 4 x 8 sheets of plywood). He had also performed in my duet, *Part of a Sextet*. In September of 1964 we shared an evening at the Moderna Museet in Stockholm in a series that featured Cunningham, Cage, Rauschenberg, Fahlstrom, Paxton, and Deborah and Alex Hay. Here Bob did *Check*, a large group work in which I performed. On the verge of making a big group piece myself (*Parts of Some Sextets*), I was very taken with *Check* (later referring to its influence in the Tulane Drama Review). So far so good. The crunch came after Life magazine covered a concert Lucinda Childs, Bob, and I had done in Buffalo in March, 1965. It had been arranged by Jill Johnston for a big arts festival there. Cindy did her beautiful *Carnation*, I did a slightly abbreviated version of my 1963 magnum opus *Terrain*, and Bob premiered his *Waterman Switch*, a powerful enigmatic tribute to Da Vinci and androgyny in which Cindy wore a man's suit and hat and Bob and I wore baby oil. Well, the Life spread showed a large full-color picture of Cindy's solo, a black-and-white photo of Bob and me locked in a tight oily embrace, and not even a mention of my MAGNUM OPUS! I still feel the sting. (To make matters worse the performing experience itself had been unpleasant; the audience — fresh from a cocktail party — was the rudest, drunkest, most loutish I had ever appeared before.) Egged on by my shrink, I lowered the boom. Either Bob had to get out of my field or I had to get out of his life. With surprising good grace he eased himself out of 'my field'. We did one more tour together — to Scandinavia in the fall of '65 — and after that Bob no longer performed or made theater work. Now that so much time has elapsed since we were together, it is easy for me to say "In a way it was too bad." His stuff was really good and affected a lot of people.

Having come more or less midstream in this chronicle and feeling a bit bushed, I would like to wind down. I notice one serious ommission: Although Merce Cunningham's name appears again and again, I say very little about him or my relationship to him. For two reasons: 1. My studies with him ran in a continuous thread from 1960 to 1967; and 2. I have already paid my respects to Merce in a piece written for a book on him put together by James Klosty. That piece appears at the end of this book as an *Epilogue.*

I hope that this imperfect recollection will shed more light on *Work 1961-73.*

JUDSON DANCE THEATRE
presents

AN EVENING OF DANCE
Judson Memorial Church
April 28, 29 - 1963

TERRAIN

Choreographed by Yvonne Rainer
performed by Trisha Brown, William Davis, Judith Dunn, Steve Paxton,
Yvonne Rainer, Albert Reid
Lighting by Robert Rauschenberg

1. Diagonal

2. Duet   Music by Philip Corner
               danced by Trisha Brown and Yvonne Rainer

3. Solo Section   Essays by Spencer Holst

               Spencer Holst #1   "On The Truth"
               Spencer Holst #2   "On Evil"
               Walking Solo
               Death Solo
               Sleep Solo

    The order of the solos changes from performance to performance.

                        INTERMISSION

4. Play   Ball Supplier - Alex Hay

               slow   fast
               game   stop
               pick-up   rest
               ball   bounce
               stance   love - (William Davis and
                                       Yvonne Rainer)

5. Bach

    Special thanks to Philip Corner, Al Hansen, Alex Hay, Robert
Rauschenberg, Lucinda Childs, Arlene Rothlein, and Linda Sidon
for their assistance and to the Reverends and staff of Judson
Church for their interest and continued support.

II Terrain

1

A one-and-a-half-hour work in five sections for six people first performed at Judson Memorial Church in New York City, April 28 and 29, 1963; later revived in an abridged version (Section 2, *Duet*, was omitted) at the Buffalo Arts Festival, March 3, 1965. The costumes for the whole evening were basically black leotards and tights with the addition of white tee-shirts or blouses worn or removed at predetermined times. During *Diagonal*, Bill, Albert, and Yvonne wore white tops; in the *Solo* section, everyone wore black; in *Play*, Judy, Bill, and Trisha wore white; in *Bach*, Bill and Steve wore white. For *Duet*, Trisha and Yvonne wore black tights and Hollywood Vassarette lace push-up brassieres.

At the very beginning of the evening the group entered upstage-right, walked briskly in a clump to the downstage-left corner where they paused for five counts, walked all the way upstage*, continuing along the upper periphery toward stage-right, then veered slightly diagonally left all the way downstage where they again paused for five counts, this time slightly to the right of the original pausing place. They then resumed walking (still in a clump) toward the downstage-right corner,   1 stopping three-quarters of the way across for another five counts, continued toward the upstage-right corner, stopping halfway for three counts, went directly into the "out-of-bounds" area at stage-right, then re-grouped in the upstage-right corner to begin *Diagonal* proper. (*See diagram page 28*).

*The pillars at Judson Church delineated at that time a natural performing area, beyond which on either side was a 4- or 5-foot space that could be used as an "out-of-bounds" type of space comparable to that on the periphery of a basket-ball court. This first up-stage walk took place in this area.

1. Diagonal

Diagonal, the first section, consisted of 10 traveling movements to be done by one to six performers (each movement designated by its own number), and 4 traveling movements to be executed by only one or two performers — each designated by a letter, A, B, C, or D. The directions of travel were limited to two upstage-to-downstage intersecting diagonals drawn corner to corner. (There were no actual indications of this pattern on the floor.)

2 *Diagonal no. 8* – Steve Paxton, William Davis, Judith Dunn

3 *Diagonal A* – Y.R., Trisha Brown

Basically this section proceeded through the calling of a single number or letter. Whoever was in the group in which the signal was called was obliged to execute the given movement with the group. Once the group had traversed the diagonal they simply walked to the upstage corner on that side of the space. While waiting for a signal you could "mill" quietly or stand still. If two signals were called simultaneously, you followed whichever one you heard more clearly. There were several ways to leave the group or split it up. One was to call a letter and simultaneously grasp the hand of a performer standing near-by, indicating that that person should accompany the "caller". If the letter "D" was called, one had four options — all of them variations on leaping. One could also not call a number or

14

4 *Diagonal No. 5* — Steve, Trisha, Y.R., Bill

letter, but simply execute any one of the designated movements alone and so leave the group. However, there was a "penalty" for such a choice: One then was obliged to stand in the out-of-bounds area until "picked-up" by another performer. One could also switch diagonals at the intersection, in which case you could also change your movement. If you were alone you would then have to go to the sidelines, but if luck were with you several others may have made the same choice, thus forming a splinter group. Sometimes two groups would start simultaneously from two different corners, nearly collide in the center, somehow work through each other, and find that they were comprised of new members who had switched groups midway.

The *Diagonal* game was intercut with another one called *Passing and Jostling.* This consisted of four activities: walking in a random floor pattern, passing at a right angle in front of another person (either walking or standing), jostling another person gently with either shoulder, and standing still. The rules were simple: You had to alternate passing and jostling; you could stand still at any time, but were not free to resume walking until someone jostled you. You could leave the *Diagonal* game at any time to start passing and jostling: however, if you chose to stand still on a diagonal and were jostled by a group you were obligated to rejoin the *Diagonal* play. This was one way of re-entering *Diagonal*; another was simply to walk to a group — either in a corner or in motion — and perform the signaled movement with that group. If I recall correctly, anyone jostled while doing *Diagonal* had to start passing and jostling. The whole section lasted about twelve minutes.

15

2. Duet

Trisha and Yvonne were the first to leave *Diagonal* so they could change costumes for the following section. *Diagonal* continued until they re-entered, at which point everyone else exited.

Duet lasted about twelve minutes. Its music was a taped collage by Philip Corner consisting of parts of Massenet's *Thais* mixed with fragments of Cecil Taylor, African music, Clementi, and ending with Massenet's *Meditation* from *Thais*, which had been filtered so that it had a thin, other-worldly quality. The dance itself was two simultaneous solos — Trisha on stage-left, Yvonne stage-right. Trisha performed movements related to romantic ballet postures, focusing on the head, shoulders, and arms, alternating or combining with movement from burlesque that focused on the pelvis and lower back. At the same time Yvonne performed an adagio learned in an intermediate ballet class conducted by Nina Stroganova at Ballet Arts in New York City. (*page 30*).

5 *Duet* as performed at Judson Hall, N.Y.C., Feb.15, 1963 — Y.R., Trisha

What happened next was a series of poses performed in the same sequence by both of us. Trisha may have started before me. By the time we were doing them, the haunting, enervated strains of the *Meditation* had probably begun, lending a goofy overtone to our cheesecake postures. (*page 30*) *Duet* ended with "palsy", followed by "wrestling". I can't remember what "palsy" was. "Wrestling" consisted of crawling under and over each other on all fours. I believe the lights faded on this image.

16

6 *Duet* – Trisha

7 *Walking Solo* – Steve

8 *Death* and *Sleep* – Albert Reid, Trisha

3. Solo Section

This section consisted of five solos, two of them accompanied by essays written by the poet Spencer Holst and spoken by the dancer as she or he executed the learned sequence of phrases. Although the essays were different, the two sequences of movement were identical. Each dancer learned two solos and performed each of the two once. This resulted in a certain amount of duplication: Trisha and Steve did *Spencer Holst No. 1* ("On the Truth"); Bill and Yvonne did *Spencer Holst No. 2* ("On Evil"); Bill, Steve, and Judy did the *Walking Solo*; Albert and Judy performed the *Death Solo*; Albert, Trisha, and Yvonne did *Sleep*. The *Spencer Holst* and *Death* solos had precise choreographed sequences, whereas the *Walking* and *Sleep* solos were comprised of learned components that could be ordered at will during the performance. No more than three solos could take place at one time, and only one *Spencer Holst* solo could be performed at a time (I wanted each essay to be heard distinctly).

Spencer Holst No. 1

On the Truth by Spencer Holst*

Over many years on many occasions I gathered bits of knowledge mostly from my father and family which gave me in fact a clear impression of my great-grandfather, on whom I wrote an essay.

Recently my sister read the essay and noticed that it was not true in some respects, which irritated me considerably.

My great-grandfather was not born in Dublin. Actually he was born in Columbus, Ohio, and his ancestors immigrated 200 years previously on the 2nd voyage of the Mayflower. He did not study in Vienna but got his medical degree at Western Reserve in Cleveland, which indicates that Ohio in those days was not too near the frontier.

Were I to change my essay to fit the facts I would not in fact, have any essay at all.

I took my predicament to a philologist friend, whose advice is granite, who had previously read and liked the essay.

"Are all the other things you said about your great-grandfather true?" she asked. "Certainly!" I answered. "His hobby was the cemetery. There's a statue of him in Weston. I've seen it with my own eyes, when I was a child. He got people to work on the cemetery by letting them pay off their doctor bills in labor. He was the only doctor then. He drained the swamp, and planted trees, redirected a stream so that it

Thirteen Essays by Spencer Holst, New York, 1960 (privately published).

18

formed a pond. He founded the first newspaper in town, which still exists. My father told me that he remembers when he was a child that my great-grandmother used to bake huge round cookies; and no matter what animal my father named, my great-grandfather could quickly bite the cookie into that shape. . .I mean, though he was not 'a man from Europe' but rather grew up in Ohio, he sounds like he grew up to become a real human being.

"Were the black swans really from Vienna?" she asked.

"I know that's true", I answered. "I read an old newspaper clipping about it, and it mentions that the swans were from Vienna."
"Oh," she said, "you read it in the newspaper. Then it must be true."
"Shall I tear up the essay?"
"Of course not. It's a convincing essay. Some other time you can write a more complete account of your great-grandfather, perhaps, but let the essay stand as it is. Philologists are always discovering things like that about old works. The philology is not important to the essay. It is irrelevant."
"Vera!" I laughed, aghast, astonished, and amazed, "what a way to use the word philology! What do you mean? What is philology? The truth?"

Spencer Holst No. 2

On Evil by Spencer Holst*

Sitting up late one night I ventured, though I had nothing to gain, to transfix the devil by some sort of solitary hypnosis or other.
I wanted to stop him for a moment, and if only for that moment, to gain a clear view of evil, to know exactly into what dimensions evil pours; for I felt evil to be all mixed up with good, and further more, I was never quite sure evil existed at all - - that perhaps it was only the absence of some good.
Yet there was the contradictory intuition, even so: that perhaps what is good is really good! And that the one thing I know about evil is: what is evil is *evil* - - - - - you understand, none of this reversaling, this "what appears to be good is really evil", etc.
A lamb crossed my daydream.
I let it go. . .
I saw a lion sitting in my mind.
I saw it sitting, and yet I was enrapt, and intent on seeing what was wrong I turned my eyes away, and let it lie there, breathing.
I saw a burning picture, a sacrifice to Blake.
An embarrassment, cogs, clashes, and clangs - - flashes in a dozen different brains - - of alarm clocks, rattling bells, and buzzered twangs, and splintering glasses - crashes.

*Ibid.

Then I fell asleep as we narrators regularly do in these stories about the devil.

I must have, for the next thing I remember was awakening from a nightmare. I went out into the kitchen and had a glass of milk, trying to shake off the dream, and vomited.

Half a dozen times that night I repeated the performance, sleeping winks between nauseating glasses of milk.

Many times I returned to my nightmares.

When finally I sat at the breakfast table across from my wife, I tried to repeat to her what I could remember of my dreams, and now those nightmares have returned to crouch in oblivion, and now that telling is all I can recall.

"You were in the dream" I said, "we were in the 2nd-story apartment of a suburban stuccoed flat. You were dancing with what's-his-name, that jerk at the party last night, and he was wearing his black suit and sun glasses. You were laughing happily, and I noticed you didn't have your dress on, and you were wearing a black slip. I walked over and took hold of your arm. He said in a low voice to both of us, "Excuse me, I must be going", and he left. Later in the dream I was walking outside the house thru what seemed to extend indefinitely like a small park. There was blackness. I heard a peculiar sound, like a puff of air, or like a giant cat spitting, or like the flap of a giant wing. . .The sound came from maybe 20 yards away, and I heard it again and again, at about 5-second intervals. . .My feet walked faster and whatever it was kept pace with me. . .it was on my right. . .traveling parallel with me. . .I turned sharply to my left, for I felt out there a horrendous presence - - what was out there was evil. . .and it still travelled on my right! Was I mad? Or was it really coming closer? The noise seemed louder. . .and as I fell forward, running, falling. . .blind. . .the sounds kept pace with me. . .never behind me. . .never in front. . .always on my right. . .and coming now obviously closer. . .not more than 10 feet away from me. . .tfff. . .tfff. . .tfff. . .I stopped stock still. .and it stopped beside me. .Yet still it sounded. . .tfff. . .tfffff. . .tfffff. . .tfffff. . .and while I waited, steadily it came closer to me. . .evil! I ran in the opposite direction and yet I could not get any further away from it. .I climbed a tree. .and it rose slowly beside me, yet coming still closer as I climbed . . .I fell. .and it dropped to the ground beside me with a small thud. . . tfff. . .tfffff. . .tfffffffffff."

I understand what the dream meant.

Now I understand, though I didn't when I dreamed.

When not performing their solos the dancers congregated casually around a street barricade which they also intermittently moved around the space. (It had been carried in after the lights came back up after *Duet*. Trisha and Yvonne had exited in the blackout to change into black leotards. They re-entered as soon as they had

20

9 Bill and Steve. In the background Albert does *Sleep*

done this and joined the group at the barricade.) Their deportment was both at ease and watchful. The solos varied in duration from five to ten minutes. The whole section must have been twenty to thirty minutes long. (*page 32*)

The *Sleep Solo* was the only one in which objects were used. There was a large patterned furry carpet bag filled with various things: a large white vase, a small sandstone turtle, a toy gun, two woolen hats, several dried mangoe pits, a glass paper weight, perhaps more that I've forgotten. The activities were eccentric: Taking things out of the bag while examining them and saying "buzz, buzz, buzz". Crouching in a deep 2nd position plié with arms stretched tautly to the side — each hand grasping a small object — and exploding vocally with "WHAMMM!" Creeping in a squat position to place an object somewhere else in the space (this solo could cover as large an area as the performer wished). Stretching arms between two objects that were too far apart to touch and shifting the gaze from one object to the other (still in a crouched position. The performer never stood erect in this solo). "Sleeping" and sitting. By simply focusing all of the attention on the objects, by never taking notice of anything else going on around one, by clutching the bag or objects to the body while simulating sleep — by all of this the performer gave an impression of an obsessed, maniacal character. The cool detatchment of the dancers who were "not performing" around the barricade contrasted strongly with the idiosyncratic behaviour in both the *Death* and *Sleep* solos. The barricade was removed when everyone had reassembled around it after finishing their solos.

21

4. Play

Play, the fourth section, was the most complicated structurally. It consisted of eleven designated units of material (for some reason *jump* did not appear on the program), each with its own restrictions governing number of participants, ways of beginning and ending, ways of combining with other units, duration, sequence (improvised or fixed). There was no prescribed order to the units themselves; this depended completely on the desires of the performers. However, there were several combinations suggested by me that we became sufficiently familiar with in rehearsal so as to go smoothly from one unit to another without interruption by stopping or calling out new signals — such as *game* could be followed by *stop* could be followed by *jump* could be followed by *rest*. Some of the units had to be initiated by a vocal signal: Any unit involving two or more people required the calling of that activity (e.g. *fast*) plus the names of the people the caller wished to be engaged in that activity (in the case of *fast* it had to be at least three names because *fast* required a minimum of four participants). Two activities — *ball* and *rest* — had priority in the sense that if your name was called while you were engaged in either of these, you were not obligated to respond. The exception was *slow*. If *slow* was called you had to stop whatever you were doing even if it was *ball* or *rest*. If anything else was called, you had to respond *unless* you were doing *ball* or *rest*, in which case you had a choice.

10

12

11, 13

10 *Game* – Y.R., Trisha

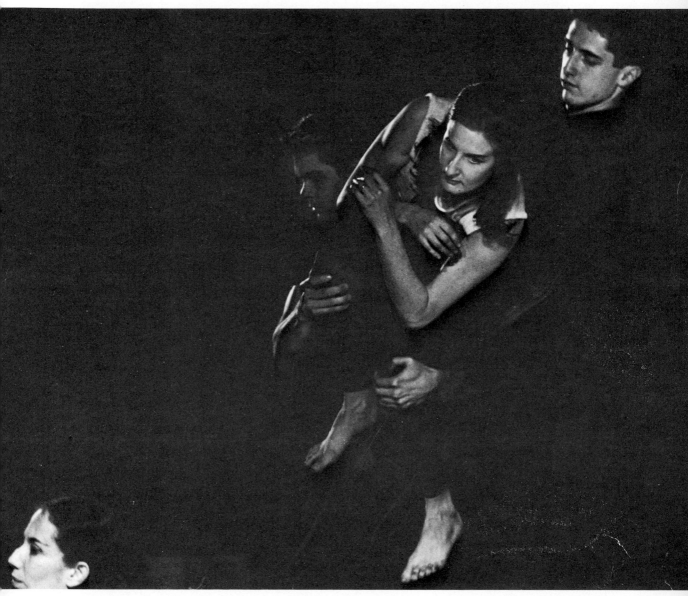

11 *Slow*

12 *Fast*

The reasoning behind the formulation of these rules was often elliptical, to say the least. *Ball* and *rest* were long drawn-out combinations of material that I wished to have seen in their entirety whenever they began. With other units of material I did not have such strong feelings against interruption.

Ball consisted of six combinations of movement, each of a different complexity and duration, all involving the manipulation of a red ball. Each one was designated by the name of one of the six performers. We all learned all six. To initiate an activity you first called "ball" and indicated you wanted a ball thrown to you by the "supplier". (At Judson Church he was in the balcony.) You then had an option of doing any of the *ball* activities alone anywhere in the space or of calling other people's names to instruct them as to which combinations to do. As far as *ball* went, the caller had more options than with any of the other units of material. The only restriction was Trisha's *ball* event, which had to be done by everyone whenever she initiated it.

In the case of other events that one could engage in alone — such as *pick-up, stance, stop, rest, bounce,* and *jump* — no call was needed. The end of *Play* was indicated when all 50 red balls littered the space. (A new ball had to be received from the supplier whenever a new *ball* event was initiated.) At this point everyone walked to the far right wall and sat down during *Love*, an erotic duet performed 14 by Bill and Yvonne, based on Kama Kala sculpture. The total duration of *Play* was thirty to forty minutes. *(page 35)*

13 *Slow*

14 *Love*

5. Bach

Bach was a seven-minute compendium, or recapitulation, of 67 phrases of move- 15 ment from the preceding three sections plus most of the traveling movements from the *Diagonal* section. It was accompanied by the second part of the Bach Cantata, "Ich habe genug," sung by Dietrich Fischer-Dieskau. Each performer repeated 10 or more of the movements in irregular sequence during the seven minutes. As the *Love* duet ended, the prelude came on and everyone took their places in a column at extreme stage-right: Trisha at the front, behind her Judy, then

positions at beginning and end

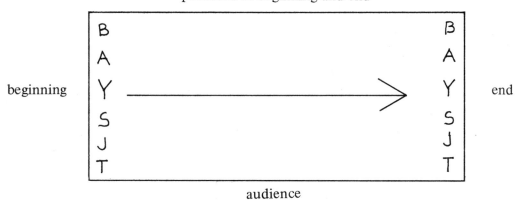

beginning   end

audience

15   *Bach* – Judy and Steve "wrestling"

26

Steve, Yvonne, Albert, Bill. We all stood in our particular *stance* from *Play*. When the basso's voice was heard, we began to do our pre-set sequences. The traveling movements invariably went in a direct line from stage-right to stage-left and back again. Whenever you returned to stage-right, you stopped just short of your previous position with the result that the whole column — with our fixed relationships within it — moved slowly from right to left. When the column had passed the midpoint of the space, a reversed procedure was followed; i.e., the traveling movements went from left to right and back again and you stopped just beyond the previous position of the column when you returned. (*see diagram below*) By the time the music ended, the column had arrived at extreme stage-left. There was a fade-out on the final bars of the music while several of us were still moving and the rest had resumed their *stance* poses. (*page 41*)

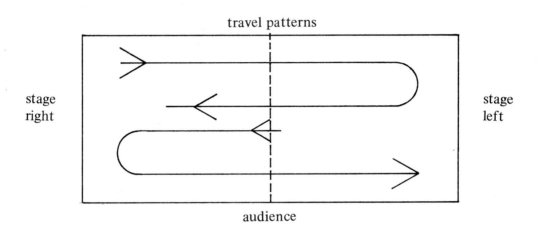

travel patterns

stage
right

stage
left

audience

1. Diagonal

Overture:

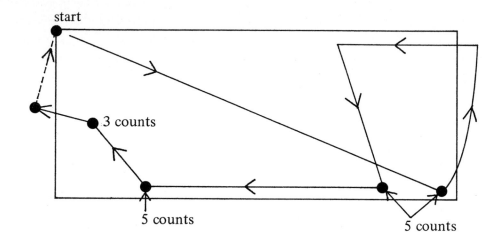

group
1. Walk
2. Run
3. Crawl - straight legs
4. Horizontal torso run with hands at ears - face d.s.
5. Stiff leg 2nd - puffed cheeks - spread fingers walk   4
6. Triplet run - left, right - then backward turn on left en route - resume triplet to finish.
7. Run. ½ way hoist "7" caller high in air.
8. Straight-leg waddle - arms high doing small windmill.   2
9. Walk - ½ way across drop into foot-over-foot squat walk.
10. 4 steps into jump - left shoulder and hip meeting - followed by r. leg thrusts forward; step on it, thrust l. leg back and across as r. elbow and shoulder blade jerk back.

for 1 or 2
A. Right arm circles twice as l. leg chassé. 3rd time bring elbow in and thrust r. arm sharply toward corner as turn skip on r. leg. Dribble walk.   3
B. R. knee turns in after 4 steps, sudden pas de bourrée, low en dehors turns on left with top of r. foot dragging as appropriate arms shoot toward corner. End on r. plié with turned-in attitude to side.
C. Movie death run ("Breathless").

28

D. Leaps
    1. Start to brush r. leg, switch to l. as
        parallel arms move down, up to r. and
        over.
    2. Parallel arms str. ahead, at peak of
        ascent, round back.
    3. Satie for 2 diagonal leap.
    4. Leading with r. knee - r. arm limply leads
        out and around, drawing back around toward
        str. l. leg behind.

2. Duet

Movements from Trisha's solo in <u>Duet</u>:

      Hip undulations

      Turns - to left on forced arch plié with right leg
in 2nd and arms in 2nd, followed by turn to right preceded by
sharp right elbow, followed by turn to left with right arm enclosing retarded head and right foot dragging arabesque on
floor.

      Small pelvis whack (both hands) combined with small
hip whack and leg shake. Stop down-stage left.

      Classic walk (like premier danseur upstage with
left arm raised) into travelling sissonne.

      Leg shimmy to d.s. left into splat walk-with-
classic arms into classic walk with hands alternating face and
shoulders with torso slowly going over.

      Big pelvis whack.   5

      Arabesque.

      Hip whack and leg shimmy going forward (twice).

      Leg shimmy longer version into splat walk to r.

      Airplane backward turn into relaxed landing.   6

      2-beat with airplane arms.

      Air version of hip whack and leg vibration in 2nd,
moving upstage. Stop still - hand on hip, back to audience.

Yvonne's adagio   5

"Fifth position, left foot front croisé. Pas de chat to tombé
croisé, pas de bourrée over, failli; soutenu with left in front,
5th (right in front) deep plié; rise bringing right hand overhead, relevé and passe left leg while raising left arm and bring
to front. Repeat pas de chat, etc. until soutenu. Extend right
leg to 2nd - arms overhead. Hold. Extend same leg forward
effacé. Turn to left and extend right leg behind in first
arabesque. Promenade. Plié, soutenu right leg behind, pas de
basque to right, pirouette en dehors on left leg, ending in plié
with right leg extended to 2nd. Pas de bourrée over. Repeat pas
de chat, etc. until failli, then soutenu behind with right leg.
Slowly lower arms."

Poses - end of <u>Duet</u>

1. Stand into right hip, look down, 1. hand on stomach.
2. Same legs, back of 1. hand on forehead - focus down left.
3. Hands crossed midsection, elbows down, head tilts back and
   to left.

30

4. Small 2nd plié, straight arms hand on knees, torso over, look to right.
5. Stand way into r. hip, l. leg bent comes across (pin up) - toes over, l. arm bent, limp wrist, look out.
6. Into l. hip, head up, mouth open, focus out, l. arm bent up front, limp wrist toward body, r. hand under l. tit, l. shoulder slightly up.
7. ½ toe - knees to l. - torso front, bent l. leg, str. parallel r. leg, r. hip up, focus out.
8. Into l. hip, hands on hips, torso slumped into hip, focus out.
9. R. knee across, hands on shoulders side view rounded spine, focus out - coy over r. shoulder and l. hand.
10. Step onto r. foot, left heel slightly off floor, r. arm bent across front, relaxed hand, l. arm bent away from body, more relaxed hand, head turned to r. and down.
11. Way into r. hip, left foot across - toes on floor, torso twisted so l. shoulder in front, r. shoulder down and back, l. hand on r. shoulder, r. hand grasps l. hand, focus out.
12. Into r. hip, l. leg slightly turned in - both hands on l. shoulder, elbows close together, focus out, head tilted to r.
13. Step forward on l. foot, right arm under chin, r. shoulder twisted to left, focus out, head tilted slightly to r., hands clasped back and to left.
14. Wilted classic - into r. hip, focus into r. armpit, r. arm crooked around head, limp l. wrist touching l. shoulder, right plié.
15. L. side of back to aud., standing on straight l. leg, focus out, head on l. shoulder, l. arm resting on l. hip, r. hand clasping l., r. leg bent, toes on floor.
16. Into r. hip, hands on head.
17. Hands on shoulders, focus out.
18. Squat, elbows on knees, hands clasped.
19. Squat, elbows on knees, r. hand under mouth.

3. Solo Section

Holst Solos

1. Somersault; slowly rise with sharp flapping of palms - arms rising to overhead; sudden plié with arms opening to side - palms out.
2. Leap, change direction in air, run 4 steps, sweep left leg back in backwards turn, end in relevé - left leg crossed in front.
3. As slowly as you can - touch shoulder with right hand - elbow at side; turn head to face left; touch right elbow with left hand; bring left foot to right knee - left knee turned in; plié; sweep head down and around to right bring right elbow to hip, drawing shoulder down as both legs straighten - left foot pointing parallel back and back becoming swayed; relevé on right foot; pas de chat back legs - bringing arms overhead - hands grasping each other.
4. Recline on back - hands grasped across stomach; bring legs straight up, bend knees to chest; roll to right with gaze directly to floor.
5. Jump - swinging right arm to side and overhead as left shoulder tries to meet left hip - legs are straight; land on right leg turned out with left straight in 2nd; slow relevé in 2nd as right arm continues circle and gently grasp left arm across midsection; bring right foot suddenly in and repeat jump, etc. 5 more times.
6. Sit - left leg cross in front; collapse - roll over out-stretched leg (in 2nd) and around and over left leg - bring right leg in so everything is coiled up - bring right foot under, rise in sudden hop, turn on right and return to collapsed position.
7. Adage - involving r. leg swing parallel cross back-pushing out left hip - arms limply in 2nd; swing around to 2nd (relevé) - arms across body - r. across left pliéd leg (turned-in right): face left as right leg moves to parallel arabesque and arms extended straight down making tiny circles.
8. Stiff leg walk - one knocking the other out to side in circle - shoot right leg and both arms forward leading with bang on left flat-foot plié - put right foot down - start descending as left leg swings back and moves to side just in time to receive squat - rise immediately.
9. Walk - weight very forward - arms swinging very loosely 1st in opposition then to other side - then relevé as arms loosely imitate bird - free leg behind. Repeat to other side.
10. Begin a sort of chassé on forced arches - right leads (straight) - both turned out - right - left - right: reverse direction so weight is into parallel plié left with right stretched behind - repeat in this direction with right leg again.

11. Hop left foot – draw right leg turned in across left as arms jazzy 2nd – hoppety to right, left foot turned in behind right – hoppety to left and circle many times on plié hopping right as left foot shakes back and forth.
12. Walk with determination 4 or 5 steps – stop short as 1. hand moves vaguely toward face – change direction. Repeat.
13. High relevé strut – legs taut and close together with turns, downward turned head, hunching torso, etc.
14. Stand, sit suddenly – legs forward, roll side to side – hip up – r., l., r. – go thru position where left leg is stretched over top right leg in crouch – rise on straight leg – torso going over – hands remain on floor – go to left extended leg – head to knee. Sudden complete arabesque – again crouch – again into huge hop on right foot.
15. 4 walks forward – r., l., r., l., – pas de chat leap leading with right – bounce into right turned out plie with left in side arabesque and forearms bent parallel to floor, limp wrists.
16. From 1st pos.: simultan. raise bent right leg to 2nd as left arm slowly sweeps out to rest on head – limp wrist – and right hand remains down to grasp under side right thigh. Torso starts to bend to left – head leading when as far as can go, bring elbow in to side.
17. Brush right leg forward while left pliés and arms open to 2nd and circle forward as right foot lands – straight leg. Begin transferring weight into forced arch shaking right. Left leg straightens back. Everything to relevé as left circles around and lands 4th front – flat feet, right hip out, casual torso.
18. Piqué, undulating torso movement ending on left knee on floor.
19. Touch toes, touch head, sit with legs outstretched, weight resting on palms, lie flat, come up in crouch, pause, run in circle, lie flat, come up in crouch – arms around knees.
20. Stiff-legged walk flat back over, gaze at feet, right hand scratches ear.
21. Watch right hand running up left arm, look inside leotard, look over right shoulder and try to peer down back, gaze follows left hand down right arm as slow parallel plié ending on left knee – right hand to chin.
22. Forearm swings with parallel leg and hip thrust.
23. Flick hair, stand into r. hip – hands on hips, undulate torso l. – front – r. – chin out. Walk in circle. Undulate again. Give additional whip and turn to right – left leg behind. Face front – stand into r. hip – slowly turn head left.
24. Airplane run – left arm extended ¼ circle, then swivel – hip walk with gyrating arms – on upst. diag. – then leap onto right leg – catching left foot with r. hand – then d.s. and across left with run – arms down – turning into swivel hip run.

Walking Solo

1. Basic beginning step - very small.
2. Basic beginning step slightly larger with ¼,½, and full turns - either with left leg flung behind to left or to right on right leg with left following. Change direction.
3. Sideways travel to r. - plié left pushing out straight right with left arm making circle or motion parallel to floor.
4. Travel forward - relevé: place foot - bent leg turned out, as other foot comes thru, turn placed foot in and straighten leg, bent arms as necessary.
5. Travel forward - one leg bent relevé, other leg straight - flat foot. Limp with bent swimming arms.
6. Travel forward.
7. Very large basic into piqué ponché attitude into lunge on left squat with str. flexed right to second on floor. Left leg swings around as weight shifts to right squat - continues around into rise and backward turns - with back undulating.
8. Large basic with right arm crooking around head in turn to right into 2nd turn to r. - r. arm leading drop plié on right - left leg trailing into preparation for tumble.
9. Walk into movement with flung right, then left, legs into bend on right - backwards turn on r. with left flung behind into relevé waddle - torso over - arms circling down - pointed at floor.

Death Solo

Turn - hold.
Sharp arm stuff into bent-over walk backwards then forward upst. half-circle with 'a-eiou' mouth. Then straight body walk - head to side - forward then back (open mouth).
Sharp arm stuff - (1st part) into quick developé left leg forward then back to lunge - reverse direction with jump - then Span stuff - then torso over - then return upright with wiggles to starting position. 1st phrase once more into arabesque with twisted mouth. Hold.
Balance on hands, fall. Balance. Stand in airplane pos. with open mouth. Promenade. Go down again into balance. Fall onto back. Jackknife stuff ending on shins facing front. Slide to r. - r. hand supporting head - 1. behind head. Roll upstage keeping arms in same position. Roll d.s. with sitting jackknife position. Death run-end stage left with arms taut overhead and skull face. Fall - stomach twiddle. Roll d.s. Walk upst. 1. Diag. d.s. r. - turning phrase ending in lopsided attitude. Promenade. Back up with vibrating arms in 2nd position - face moving thru twisted mouth, skull, wide open mouth. Move foot - over - foot to left. Drop. Do head-foot stuff.

4. Play

Ball Movements

Steve - Stiff leg balances from one foot to the other while passing ball hand to hand. Pitching phrase - sudden battement l. leg; shoot ball arm str. thru, face l. Jump with torso over, turns inside on r. leg - impetus in ball-changing arms. Bounce ball with left hand toward r. side, grab with r. hand and spin to l. Run, sissonne, bring l. foot sharply in.

Trisha - Incomplete arm and torso thrusts, standing in one place. Rule: No one can do her phrase until she has done it. When she starts to do it, as soon as each person becomes aware that she is doing it, he goes to appointed place and does it until she stops doing it.

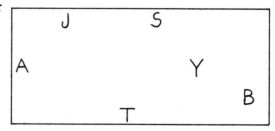

Al - Assemblé, sissonne, wiggle r. leg, lunge into 2nd r. plié, turn - torso over - to left on l. leg, tombé, swirl l. behind, come up - lifting r. leg around high, tombé, parallel triplet, run - l.r., hop off r. lifting l. to passé and wiggle out to 2nd while in air - step l. do Trisha's leg shimmy - r. leg - twice. 2nd time go over, walk on all fours.

Bill - Arrange at will. 1.Trot. 2.Sudden hard stop on 2 feet plié with l. arm shooting straight to side, fast turn to r., repeat, stop, etc. 3.Sudden soft stop, falling back and bringing both arms up. 4.'Skip'. 5.R. battement, turned in, to side, preceded by ball r. arm, turn to l. as r. transfers ball to l. which stretches out to side. Step r., reverse direction. Repeat - always same leg. 6.Turn - with swimming arms, left forced arch plié, r. leg sort of peddling body, around as it makes pas de cheval and straightens. Rule: When people become aware that Bill is doing his skip on diag, all must join in and do it until he stops. In doing Bill's phrase, no one can do the skip on the diagonal. However, one can do it in any other floor pattern.

Yvonne - Bouncing ball along "crack". Walk takes off perpendicular to horizontal line. 1st arabesque: torso sideways, gaze at ball in left hand stretched back. 2nd: l. hand comes down forward and toward r. shoulder as promenade en dehors. Gaze follows ball. 3rd: both arms back; bring l. leg forward bent knee high as arms swoop down and back with backbend and taut relevé r. 4th: l. leg comes down, also l. arm - preparation for flying hop on r. leg as l. arm "throws" ball overhand; change ball hand as r. leg battement to 2nd - face front and l. foot

relevé; change ball hand again as r. leg crashes down parallel
- torso still front - kicks back as l. leg reverses direction.
This last (battement to 2nd, etc.) can be done alone to other
side. 5th: same as 4th except after jump switch ball, relevé
l., bring r. passé in back, float torso and arms up and to l.
(facing d.s.) travels to r.

Judy - Airplane turn, right arm thru, then right leg over, step
onto left - face left, straight legs, right tendu back, both
hands on ball stretched forward; wind up, airplane to left on
straight left, body over, airplane right and plié right. (Repeat
2½ times. Wind up to right facing right, parallel legs; back up
handing ball back and forth, big sweep of right leg turn, step
left back on right, repeat; come suddenly front - vibrate.
Jerky lunge 2nd right leg plié - hands with ball down, side
right and overhead into left plié, right croisé straight.
Concentrate - fall, softly wobble, smoothly return. Repeat 4
times. Fourth time leave left leg to side, slowly straighten.
Promenade.

Game
(for 2
people)   Catch. One squats while other pretends to throw
ball - sharp jerky movements. Running back and
forth passing ball, slowly shortening distance
between the 2 until activity takes place a foot
apart. Finally person without ball signals
supplier for ball. Can be followed by

Stop   Run in unison d.s. left diagonal; do "soft stop"
(a jump with soft landing in semi-squat). Run upst.
and   center, do "stop" facing right and inclining torso
sideways toward upst. Run d.s. right, do stop.
Jump   Back up toward stage left 5 steps; do backward
can be   stop. 5 steps forward to stage right, do forward
done   stop. Turn, running big arc to upst. left, sideways
separately   stop toward upst. Run directly d.s.; do d.s. side-
by any   ways stop facing left. Run in big arc around to
number of   d.s. right - sharp battement right leg - tonlevé
people   left; land left; shift immediately to right as left
thrusts parallel to side and left arm thrusts down
front. Shift direction - still on right plié - to
upst. left - left leg now turned out tendu front -
arms parallel down, shift direction d.s. -
completing circle - torso inclined to left side,
face to ceiling, left arm wrapped around head, l.
foot cou de pied in back. Straighten r. leg as
torso inclines r., straighten and take weight on
l. leg as torso inclines forward and r. foot comes
to cou de pied front. "Skip" to left sideways on r.
foot as torso returns and arms circle overhead.

10

36

Repeat shuffle with torso moving r. side, front, l. side back on each weight shift - plus skip - so that shuffle and skip repeat <u>3 times</u> in their entirety. Then shift direction to upst. and weight to l. foot and ball to left hand to do Bill's skip to upst. diagonal l. Skip is done twice. Then lie down to do rest phrase.

Rest Phrase (individual activity - not called)
Lie on back. Grasp ball both hands - raise straight up. Take ball in d.s. hand and extend out on floor as gaze follows and other remains in air - hand drooping. Curl up on side, bring ball in front of face with both hands. Prop body up slightly on forearm head erect, as other hand holds ball over-head. Bring ball in front of eyes. Drop ball. Roll onto stomach, looking at ball. Rest chin on ball. One can refuse to participate in a called activity if one is doing <u>rest</u> (unless <u>slow</u> is called).

Pick-up (not called)
Running in circular perimeter of space, occasional-ly jumping in air. "Pick Up" whoever is in path. When there are an odd no. of people - 3,5 - the center person must get out from the center and go to an end position. It is obligatory to join if picked up.

Slow
A series of tableaux assembled and disassembled in slow-motion, performed by three and four people, always in the same order. *I can't remember if everyone learned all the parts or whether every-one simply was aware of the over-all configuration of each tableau. Where names are mentioned below it simply means that when that person was called on to participate in* <u>Slow</u> *he or she always assumed that exact position in a particular tableau. I seem to recall soft talking through some of it, as though we had to check with each other about the next move. Judy had a special instruction if she were involved: In those tableaux that required only 3 people she was to work alone in the immediate vicinity of the group doing a slow-motion roll from down-stage to up and back again, ready to rejoin the group when a fourth person was needed. The whole episode took place downstage right.* <u>Slow</u> *required the presence of whomever was called regardless of what they had been doing.* <u>Slow</u> *could not be abandoned until the caller chose to end it. The order of events was as follows:*

1. Trisha, (if she is present) lying   13
sideways on shoulder.

2. 4 people.

3.

4. Steve, lying sideways on shoulder.

5. Circle of 4, holding hands and descending to
the floor via stiff legs and breaking at the
hip until sitting on the floor, feet touching
at center.
6. Circle of 3 same as above.

7. Two men lifting Trisha to sit on their adjacent   11
shoulders. After holding this pose for a short
time she says "OK". As they each take a step to
the side she plummets to the floor.

Stance   Standing anywhere in the space in a relaxed
position. *Each person had a different position,
based on how she or he seemed most relaxed. Each
position, once decided on, was fixed.*

Bounce   Stand anywhere in the space and bounce ball.
(Bounce and Stance are individual activites, not
called.)

Fast   Minimum of 4 people: Huddle, moving rapidly in a
clump to opposite side of space while passing
ball hand to hand. Object is to grab ball and
break out, running toward whichever side is
furthest away. Group then joins hands and
gives chase to corral the fugitive back into   12
huddle. Game resumes as before. Can be left by
anyone anytime.

Love (done last by Yvonne and Bill)

Face diag. d.s. 1. Y. bends over, bouncing ball. B. grasping her
hips pulls her back and forth. Y. loses ball, bends all the way
over - straight legs - B. turns Y. around to face him in squat -

she grasps his legs, looks up, begins dialogue "I love you". Y.
shifts onto l. shin grasping B.'s r. leg her head against his
leg. Coils around his leg by pushing 1st knee thru until sitting
facing him again. B. pulls Y. up to standing. Embrace. Each
raises r. leg around the other. Slow descent - Y. backwards -
until reach floor - Y. l. leg extended, r. shin bearing his
weight. B. extends r. leg as roll d.s. ½ turn. Sit in embrace as
Y. pulls legs up to sit facing B. between his bent legs. Fall
over d.s. as maneuver to arrive face to face recline - B. on top
- heads toward stage. R. roll upst. hesitating on sides each
time as Y.'s leg bends around B.'s hips. Leg straightens diving
roll, then other leg bends, etc. About 3 revolutions. End B. on
top. Both draw up legs - Y.'s around B. Begin counterclockwise
rolls, B. arching back each time he is underneath. Full circle -
end Y. on top, heads s.r Y. eases off as B. arches back to allow his knees to fit thru hers. Both exert pull backwards as
hard as possible to facilitate rise to standing position. Both
look at feet activity: each tries stepping on other's feet as
hands vaguely grope over each other. B. pulls up Y.'s l. knee,
holds it as she sways on relevé - again vague grasping with
hands. B. grasps her around waist as Y. wraps other leg around
him - front piggyback. B. slowly plié as far as he can. Just   14
as Y's toes touch floor he sits, slides backwards. Both give
strong push backwards so that they sit facing each other,
toes touching - each in 2nd. Begin inching forward - dialogue
very rapid at this point. Y. bends knees so that B.'s legs
can go under. Arrive Y. sitting between B.'s legs, her legs
scrunched up. During "inching" alternate with soft quick
slapping of each other's face. When arrived, nuzzle until B. begins to raise Y. to stand. B. passes his head thru Y.'s gets up
to stand in back of her - both facing s.r. B. pushes Y out by
hips, catches her weight by placing his hands on her breasts, Y.
swings her arms loosely forward, places hands on B.'s hands as
he catches her. Repeat twice more. On 4th time Y. turns - arms
coming overhead - to face B. Hands on each other's shoulders descent to floor in squat - weight falling away. Rise, embrace, Y.
turns. Repeat twice more. 3rd time stay in squat. Grasp each
other's knees. Y. inches into sit scrunched up around B.'s l.
foot. B. sits, opens Y.'s l. knee as he slides to rear of her,
pulls her back to recline on him in languid sit as his r. hand
glides over her shoulder and rests on her crotch - both her
knees now open. B.'s r. arm grasps Y.'s waist, his l. straight
leg, slides under her as they shift onto l. side - feet d.s.
Y. moves forward from waist, draws B.'s knees into her own
- cocoon-like. Both straighten legs toward stage r. as shift onto Y.'s belly - B. belly down on top. B.'s hands slip under
Y.'s shoulders as they roll d.s. 1½ times - end Y. on top - feet
toward s.r. Y. draws bent legs up - shins on floor, sits up,
sways back as torso goes all the way over until face is on floor
between B.'s feet. B. sits up, moves hands over Y.'s body, slides
hands under her shoulders and pulls her up. Lets her down again
by arms, pulls her up same way, again same descent - this time

when she arrives down, her legs extend straight back: As B.
pulls her up, legs flex again. B. places hands flat on Y.'s mid
section for final descent, lays her straight out, as Y. reaches
floor her legs straighten and B. pulls her back by hips so that
their crotches are in contact. His hands slide up underside of
her body until he grasps her shoulders. Pulls her up. As Y.
sits, both draw legs up - Y. by contracting pelvis - so that Y.
sits cradled in B.'s lap. B. grasps Y.'s waist with r. arm as
they roll d.s. onto l. side - remaining in same position - then
onto knees - dog fashion. B. sits up in squat, pulling Y. onto
his lap - both facing s.l. Bach begins.

*The above duet was accompanied by an irregularly timed dialogue
consisting of variations on "I love you", such as "Why don't
you love me?", "I've always loved you", "Say you love me", etc.*

5. Bach

1. Hunchback
2. Elbow swings with 1. hip and parallel leg action.
3. From Duet Sec: Trisha's first movements - hip undulations, etc.
4. Turns
5. Pelvic whack
6. Leg shimmy
7. Hip whack with vibrating leg in 2nd
8. Airplane arms - bent over 2 beat
9. Splat walk in small circle
10. Classic walk in small circle with classic arms, hands on face, on shoulders, torso going slowly over.
11. 1st 6 cheesecake
12. 2nd 6 cheesecake
13. Last 7 cheese
14. Grand plié from adage with relevé and passé.
15. Small steps, romantic arms from adage.
16. R. leg ext: 2nd, effacé, arabesque-promenade
17. Bumpy stuff - including airplane turn
18. Palsy
19. Spencer Holst somersault
20. S. H. leap and reverse
21. S. H. r. hand to r. shoulder, etc.
22. S. H. lie on back and roll over
23. S. H. jump with r. arm swinging overhead
24. S. H. sit coil up, jump - coil up.
25. S. H. parallel descent to floor.
26. S. H. opposition arms - stepping forward
27. S. H. jazz step
28. S. H. strut with torso bumps
29. S. H. sit, roll from hip to hip, etc.
30. S. H. r. knee to 2nd, slow bend to 1.
31. S. H. vibrating r. foot phrase.
32. S. H. touch head, touch floor
33. S. H. look into leotard
34. Death Solo 1st turn
35. D. S. head to side - 1st movement
36. D. S. forced arch walk with vague hands and head to side
37. D. S. crouch on hands with falling over
38. D. S. jacknife rolls
39. D. S. skull position into fall on stomach
40. D. S. walking side to side with vibrating arms and changing expressions.
41. D. S. airplane arms, mouth open, careful walk in circle
42. D. S. final positions
43. Ball - Bill's phrase with flung leg
44. Ball - Steve's pitch, fling, jump, turn
45. Trisha ball movement

46. Yvonne ball arabesques
47. Yvonne ball - 1. leg swing to 2nd, letting drop, kick out
    as body changes direction r. foot comes parallel -
    facing 1.
48. Judy - ball - variation on 1st part: backward turn, etc. up
    to thrust; then big swing of r. leg to arrive at point
    where repeat from beginning.
49. Ball - Judy - wing - spread turns.
50. Judy - vibrating - staccato shift of weight into fall and
    shift.
51. Judy - same phrase done smoothly.
52. Last part of 50 into promenade.
53. Rest phrase
54. Staccato "pretend-throw"
55. "Catch" footsy stuff done slowly without skip
56. Ball bounce
57. Rest stance arms crossed
58. "55" done fast
59. Walk solo preparation and tumble phrase
60. Walk solo preparation into lunge over - no turns
61. Ball - Bill's turning-treading phrase
62. Duet section wrestling
63. Duet section - flung way out turn
64. Spencer Holst forced arch step, reverse with 1. arm out,
    up, and down chest
65. Arabesque with grimace
66. Ball skip
67. Diagonal section r. 1. flung jump into going over and
    battement

15

Score for Al's sequence in *Bach*. Each performer had an individual score. The numbers at the left correspond to the numbered movements beginning on page 41; the short lines next to them are in ten different colors which recur in the bottom half of the score; "− − −" indicates slow speed, "ΛΛ" fast, and "——" normal speed; the circled numbers refer to length (number of counts) of stillness following a particular movement. The arrows show how far across the space the performer is to go. The numbers or letters over the arrows refer to *Diagonal* movements. (*page 28*).

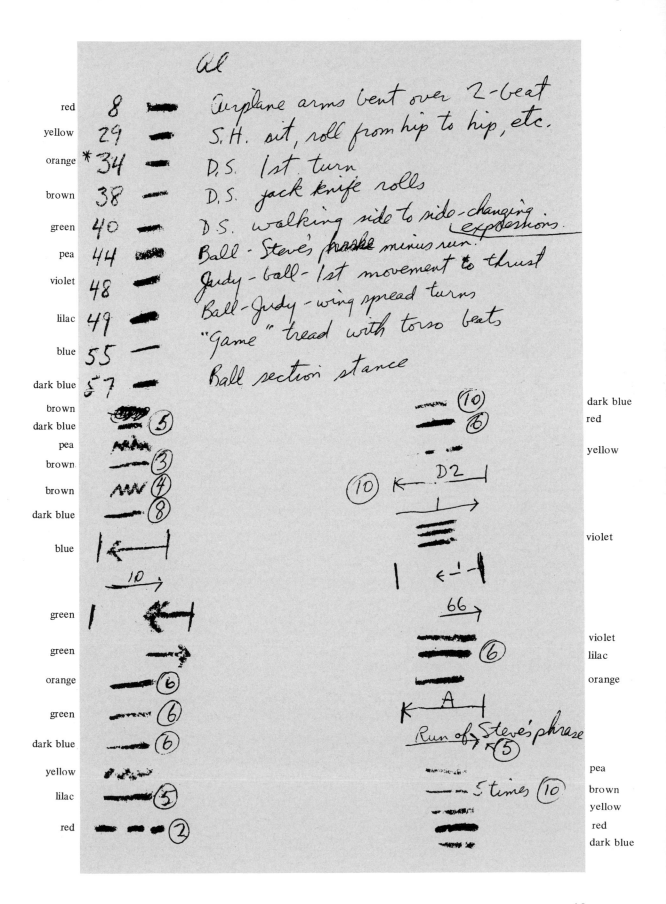

al

red	8	Airplane arms bent over 2-beat
yellow	29	S.H. sit, roll from hip to hip, etc.
orange	*34	D.S. 1st turn
brown	38	D.S. jack knife rolls
green	40	D.S. walking side to side-changing expressions.
pea	44	Ball - Steve's phrase minus run.
violet	48	Judy - ball - 1st movement to thrust
lilac	49	Ball - Judy - wing spread turns
blue	55	"Game" tread with torso beats
dark blue	57	Ball section stance

43

16   Activities nos. 5, 3, 22 at the Wadsworth Atheneum, Hartford, Conn., March 6, 1965

III Parts of Some Sextets

Some retrospective notes on a dance for 10 people and 12 mattresses called *Parts of Some Sextets*, performed at the Wadsworth Atheneum, Hartford, Connecticut, and Judson Memorial Church, New York, in March, 1965.*

1. **Origins of piece.** Earliest recollections go back to April '64 concert in Philadelphia where I did *Room Service, (page 294)* a big sprawling piece with 3 teams of people playing follow-the-leader thru an assortment of paraphernalia which is arranged and re-arranged by a guy and his two assistants. At this performance it spilled off the stage into the aisles, into the seats — displacing audience — and out the exits. I was excited by a particular piece of business: 2 of us carrying a mattress up an aisle, out the rear exit, around and in again thru a side exit. Something ludicrous and satisfying about lugging that bulky object around, removing it from the scene and re-introducing it. No stylization needed. It seemed to be so self-contained an act as to require no artistic tampering or justification.

Later — May or June — at a Judson Church concert in which half the evening was devoted to individual improvisation, I invited Bob Morris to help me do some "moving". We moved all the furniture in the lounge into the sanctuary (which was the playing area), including the filthy dusty carpet. Thoroughly irritated everybody interfering with their activities, broke a leg off the couch, spilled ashes and sand inadvertantly all over my black dress. This situation was definitely not satisfying. Was the difficulty in the nature of the materials? Could it be that a living room couch is not as "plastic" as a mattress? Hard materials versus soft — or more flexible — materials? (An absurd area of speculation? — like comparing the virtues of plastic or wood toilet seats?) Having completed the job I found myself with no ideas. In exasperation Bob left and in desperation I fell back on some of my more eccentric improvisatory techniques. (At that time I had not yet made the decision to abandon the loony bin and the NY subways as sources of inspiration.)

Decided to stick to mattresses. Began thinking about a sextet, six people plus a stack of single mattresses the height of a man. Meanwhile was working on a duet with Bob Morris. Material for a man and woman, mildly gymnastic, implicitly sexual, that when condensed could be a duet (there was a performance opportunity coming up at which I wan-

*First published in Tulane Drama Review, Vol. 10, No. 2, Winter 1965

ted to present something new) or when broken up could go into a pot for six people. Duet was called *Part of a Sextet* (By the time it was finished, the larger projected piece had expanded to ten people, but I liked the corny pun on sex.)

August — went to Stockholm with Bob. Shared a concert at the Moderna Museet in which I did solos and the duet; he did — among other things — *Check*, a piece for 40 Swedes. I was very excited by that piece, never having experienced those exact circumstances before: A huge room 300 feet long by about 100 feet across — the center filled with chairs, most of them empty; on the periphery and also in the sea of chairs standing and sitting the audience — about 800 strong; simple activities alternating in different parts of the room; Bob and I getting in and out of a box with a dozen faces looming over us; twelve people out of 800 knew what we were doing; the 40 performers assembling at a signal into 2 groups marching determinedly thru the audience; darkness: a man running back and forth on a wooden platform at one end while I moved slowly in front of an image with vertical lines thrown by a slide projector at the opposite end of the space from where the man was running. Simple, undistinctive activities made momentous thru their inaccessibility. A "cheap trick" to play on an audience in excluding them from the action? Or rather another device designed to counter the venerable convention of serving it all up on a platter?

2. **The work.** We next spent six weeks in Dusseldorf. Bob prepared sculpture for a show. I went every day to a tiny sixth-floor walk-up ballet studio in the Altstadt; I could see the Rhine beyond the old rooftops. One day there was a fire in the next block. Much smoke and scurrying around. I felt like a cuckoo in a Swiss clock observing an intricate mechanized toy go thru its paces. All those little firemen and townsfolk seemed wound up. And in the distance that flat river and green-washed Rhinemeadow. The whole scene was decidedly depressing.

Since there was nothing else to do, I worked. Worked mechanically and at times despairingly on movement. It was necessary to find a different way to move. I felt I could no longer call on the energy and hard-attack impulses that had characterized my work previously, nor did I want to explore any further the "imitations-from-life" kind of eccentric movement that someone once described as "goofy glamour." So I started at another place — wiggled my elbows, shifted from one foot to the other, looked at the ceiling, shifted eye focus within a tiny radius, watched a flattened, raised hand moving and stopping, moving and stopping. Slowly the things I made began to go together, along with sudden sharp, hard changes in dynamics. But basically I wanted it to remain undynamic movement, no rhythm, no emphasis, no tension, no relaxation. You just *do* it, with the coordination of a pro and the non-definition of an amateur. It's an ideal, still to be worked on.

I was also doing a lot of thinking about my group piece. The impact of *Check* had become a strong reference point. I wanted to make a piece that had the same effect, but I wanted the whole situation to take place directly in front of the audience. In other words, something completely visible at all times, but also very difficult to follow and get involved with. How I decided upon the system that I ultimately used is now not too clear to me, especially since in retrospect it seems there were many solutions that might have more successfully achieved what I had in mind. However, it *was* clear that there must not be a flowing or developmental type of progression in the action, but rather whatever changes were to take place must be as abrupt and jagged as possible, perhaps occurring at regular brief intervals. So I resorted to two devices that I have used consistently since my earliest dances: repetition and interruption. In the context of this new piece, both factors were to produce a "chunky" continuity, repetition making the eye jump back and forth in time and possibly establishing more strongly the differences in the movement material – especially the "dancey" stuff – that some of the movement episodes were simply small fragments used randomly and some were elaborate sequences made from consecutive phrases. Interruption would also function to disrupt the continuity and prevent prolonged involvement with any one image. So it began to take shape in my head: dance movement of various kinds; activities with mattresses; static activities (sitting, standing, lying); continuous simultaneous actions changing abruptly at perhaps thirty-second intervals, sometimes the whole field changing at the same time, sometimes only a portion of it, but every thirty seconds something changing. Thirty seconds began to seem like the right interval-length. I did not realize until much later that a given duration can *seem* long or short according to what is put into it. So my scheme, when applied to the diversity of materials that finally filled it out, did not really produce the insistent regularity I had thought it might. However, by the time I made this basic discovery I had begun to like the irregularities of the piece.

Returned to New York beginning of Nov. 1964. Had already decided on the soundtrack for the piece. Spent the next five weeks in the N.Y. Public Library perusing the index of and copying excerpts from the *Diary of William Bentley, D.D.* (*page 55*), a late 18th-century Episcopal minister who lived in Salem, Mass. and kept careful stock of the local goings-on during his forty-year tenure. Continued to work on movement material. Began to assemble the chart that would dictate the final arrangement of materials and people. (*page 52*)

The chart, reading down, lists 31 choices of material; reading across, numbers consecutively thirty-second intervals 1 thru 84. The piece is as long as two sheets of 22 x 17 inch graph paper allow with one-half inch of ruled space equivalent to thirty seconds. The chart is divided into squares, each indicating the juncture of a given piece of material with a given interval in time. The physical space of the dance – where the material would take place – was to be decided by necessity and whim as rehearsals progressed.

The 31 possibilities as briefly described on the chart are: 1. Duet: Corridor Solo; 2. Duet: Bob's entrance thru Y's squeals; 3. Duet: Leaning away thru 1st embraces; 4. Duet: Diagonal run to end; 5. Bird run; 6. Running thru; 7. Racing walk; 8. Solo beginning with shifting of weight; 9. Standing figure; 10. Bent-over walk; 11. Quartet; 12. Rope duet (with rope); 13. Rope movements 1 thru 4; 14. Rope movements 5 thru 8; 15. Rope movements 9 thru 13; 16. One vertical mattress moving back and forth on single layer; 17. "Swedish werewolf" (always off-stage); 18. Human flies on mattress pile; 19. Formation no. 1 (fling); 20. Formation no. 2 (with "bug squash"); 21. Move pile to other side; 22. Peel one at a time; 23. Crawl thru below top mattress; 24. Standing figure on top of pile; 25. House lights; 26. One person running another into pile; 27. Bob's diagonal; 28. Sitting figure; 29. Sleeping figure; 30. Vague movement; 31. Formation no. 3 (pile-up). 16 16 18 19 16, 17

In December began asking people to perform in the piece. The cast materialized as Lucinda Childs, Judith Dunn, Sally Gross, Deborah Hay, Tony Holder, Robert Morris, Steve Paxton, Me, Robert Rauschenberg, Joseph Schlichter. Joe's wife, Trisha Brown, considered being involved for awhile, even though she was pregnant, and even came to a few of the earlier rehearsals. I had very much wanted her to participate, especially in the very pregnant condition we thought she would have been in by the time of the performance. The idea was that there were no stars in this dance — just people — and if one of them was pregnant,

17 *Corridor Solo* and *Crawling Through* at the Wadsworth Atheneum

48

18 *Rope Duet* performed independently at Judson Church, Jan. 10, 1966 – Y.R., Alfred Kurchin

19 *Fling* at Judson Church, March 1965 – Steve

well — that would be a pregnant one. Thinking about it now, I feel that a "pregnant one" would have stood out as the only one whose activities were restricted to the less strenuous material. (Trisha's decision to withdraw was fortunate: she gave birth to a boy less than a week before the concert.)

Began teaching the dance material. (The non-trained people, Morris, and Rauschenberg, learned everything except "Quartet".) Had been putting off the actual filling in of the chart, but now with the mattresses bought and rehearsals proper ready to start, there could be no more delay. So one night I took the plunge and with a pencil made random marks all over the chart paper. Mostly in isolated squares, but sometimes in two, three, or even four consecutive ones.*

Then the work began: in column no.1 (the first thirty seconds) marks fell in the square indicating Duet: Corridor Solo, Bird run, Bent-over walk, Quartet, Peel one at a time, House Lights, Sitting Figure. The remaining decisions to make were who — and how many — were to do these and where they were to do them. Column by column I filled in initials of the cast. The decisions were based both on expediency (e.g., "do the rope movements wherever you happen to be" or "J. can't continue doing that because she has to do Corridor Solo here," etc.) and my feeling about the constantly shifting churned-up quality I was after. So when one activity went on for more than two columns (one minute), I usually added to or reduced the number of people doing it or even replaced them half way thru.

The final problem was that of cues. Eventually we would take word cues from the taped reading of the diary, but I hadn't yet made the tape because I thought it would be too difficult to learn movement sequences and cues at the same time. So I made a work tape with my voice saying "change" every thirty seconds. Now I feel that using the double learning process from the very beginning would have meant a considerable saving in time and work. As things stood, after we had learned the dance with the work tape, we had to plod thru it innumerable times for the extra familiarizing process involving the cues in the reading.(*pages 54, 56*)

The dance took eight weeks to learn. For the first four weeks we rehearsed four times a week; after that two or three times a week. It proved to be dry, plodding work, partly due to the length and repetitiousness. Also, since there was no "organic" or kinesthetic continuity, some of us found it extraordinarily difficult to learn and ended up memorizing it by rote, like multiplication tables or dates in history.

For a while I couldn't decide whether to keep the same consistency of texture from beginning to end, thru forty-three minutes of activity, or introduce changes midway. It might be said that I "chickened out" of

*It is apparent that the placement of the marks was not truly "random," as my choices were intuitive and subliminally aesthetic. "Randomness" precludes motivation and the exercise of taste.

the first alternative, but only slightly. What actually happened was that on the second half of the chart I made more deliberate choices, with an eye to larger and simpler configurations, one of which was two groups alternating Racing walk, Human fly, Werewolf, and Solo shifting weight. In the last thirteen minutes I had "YJPJo" (chart abbreviation for "Yvonne, Judy, Paxton, Joe") do Quartet and Solo shifting weight in staggered unison from beginning to end, while "CB" ("Cindy, Bob in staggered unison from beginning to end, while "CB" (Cindy, Bob) did Rope duet. The Quartet, etc., lasted half that time, permitting the Rope duet to be the next-to-last image. The dance ended with all of us perched on the single stack of mattresses.

3. Postscript. All I am inclined to indicate here are various feelings about *Parts of Some Sextets* and its effort in a certain direction — an area of concern as yet not fully clarified for me in relation to dance, but existing as a very large NO to many facts in the theatre today. (This is not to say that I personally do not enjoy many forms of theatre. It is only to define more stringently the rules and boundaries of my own artistic game of the moment.)

NO to spectacle no to virtuosity no to transformations and magic and make-believe no to the glamour and transcendency of the star image no to the heroic no to the anti-heroic no to trash imagery no to involvement of performer or spectator no to style no to camp no to seduction of spectator by the wiles of the performer no to eccentricity no to moving or being moved.

The challenge might be defined as how to move in the spaces between theatrical bloat with its burden of dramatic psychological "meaning" — and — the imagery and atmospheric effects of the non-dramatic, non-verbal theater (i.e., dancing and some "happenings") — and — theater of spectator participation and/or assault. I like to think that *Parts of Some Sextets* worked somewhere in these spaces, at the risk of losing the audience before it was half over (but that is yet another matter of concern, not to be investigated here). Its repetition of actions, its length, its relentless recitation, its inconsequential ebb and flow all combined to produce an effect of nothing happening. The dance "went nowhere," did not develop, progressed as though on a treadmill or like a 10-ton truck stuck on a hill: it shifts gears, groans, sweats, farts, but doesn't move an inch.

Perhaps next time my truck will make some headway; perhaps it will inch forward — imperceptibly — or fall backward — headlong.

	1	2	3	4	5	6	7	8	9	10	11	12	13	14	15	16	17
1. Duet: Corridor Solo	−↑/J				Y					J							
2. Duet: Bob's entrance thru Y's squeals						sR				sR							
3. Duet: Leaning away thru 1st embraces			cT									cT	cT	cT	cT		⇒cT
4. Duet: embraces to end (diag. run)																	
5. Bird run	SPJo								BY	BY		BY					
6. Running thru		RJo	JJo	JJB	B		Rc										
7. Racing walk								D				Jo					
8. Solo beginning with shifting weight			S	S					P	PJo	S	J					
9. Standing figure					R	DB								J			
10. Bent-over walk	→4c										J			YR			
11. "Quartet"	TJ	DTP	YPD		CS							PS		JY			
12. Rope Duet (with rope)																	
13. Rope movements 1 thru 4						SP	S			R			J				
14. Rope movements 5 thru 38												R	R	R			
15. Rope movements 9 thru 13					Jo		Jo		B								
16. 1 vertical mattress moving back & forth on single layer		JXCS															
17. "Swedish were-wolf" (always outside)			Y						T								
18. Human flies on mattress pile								PBJo			SPTD	D					
19. Formation #1 (fling)											PJT/D						
20. Formation #2 (with "bug squash")				PDc													
21. Move pile to other side							YTo	YoY	JY	TY							
22. Peel 1 at a time	B	B	R														
23. Crawl thru below top mattress on pile				J				C									
24. Standing figure on top of pile														P			
25. House Lights	R									Cdb							
26. 1 person running another into pile								RJo	RJo								
27. Bob's Diagonal																	
28. Sitting figure	K						JC										BYNJ
29. Sleeping figure											C	CRJo					
30. Vague movements														Y			
31. Formation #3 (pile-up)												PBJoS/D	PRJo/SD	RJo/SD	PJoS/D		

20	21	22	23	24	25	26	27	28	29	30	31	32	33	34	35	36	37	38	39
	J̄							Ȳ J̄											
S̄R	S̄R							S̄R							-K̄				ĒR
																C̄T			
		B̄Y	B̄Y	B̄Y				B̄Y											
									R̄B̄ / YTP	Y	Y	Y	Y	Y	Y	Y			
	S											TR̄							
		J̄		J̄				YD̄ / JoJS	D̄										
			RTJ / PL̄Jo		J̄D										R̄				
D̄										ȲT / RB									
	PJ̄YD															Jō			
							P̄		P̄										
			PT̄		PT̄			T̄ / CP̄R		J̄									
	JōTR																		
						R̄		T̄											
			R̄PT̄ / Jō																
B̄YCJo										P	C	P							
		PBRT / S							JōC		BSD / PLōT	BSD / CR̄J	PBC / TJō						B̄Y
						JJo / TS	JJo / TS												
				B̄															
	Jō		Ȳ														B̄Ȳ		
																CL̄P / R̄			
Ȳ / JY								D̄ou											HB̄
T̄P			B̄D																
J̄	C			Ȳ			B̄												
		C	C	C					D̄										
			S̄						S̄J										
	B̄	D̄													SS̄J				

(16½' from beginning

1 water now is as of a
2 it was taught
3 waxwork of same name
4 (2 owls) who gave us
5 Newbury, & the note
6 1800, attended
7 want of a small boat
8 misery at Manchester
9 (Little egg) Rock lies
10. round which is the
11. is a living (spring)
12 A Moose
13 tide at Salem
14 fence & partly buried
15 we are anxious
16 Mattoon aged 78
17 intelligible. He was
18 she comforted him
19 that they were given
20 (7 seconds after song)
21 D. leaves vague movemts.
22 Quartet disperses
23 Steve leaves sit
24 hi note in song
25 Bowen in Salem
26 We found a most
27 He was introduced

28 antiques in plates
29 Northfield,
30 places. They
31 funeral of my father's
32 it ran parallel
33 discovered (Aug. 4)
34 Charity House was
35 & one horse (killed)
36 & it will be re-
37 The last fear.
38 20 years ago I
39 intoxicated
40 comparative use
41 sun during
42 the stars seen
43 the passing off of
44 2500 dollars
45 but not succeeding
46 Essex, was son
47 on which the millpond
48 the inhabitants
49 Crowninshield
50 to perform
51 Sat. & died on
52 Charity House
53 January

Cues from Bentley tape (at 30-second intervals)

54

Excerpts from the taped reading from the *Diary of William Bentley, D.D.* that accompanied *Parts of Some Sextets*

2-2-1786

A note to John Brown to join the Wednesday night singers. On Monday evening a fire broke out in Marblehead, by which was consumed a large Store, the chamber of which was a Sail loft, containing many suits of Sails belonging to fishermen. In the Store was a large quantity of fish, part of which was destroyed. The Town of Salem was alarmed, but on account of the storm the preceding day, which continued thru the evening, and the great drifts of snow, the engines did not arrive soon enough to give any assistance. The engines went on to Cross Roads. On Wednesday, Mr. John Brown and Caleb Bengs, and Joseph Loring, joined the New Singing School. Lent Dr. Nuttig a dollar. Invited James Cushing to attend Singers.

3-18-1789

A Building the property of the family of Lambert, having one room upon a floor, and the entrance in a range with the Chimney at the eastern end, the whole building facing the western end of English's Lane, nearly taken down.

3-18-1790

In the Worcester Gazette is an authenticated account of a person cutting down a hollow tree, in which were found a large no. of swallows in a torpid state, the quantity was said to be two barrels, but that upon being carried near the fire they speedily revived and soon flew about the house. A late memoir in the 1st Volume of the American Academy respecting swallows being found in the water, has made this a subject of enquiry.

12-17-1790

Last night departed from life Old Grandame Whitefoot, above one hundred years old, being christened in 1690, among other children of the same parents, and then not the youngest. She was very small of stature, small face, quick temper, but soon reconciled. Always singing and dancing, not modest in her conversation, and aimed at jocose wit. Her whole habit was thin, and nothing made a deep impression on her mind. She was addicted to Smoaking which easily intoxicated her, and rendered her troublesome. She went abroad till nearly the time of her death and she sunk away in insensibility. She was a woman who neglected reading altogether, and for many years public worship, but never professed any aversion, but a carelessness. These facts have come within my own knowledge.

7-31-1792

Anti-Morgan made his appearance again. There is much speculation who his antagonist may be as it is yet unknown even to himself. He has taken no pains to satisfy this curiosity. There is a pertinent hint to Marblehead Academy about spouting. So much talk has been in the

1. Bent over walk   water now is of a
2. Vertical Mattress   it was taught
3. Quartet (P & D)   way work of same
4. Werewolf   2 owls w   gave us
5. Corridor Solo   Newbury & the notes
6. Move pile (T)   1800 attended
7.   "   "   want of a small boat
8.   "   "   misery at Manchester
9. Remove top 3 for C   Little Egg Rock
10. Bird run (B)   round which it lay   Digest
11.   "   "   / is a living (spring)
12. —   a moose
13. Bird run   tide at Salem
14. Vague movements / fence & partly burieds
15. Quartet (J)   We are anxious
16. Bent-over walk   Mattoon aged 78   intelligible, He was
17. Sitting fig.   Return object
18. Rope movements (III)   she com- / forted him
19. Racing walk (that they were given
20. Formation #1 (fling)   Her song
21. House lights + Quartet   visual
22. Duet diag. with B.   cues
23. Continue duet   Steve
24.   "   "   hi note
25. Crawl thru matt.   Bowen in Salem
26. Bob's diag.   We found a most   He was introduced
27. —   antique plaster
28. Duet (from   walk H.S.)
29. —   Northfields
30. Solo shifting weight   places, They
31. Corridor (J.)   funeral of my father's
32. Running thru   it ran parallel
33. Bent-over walk   discovered
34. Running thru   Charity House, was
35.   "   & one horse killed
36.   "   & it will be re-
37.   "   The last 3 fear
38.   "   20 years ago I
39. House lights   intoxicated
40. Running thru   comparative use

41. Bent over walk   sun during
42.   "   The stars seen
43. Duet   the passing off of
44. — $2500
45. Fling (P) & Bird run   but not succeeding
46. House lights (stay offstage   Essex, was son
47. Solo shifting weigh   on which the mill and
48. Duet (B)   the inhabitants
49.   Crows instructed
50. Sitting fig.   to perform
51. Human fly   Sat. & died on
52. Racing walks.   Charity Houses
53. Bird run + human fly   January
54. Human fly   himself
55.   "   conversation
56.   "   but we are (a being)
57. Quartet   food, & air (healthy)
↓
63. Solo shifting weight   upper jaw
68. Quartet   results to the

Cues with corresponding activities

56

country about Theatrical entertainments that they have become the pride even of the smallest children in our schools. The fact puts in mind of the effect from the Rope flyers, who visited N. England, after whose feats the children of seven were sliding down the fences and wounding themselves in every quarter.

11-28-1793

The day appointed for the public correction of some offenders in the Gaol. The Subjects were two men and a woman. The woman and man were Irish, the young man, Smith, of this Town, for Theifts. The whole was conducted by the Deputy Sheriffs without any order. The prisoners were audacious beyond example. Upon mounting the Gallows on which they were to sit, through intoxication one of them fell off, and was carried away senseless. After insulting the spectators, and the most profane words and indecent behaviour, the woman and man were whipped, but the ladder was filled with spectators, and the Sheriff had not room to move his arm. The whipping produced a few tears from the culprits, or rather the Cold. My old chum Herrick has repeatedly called on me for the loan of 6 pounds. I tried to draw it out of Mr. Bernhard, but without success. I begged it however of Capt. B. Hodges, giving my note, paying immediately, and taking Herrick's to be paid, when I can get it. But let us encourage one another.

10-18-1796

In company with Capt. Collins of Liverpool, Nova Scotia. He faults Des Barres Charts, because they have changed and neglected the old names by which places are laid down upon that Shore. Because he has placed too far southerly Cape Sable and the Island, 20 miles. Because he has placed the island before Liverpool, almost in the middle of the Entrance. He gives the preference to Cooke's drafts of the Labrador Shore, which he had found to be particularly accurate. The same Cooke, who was afterwards circumnavigator.

12-4-1796

Sunday, Madame Gardner gave me some account of Mr. Robert Stanton. He had a piercing eye, was tall, graceful, ready in conversation, chearful, open, and censured without real blame. Was rather too gay for a minister. He was athletic, could leap with great ease, and move with great activity. He was fond of gunning, as his sport. He was blamed as imprudent. A Goody Beadle, who lived in Essex Street in a house from the street, between Curtis and Herbert Streets, was notorious for her shrill voice in calling her son Jonathan at Stage Point. The Parson incurred the displeasure of the good woman by an exact imitation both of the loudness and shrillness of her voice. She would never be reconciled. He lived in the house of the parent of my informant, before he married, and was very apt to divert himself with the little incidents of life. Upon seeing a sick child of which he was fond, he burst instantly into tears. He was much beloved. He married a g. daughter of Barton, of Boston, near Barton's point, and died of a violent fever. Upon being quoted by a clergyman for what he never said, to the disadvantage of his interest, when told of it he replied, I will not unnecessarily contradict it. He was from Stoneington in Connecticut.

7-14-1797

Showers, which were gentle and kind, and the thunder continual, but not severe. We had no idea of the Storm in the S.W., but the evening Master Lang came to my house with a mass of hail stones in a state of congelation as large as his handkerchief could conveniently hold, which he has brought in the heat 12 miles from Malden. He declared, and his Son the Doctor attested, that they saw a gentleman from curiosity wade to his knees in the pile in the road. The extent of the damage is not known. We may expect particular account on the morrow. I spent the evening in carrying the hail stones in a plate round to be viewed by my friends.

7-26-1797

Upon our return I had the great pleasure of seeing Calvin, a dwarf child from Bridgewater, which has lately been exhibited at Boston. It is in the finest natural proportions and a perfect miniature. Its muscles are free, the motions regular, the passions strong, the tongue at liberty, and yet at 7 years is only 26 inches high and weighs 12 pounds. It is carried about by its relatives, who are unacquainted with any arts, and who plead the poverty of its parents. They have taught it only the childish amusements of ball, play at marbles, and with a whip, having no acquaintance with the fine arts or any other than country amusements. Such a sight was novel. Mrs. Leach of Beverly who lived above 60 years had an head of the usual size, but the substance of the bones was cartilaginous. She was deformity itself. But here nature has varied from her plans, not in proportions, but in dimensions. And we see harmony, while we see very far below the usual growth. The reason offered for so little attention to its mind, are its impatience, and obstinacy, and the design of exhibiting him continually to the public.

8-30-1797

Went to the Market House to see the elephant. The crowd of spectators forbad me any but a general and superficial view of him. He was 6 feet 4 inches high. Of large Volume, his skin black, as tho lately oiled. A short hair was on every part, but not sufficient for covering. His tail hung 1/3 of his height, but without any long hairs at the end of it. His legs were still at command at the joints, but he could not be persuaded, to lie down. The Keeper repeatedly mounted him but he resisted in shaking him off. Bread and Hay were given him and he took bread out of the pockets of the spectators. He also drank porter and drew the cork, conveying the liquor from his trunk into his throat. His Tusks were just to be seen beyond the flesh, and it was said had been broken. We say "his" because the Common language. It is a female and teats appeared just behind the forelegs.

11-3-1797

Mr. Harris told us at Dorchester, that digging a well on the hill near his house, 80 feet deep, at the greatest depth he came to sand and stones, exactly resembling the shore, and to marsh, which had the same effluvia as on the shore, tho a more perished appearance, but of the same color. That the Well for a time became useless from the stench of the waters,

and at last they ceased to pump it out or draw it and used the well only to hang down meat so to preserve such things cool. That by accident a string broke and 18 lb. of Beef fell into the well. Attempts were made in vain to recover it. Soon afterwards a frothy substance appeared on the surface of the water, which gradually disappeared and the water now is of as agreeable a taste and as clear as any which can be drunken. I drank of it in his house not knowing its history, with great pleasure.
3-12-1798

I went to Boston to attend a Committee of the Grand Lodge. Upon my arrival and for a moments amusement I visited the Learned Pig and the exhibition greatly exceeded my expectations. It was taught to discover the cards, to assort the letters of words, and to bring numbers for any purpose. I afterwards visited Bowens Museum and tho' the arrangement by no means met my wishes, yet I could select many things to give me pleasure. The wax work is extensive, but I can pronounce nothing. The tapestry obliged my attention. The painting, Death of Lewis, from which the waxwork of the same event is taken, was good, but the resignation of Washington interested me. There are many portraits which are interesting. The musical clocks discover ingenious mechanisms but the notes of the clock describing the Organ and Charonets were captivating. In the menagery was a bear sleeping and slumbering with an insolent contempt of every visitor. A Babboon, more fond of entertaining his guests, an affronted porcupine, and 2 owls who gave us no share of their notice.
12-23-1800

This morning died in Walnut Street, Hubartus Mattoon, aged 78. He removed from Newcastle, N.H. after his marriage and was a zealous follower of Whitaker and an Elder of his Church, and he never renounced his attachment. He was as far from beauty as he could be without deformity, and as brutal in his zeal as he could be without persecution. He was ignorant, noisy, petulant, but happily neither his organs nor his abilities make him intelligible. He was a Blacksmith with the same fame as he was religious. There was no polish, no invention, and no praise in what he did, more than in what he said. He declined at last into intemperance, dishonesty, and derangement, and died of a cancer which took away all his face, and made him as ghastly to behold as he was terrible to hear. His wife was glad he was dead and even Charity had not a tear, tho' she comforted him in his sickness and carried him to the grave. The race is extinct, and like the Mammoth nothing is left but his bones.
12-29-1804

This day died in real truth poor blind Caesar in the Charity House. Upon the death of the last negro, poor Caesar's name was given out among the dead. The last fear of this poor creature was that he should not get well soon enough for New Years' Day. He had a surprising memory by which he got a decent support, while his health lasted and which he retained without losing it, so as to bring it to a common size till his death. He employed it soberly upon one subject, the ages of persons, and no example have I ever known for such retention of this favorite subject. Twenty years ago I gave him the age of my parents and kindred of 3 generations with the promise of a reward upon every notice of their birthday. I have never known that he lost one or confounded it with any other. I shall save my pennies and miss Caesar. Tho' often at my door, he never was troublesome. In the close liquor easily overpowered him, but did not enslave him. He was peaceable and disposed to behave well, he never meant to be intoxicated.

5-25-1805

The use of Coffee, which 1st appeared in Europe in 1657, but not much used for 30 years afterwards. In 1764 above a millions weight was exported from St. Domingo, from the Cape only and above 3 millions from other parts. Tea has had great use, but Coffee is continually supplanting it. The comparative use of Tea at present is small. No house is without Coffee. Tea is rarely asked for Travellers, even females.

6-16-1806

All attention was directed to the Eclipse of the Sun. I am sorry to say that without a regulated clock or any other preparation I was a mere gazer on the Sun during this singular phenomenon. It did not begin as early by 10 minutes as the calculation according as the clocks then stored in town, and the clocks were in the same state in Boston. Nothing incommon took place till the total observation. Then the disk of the sun was completely covered but an irradiation was like a glory around. A few stars appeared and Venus was visible thruout. The stars seen were near the sun, excepting one planet in the east far above the horizon. As soon as the total eclipse begun the horizon lighted up around above 20 degrees as bright as the twilight ever appears so that the obscuration was not beyond the degree in which the atmosphere is darkened by thick vapor or heavy rain and by no means in the degree of the dark day. The return of light was instant upon the passing off of the moon and the return of light put an end to every thing wonderful to the sight in this event.

8-30-1811

We are full of reports of war so that scarcely anything else is mentioned. The reports are vague but we are to expect anything from British vexation. The nation is in great trouble and they will keep the world in the same condition. The Gov. and Council keep their secrets absolutely. No one pretends to have such influence as to have any secret communications. The many appointments upon the new order of things has made this a very interesting moment to speculators. It is intended, whatever be the event, to free the administration from the support of its opposers.

7-29-1817

We learn that the Elephant exhibited as a Curiosity in this town lately, was shot in open day by a villain at Alfred, Maine. We have such wretches in our country who have all the lawlessness of our Savages and a full share of them in Maine. It is said the pretense was that money should not be raised in that way in that neighborhood. Even in Salem it has not been uncommon to deface what appears to have been a display of the taste and elegance of the Town as of private citizens. The monument on the hill had been repeatedly pulled down. Fences often daubed, etc. We believe our manners very correct generally, but we have Savages still.

9-24-1818

Went in a Horse and Chaise for Andover to visit some female friends of Hodges family living at Ballard's. We found the situation at Ballard's romantic and the Shawsheen as delightful as I found it above and below formerly. Immediately upon our arrival we began our walk. We passed the bridge which was more delightful from the great height of the river and extended sheet of water, forming several small islands in the river among the meadows. We passed eastward from the mills, found the cranberries plentiful and at length reached the pond. South of the pond we found the Boston road and passed partly down it and then turned to the mills and reached home. At table we had roast fowles, the greatest luxury of N. England and Beef a la mode the richest dish we have borrowed which all know how to prepare. Our pastry and puddings excellent, and our fruit the best, pears melons and apples. Soon after dinner we had an excellent dish of tea with bread of wheat, or rye, or rye and indian and all of the first quality as our Landlord is rich and has the best which our farms can produce.

8-3-1819

Yesterday the Sea Serpent was seen off Marblehead. B. Stone at Marblehead Neck saw him near the Inner Pig rock at 7 A.M. about 2 hun. yds. from the beach, resembling a row of porpoises. He viewed him from 7 to 11 A.M. A Mr. J. Hathaway of the farms with him. They thought they saw 20 protuberances. Several at Marblehead at noon saw him off Tinker's Island with a glass, Length supposed 100 ft.

IV The Mind is a Muscle

A Quasi Survey of Some "Minimalist" Tendencies in the Quantitatively Minimal Dance Activity Midst the Plethora, or an Analysis of *Trio A.**

Objects	Dances
eliminate	
or	
minimize	

Objects	Dances
1. role of artist's hand	1. phrasing
2. hierarchical relationships of parts	2. development and climax
3. texture	3. variation: rhythm, shape, dynamics
4. figure reference	4. character
5. illusionism	5. performance
6. complexity and detail	6. variety: phases and the spatial field
7. monumentality	7. the virtuosic feat and the fully extended body

substitute

Objects	Dances
1. factory fabrication	1. energy equality and "found" movement
2. unitary forms, modules	2. equality of parts, repetition
3. uninterrupted surface	3. repetition or discrete events
4. nonreferential forms	4. neutral performance
5. literalness	5. task or tasklike activity
6. simplicity	6. singular action, event, or tone
7. human scale	7. human scale

Although the benefit to be derived from making a one-to-one relationship between aspects of so-called minimal sculpture and recent dancing is questionable, I have drawn up a chart that does exactly that. Those who need alternatives to subtle distinction-making will be elated, but nevertheless such a device may serve as a shortcut to ploughing through some of the things that have been happening in a specialized area of dancing and once stated can be ignored or culled from at will.

*Written in 1966, previously published in *Minimal Art, A Critical Anthology* edited by Gregory Battcock, New York, 1968.

It should not be thought that the two groups of elements are mutually exclusive ("eliminate" and "substitute"). Much work being done today — both in theater and art — has concerns in both categories. Neither should it be thought that the type of dance I shall discuss has been influenced exclusively by art. The changes in theater and dance reflect changes in ideas about man and his environment that have affected all the arts. That dance should reflect these changes at all is of interest, since for obvious reasons it has always been the most isolated and inbred of the arts. What is perhaps unprecedented in the short history of the modern dance is the close correspondence between concurrent developments in dance and the plastic arts.

Isadora Duncan went back to the Greeks; Humphrey and Graham* used primitive ritual and/or music for structuring, and although the people who came out of the Humphrey-Graham companies and were active during the thirties and forties shared socio-political concerns and activity in common with artists of the period, their work did not reflect any direct influence from or dialogue with the art so much as a reaction to the time. (Those who took off in their own directions in the forties and fifties — Cunningham, Shearer, Litz, Marsicano, et al. — must be appraised individually. Such a task is beyond the scope of this article.) The one previous area of correspondence might be German Expressionism and Mary Wigman and her followers, but photographs and descriptions of the work show little connection.

Within the realm of movement invention — and I am talking for the time being about movement generated by means other than accomplishment of a task or dealing with an object — the most impressive change has been in the attitude to phrasing, which can be defined as the way in which energy is distributed in the execution of a movement or series of movements. What makes one kind of movement different from another is not so much variations in arrangements of parts of the body as differences in energy investment.

It is important to distinguish between real energy and what I shall call "apparent" energy. The former refers to actual output in terms of physical expenditure on the part of the performer. It is common to hear a dance teacher tell a student that he is using "too much energy" or that a particular movement does not require "so much energy". This view of energy is related to a notion of economy and ideal movement technique. Unless otherwise indicated, what I shall be talking about here is "apparent" energy, or what is seen in terms of motion and stillness rather than of actual work, regardless of the physiological or kinesthetic experience of the dancer. The two observations — that of the performer and that of the spectator — do not always correspond. A vivid illustration of this is my *Trio A*: Upon completion two of us are always dripping with sweat while the third is dry. The correct conclu-

---

*In the case of Graham, it is hardly possible to relate her work to anything outside of theatre, since it was usually dramatic and psychological necessity that determined it.

sion to draw is not that the dry one is expending less energy, but that the dry one is a "non-sweater".

Much of the western dancing we are familiar with can be characterized by a particular distribution of energy: maximal output or "attack" at the beginning of a phrase*, recovery at the end, with energy often arrested somewhere in the middle. This means that one part of the phrase — usually the part that is the most still — becomes the focus of attention, registering like a photograph or suspended moment of climax. In the Graham-oriented modern dance these climaxes can come one on the heels of the other. In types of dancing that depend on less impulsive controls, the climaxes are farther apart and are not so dramatically "framed." Where extremes in tempi are imposed, this ebb-and-flow of effort is also pronounced: in the instance of speed the contrast between movement and rest is sharp, and in the adagio, or supposedly continuous kind of phrasing, the execution of transitions demonstrates more subtly the mechanics of getting from one point of still "registration" to another.

The term "phrase" can also serve as a metaphor for a longer or total duration containing beginning, middle, and end. Whatever the implications of a continuity that contains high points or focal climaxes, such an approach now seems to be excessively dramatic and more simply, unnecessary.

Energy has also been used to implement heroic more-than-human technical feats and to maintain a more-than-human look of physical extension, which is familiar as the dancer's muscular "set." In the early days of the Judson Dance Theatre someone wrote an article and asked "Why are they so intent on just being themselves?" It is not accurate to say that everyone at that time had this in mind. (I certainly didn't; I was more involved in experiencing a lion's share of ecstacy and madness than in "being myself" or doing a job.) But where the question applies, it might be answered on two levels: 1) The artifice of performance has been reevaluated in that action, or what one does, is more interesting and important than the exhibition of character and attitude, and that action can best be focused on through the submerging of the personality; so ideally one is not even oneself, one is a neutral "doer." 2) The display of technical virtuosity and the display of the dancer's specialized body no longer make any sense. Dancers have been driven to search for an alternative context that allows for a more matter-of-fact, more concrete, more banal quality of physical being in performance, a context wherein people are engaged in actions and movements making a less spectacular demand on the body and in which skill is hard to locate.

It is easy to see why the *grand jeté* (along with its ilk) had to be abandoned. One cannot "do" a *grand jeté*; one must "dance" it to get it

---

*The term "phrase" must be distinguished from "phrasing." A phrase is simply two or more consecutive movements, while phrasing, as noted previously, refers to the manner of execution.

done at all, i.e., invest it with all the necessary nuances of energy distribution that will produce the look of climax together with a still, suspended extension in the middle of the movement. Like a romantic, overblown plot this particular kind of display — with its emphasis on nuance and skilled accomplishment, its accessibility to comparison and interpretation, its involvement with connoisseurship, its introversion, narcissism, and self-congratulatoriness — has finally in this decade exhausted itself, closed back on itself, and perpetuates itself solely by consuming its own tail.

The alternatives that were explored now are obvious: stand, walk, run, eat, carry bricks, show movies, or move or be moved by some *thing* rather than oneself. Some of the early activity in the area of self-movement utilized games, "found" movement (walking, running, etc.), and people with no previous training. (One of the most notable of these early efforts was Steve Paxton's solo, *Transit*, in which he performed movement by "marking" it. "Marking" is what dancers do in rehearsal when they do not want to expend the full amount of energy required for the execution of a given movement. It has a very special look, tending to blur boundaries between consecutive movements.) These descriptions are not complete. Different people have sought different solutions.

Since I am primarily a dancer, I am interested in finding solutions primarily in the area of moving oneself, however many excursions I have made into pure and not-so-pure thing-moving. In 1964 I began to play around with simple one- and two-motion phrases that required no skill and little energy and contained few accents. The way in which they were put together was indeterminate, or decided upon in the act of performing, because at that time the idea of a different kind of continuity as embodied in transitions or connections between phrases did not seem to be as important as the material itself. The result was that the movements or phrases appeared as isolated bits framed by stoppages. Underscored by their smallness and separateness, they projected as perverse *tours-de-force*. Everytime "elbow-wiggle" came up one felt like applauding. It was obvious that the idea of an unmodulated energy output as demonstrated in the movement was not being applied to the continuity. A continuum of energy was required. Duration and transition had to be considered.

Which brings me to *The Mind is a Muscle, Trio A*. Without giving an account of the drawn-out process through which this four-and-a-half-minute movement series (performed simultaneously by three people) was made, let me talk about its implications in the direction of movement-as-task or movement-as-object.

One of the most singular elements in it is that there are no pauses between phrases. The phrases themselves often consist of separate parts, such as consecutive limb articulations — "right leg, left leg, arms, jump," etc. — but the end of each phrase merges immediately into the beginning of the next with no observable accent. The limbs are never in a fixed, still relationship and they are stretched to their fullest extension only in transit, creating the impression that the body is constantly engaged in transitions.

Another factor contributing to the smoothness of the continuity is that no one part of the series is made any more important than any other. For four and a half minutes a great variety of movement shapes occur, but they are of equal weight and are equally emphasized. This is probably attributable both to the sameness of physical "tone" that colors all the movements and to the attention to the pacing. I can't talk about one without talking about the other.

The execution of each movement conveys a sense of unhurried control. The body is weighty without being completely relaxed. What is seen is a control that seems geared to the *actual* time it takes the *actual* weight of the body to go through the prescribed motions, rather than an adherence to an imposed ordering of time. In other words, the demands made on the body's (actual) energy resources appear to be commensurate with the task — be it getting up from the floor, raising an arm, tilting the pelvis, etc. — much as one would get out of a chair, reach for a high shelf, or walk down stairs when one is not in a hurry.* The movements are not mimetic, so they do not remind one of such actions, but I like to think that in their manner of execution they have the factual quality of such actions.

Of course, I have been talking about the "look" of the movements. In order to achieve this look in a continuity of separate phrases that does not allow for pauses, accents, or stillness, one must bring to bear many different degrees of effort just in getting from one thing to another. Endurance comes into play very much with its necessity for conserving (actual) energy (like the long-distance runner). The irony here is in the reversal of a kind of illusionism: I have exposed a type of effort where it has been traditionally concealed and have concealed phrasing where it has been traditionally displayed.

So much for phrasing. My *Trio A* contained other elements mentioned in the chart that have been touched on in passing, not being central to my concerns of the moment. For example, the "problem" of performance was dealt with by never permitting the performers to confront the audience. Either the gaze was averted or the head was engaged in movement. The desired effect was a worklike rather than exhibitionlike presentation.

I shall deal briefly with the remaining categories on the chart as they relate to *Trio A*. Variation was not a method of development. No one of the individual movements in the series was made by varying a quality of any other one. Each is intact and separate with respect to its nature. In

---

*I do not mean to imply that the demand of musical or metric phrasing makes dancing look effortless. What it produces is a different kind of effort, where the body looks more extended, "pulled up," highly energized, ready to go, etc. The dancer's "set" again.

a strict sense neither is there any repetition (with the exception of occasional consecutive traveling steps). The series progresses by the fact of one discrete thing following another. This procedure was consciously pursued as a change from my previous work, which often had one identical thing following another — either consecutively or recurrently. Naturally the question arises as to what constitutes repetition. In *Trio A*, where there is no consistent consecutive repetition, can the simultaneity of three identical sequences be called repetition? Or can the consistency of energy tone be called repetition? Or does repetition apply only to successive specific actions?

All of these considerations have supplanted the desire for dance structures wherein elements are connected thematically (through variation) and for a diversity in the use of phrases and space. I think two assumptions are implicit here: 1) A movement is a complete and self-contained event; elaboration in the sense of varying some aspect of it can only blur its distinctness; and 2) Dance is hard to see. It must either be made less fancy, or the fact of that intrinsic difficulty must be emphasized to the point that it becomes almost impossible to see.

Repetition can serve to enforce the discreteness of a movement, objectify it, make it more objectlike. It also offers an alternative way of ordering material, literally making the material easier to see. That most theatre audiences are irritated by it is not yet a disqualification.

My *Trio A* dealt with the "seeing" difficulty by dint of its continual and unremitting revelation of gestural detail that did *not* repeat itself, thereby focusing on the fact that the material could not easily be encompassed.

There is at least one circumstance that the chart does not include (because it does not relate to "minimization"), viz., the static singular object versus the object with interchangeable parts. The dance equivalent is the indeterminate performance that produces variations ranging from small details to a total image. Usually indeterminacy has been used to change the sequentialness — either phrases or larger sections — of a work, or to permute the details of a work. It has also been used with respect to timing. Where the duration of separate, simultaneous events is not prescribed exactly, variations in the relationship of these events occur. Such is the case with the trio I have been speaking about, in which small discrepancies in the tempo of individually executed phrases result in the three simultaneous performances constantly moving in and out of phase and in and out of synchronization. The overall look of it is constant from one performance to another, but the distribution of bodies in space at any given instant changes.

I am almost done. *Trio A* is the first section of *The Mind is a Muscle*. There are six people involved and four more sections. *Trio B* might be described as a VARIATION of *Trio A* in its use of unison with three people; they move in exact unison thruout. *Trio A* is about the EF-FORTS of two men and a woman in getting each other aloft in VARIOUS ways while REPEATING the same diagonal SPACE pattern throughout. In *Horses* the group travels about as a unit, recurrently REPEATING six different ACTIONS. *Lecture* is a solo that REPEATS the MOVEMENT series of *Trio A*. There will be at least three more sections.

There are many concerns in this dance. The concerns may appear to fall on my tidy chart as randomly dropped toothpicks might. However, I think there is sufficient separating-out in my work as well as that of certain of my contemporaries to justify an attempt at organizing those points of departure from previous work. Comparing the dance to Minimal Art provided a convenient method of organization. Omissions and overstatements are a hazard of any systematizing in art. I hope that some degree of redress will be offered by whatever clarification results from this essay.

This article was written before the final version of *The Mind is a Muscle* had been made. (*Mat, Stairs,* and *Film* are not discussed.)

THE MIND IS A MUSCLE
by
YVONNE RAINER

at the Anderson Theater April 11, 14, 15, 1968

with

Becky Arnold	William Davis	Harry De Dio
Gay Delanghe	David Gordon	Barbara Lloyd

Steve Paxton   Yvonne Rainer

The approximate running time of the evening is one hour 45 minutes.

interlude #1: Conversation (*Lucinda Childs, William Davis*)

1. Trio A . . . . .William Davis, David Gordon, Steve Paxton
2. Trio B . . . . .Becky Arnold, Gay Delanghe, Barbara Lloyd

interlude #2: Dimitri Tiomkin (*Dial M for Murder*)

3. Mat then . . . . .Becky Arnold, William Davis
      Stairs . . . . .David Gordon, Steve Paxton, Yvonne Rainer

interlude #3: Henry Mancini (*The Pink Panther*)

4. Act . . . . Harry De Dio
      Group

INTERMISSION

interludes #4: The Greenbriar Boys (*Amelia Earhart's Last Flight*)
      #5: Silence (6 minutes)
      #6: Frank Sinatra (*Strangers in the Night*)
      #7: Conversation (continued)

5. Trio A^1 . . . . William Davis, David Gordon, Steve Paxton
6. Horses . . . . Group

interlude #8: John Giorno (*Pornographic Poem*)

7. Film . . . . Group
      Foot Film by Bud Wirtschafter; Hand Film by William Davis
8. Lecture . . . . Yvonne Rainer

interlude #9: Jefferson Airplane (*She Has Funny Cars*)

STATEMENT

(It is not necessary to read this prior to observation.)

The choices in my work are predicated on my own peculiar resources — obsessions of imagination, you might say — and also on an ongoing argument with, love of, and contempt for dancing. If my rage at the impoverishment of ideas, narcissism, and disguised sexual exhibitionism of most dancing can be considered puritan moralizing, it is also true that I love the body — its actual weight, mass, and unenhanced physicality. It is my overall concern to reveal people as they are engaged in various kinds of activities — alone, with each other, with objects — and to weight the quality of the human body toward that of objects and away from the superstylization of the dancer. Interaction and cooperation on the one hand; substantiality and inertia on the other. Movement invention, i.e. "dancing" in a strict sense, is but one of the several factors in the work.

Although the formal concerns vary in each section of THE MIND IS A MUSCLE, a general statement can be made. I am often involved with changes as they are played against one or more constants: Details executed in a context of a continuum of energy (Trio A, Mat); phrases and combinations done in unison (Trio B); interactive and mutually dependent movements done in a singular floor pattern (Trio A^1); changing floor patterns and movement configurations carried out by a group moving as a single unit (Film, Horses); changes in a group configuration occurring around a constant central area of focus (Act); and more obvious juxtapositions that involve actual separations in space and time.

The condition for the making of my stuff lies in the continuation of my interest and energy. Just as ideological issues have no bearing on the nature of the work, neither does the tenor of current political and social conditions have any bearing on its execution The world disintegrates around me. My connection to the world-in-crisis remains tenuous and remote. I can foresee a time when this remoteness must necessarily end, though I cannot foresee exactly when or how the relationship will change, or what circumstances will incite me to a different kind of action. Perhaps nothing short of universal female military conscription will affect my function (The ipso facto physical fitness of dancers will make them the first victims.); or a call for a world-wide cessation of individual functions, to include the termination of genocide. This statement is not an apology. It is a reflection of a state of mind that reacts with horror and disbelief upon seeing a Vietnamese shot dead on TV — not at the sight of death, however, but at the fact that the TV can be shut off afterwards as after a bad Western. My body remains the enduring reality.

Yvonne Rainer
March, 1968

Interlude No. 1   (first event in the M is a M)

Conversation (on tape)

He	You have a strong belly.
She	Oh, yes . . . hm. Yours is pretty hard . . . What did you like about that movie?
He	Well, when I first saw it I thought I liked — uh — the camera, the — the way the image kept moving around all the time, kept very close up.
She	M-hm . . . like running? . . the running in the begin . . .
He	Well, when that guy was on the bicycle.
She	Oh yeh, yeh . . . like you didn't know what happened to him . .
He	Yeh.
She	. . . the camera went *with* him.
he	And I guess I liked — uh — the fact that the story really developed into some kind of plot and yet there were no real incidents in the showing of anything that made that plot develop that way, it seemed.
She	M-hm.
He	You didn't see those moments you usually see that account for a plot.
She	You didn't see the moments between the man and the woman that made for that outcome.
He	Yeh, but you saw scenes between them.
She	Yeh yeh, that was curious. Usually that would strike you as — as being unreal — that the plot didn't lead up to that.
He	Yeh, I know, but this doesn't — or didn't . . .
She	No.
He	. . . because you had a sense of it somehow, or — it — I don't know — it seemed to feel like you could be convinced of the plot.
She	M-hm. It really had some beautiful things in there, like playing of Verdi . . .
He	Yeh.
She	. . . Macbeth — and the action takes place in the Opera House and all — in the audience — and they applaud — and out in the — out in the lobby and the aisles and all that . . .
He	Yeh.
She	. . . but the opera just goes on . . .
He	Yeh.
She	. . . just like a recording of the opera superimposed over the whole environment of opera, like the whole place — you get — is saturated with the music.
He	I thought they used it just about as good as *Sandlot's Flight*.
She	Yeh (laughter). I was thinking of that . . . say . . . aria — there's

72

a particular aria . . . Hey! Are you putting some propaganda here? No wonder you said that. (Raucous laughter from both) Come on, please.

He   Oh, what I really liked was seeing the car go by all those villas and — and then accounting — or — you know, like — you got a picture of that room by just those things she said and it had absolutely nothing to do with the action, but you're just looking out this car window.

She   I don't even know what she was saying at that point.

He   She was saying don't — don't probe . . .

She   O yeh yeh.

He   . . . and she was realizing that he was in love with her and that . . .

She   Yeh.

He   . . . he hadn't said anything, but he just looked at her in a certain way and . . .

She   Yeh yeh.

He   . . . she was saying I don't know what it means and — and — like she was pessimistic from the very beginning.

She   Yeh yeh, but that's been done — all that looking out of the car and talking.

He   But you didn't see them at all.

She   I mean, what goes by the car window.

He   Well, I liked seeing that — those villas.

She   What I liked was when the old guy — Puck . . .

He   Yeh, I liked that too.

She   . . . when he's talking about all this is going to be gone and no more guns and no more hunting and no more poplar trees.

He   Yeh — it was so grandiose.

She   And you get all these different images of that country and all of a sudden . . .

He   Yeh.

She   . . . an aerial view of it too while he's still on the ground . . . mm . . . But I found that pretty erotic — the . . . I mean that was the turning point for me. It started out as another . . . like a very Antonioni-ish . . .

He   Yeh. Well I guess it was — a lot of those elements were very much like . . .

She   . . . serious young man and his . . .

He   . . . Antonioni . . .

She   . . . conversations.

He   . . . and certainly she was like an Antonioni woman . . .

She   Yeh.

He   . . . I mean, she didn't know what she wanted.

She   Yeh — that kind of non-sequitur talking . . .

He   Yeh.

She   . . . and laughing and . . .

He   Yeh — and non-sequitur actions . . .

She	Yeh — the — yeh — the — the eyeglasses . . .
He	. . . going with that guy to that hotel.
She	Mm, m-hm — yeh. Why'd she do that — what — yeh. Yeh, what was she all about? I mean, that . . .
He	She didn't know . . .
She	. . . because that's a . . .
He	. . . except that she — well, she — you knew that she was a bored rich lady.
She	Well, did you know that?
He	Sure. When he said "What do you do in Milan," she said "Nothing." She plays the triangle, she takes baths, she — you know.
She	That was a pun, you know, because evidently she was going with a married man — the guy she called — there was some reference to his family, his wife.
He	Oh no, but I thought that was her psychiatrist, because . . .
She	Ohhh.

Some non-chronological recollections of *The Mind is a Muscle*

Trio A was first performed at Judson Church, Jan. 10, 1966, as *The Mind is a* 20
Muscle, Part 1. My memories of rehearsing it for that particular performance have
merged with other rehearsal memories, some very recent. At that time it was performed by Steve Paxton, David Gordon, and me. I remember showing it to David
for the first time; he expressed doubts about being able to execute it in the
proper style. Now I say anyone can master the style, or just about anyone. I
didn't have a concept of that possibility in 1966. At one session something David
was doing looked strange to me. I asked him what kind of imagery he was using.
He said "I'm thinking of myself as a faun." I said "Try thinking of yourself as a
barrel." More recently I had a similar experience with John Erdman, only at a
different point in the dance. John had learned part of *Trio A* from Barbara Lloyd,
who is the only person, to my knowledge, who was never officially 'taught'
Trio A, but, rather, picked it up entirely on her own by observing me, Steve,
David, and Becky Arnold. On inquiring how Barbara had described a particular
movement, John said "bird-like". I re-taught it to him as "airplane-like."

The photo of that early performance shows wooden slats on the floor. They were
hurled one at a time with metronome-like regularity from the balcony of the
church for the duration of the dance (nine minutes, or *Trio A* done twice). They
constituted the original 'music' for *Trio A*. Audience members complained afterwards about the relentlessness of this 'music'. It may have been at this performance that a man sitting in the front row picked up a slat, attached a large white
handkerchief to it, and waved it over his head. I retained the slats as an accompaniment for *Trio A* through the Anderson Theater performance (Apr. '68).
Even before that *Trio A* had begun the first of its many transmogrifications. At
Judson (5-24-66) it was done by David, Bill Davis, and me as the first section of a
four-part *Mind is a Muscle*. The slats were reserved for the fourth section called
Lecture, which was a special version of *Trio A* tailored to the balletic talents of 21
Peter Saul. While teaching it to him, wherever possible I stuck in a pirouette or
jump. Peter was unavailable for the Anderson show. I was stuck. I had grandiose
fantasies of Jacques D'Amboise appearing at the end from nowhere to do a bra-
vura *Trio A*. Next in line (in my fantasy dance) was Merce Cunningham. I became
obsessed with this idea and eventually proposed it to him at a party. He laugh-
ingly declined. I finally did it myself in tap shoes (minus the balletic furbelows)
with the slats shot in from a ladder in the wings, and with a wooden grid that
filled the proscenium space descending in the middle of the solo. It stayed down 22
for one minute, then ascended out of sight. I had the same ambivalence about
decor I had about music: It shouldn't hang around too long, and the more grand
the effect the briefer the appearance.

20 First performance of *The Mind is a Muscle*, Part I, Judson Church, Jan. 10, 1966 – Steve, David, Y.R.

21 *Lecture* in the short version of *The Mind is a Muscle*, Judson Church, May 24, 1966 – Peter Saul

In the final version of *The Mind is a Muscle* the white motif appeared again: In each section a different person wore all white. Everyone had a chance to be a 'star' — at least in appearance. Another carry-over from *Terrain* was the business of inactive performers watching — in view of the audience — the active performers. I hated the 'magic' of entrances and exits, the nowhere or imaginary 'somewhere' of the wings, or off-stage area. In *Terrain*'s *Solo Section* the street barricade had provided an expedient and decorative observation post. At the Anderson Theater the inactive ones simply stood quietly at the back of the stage. I seem to have persisted with this device despite the complaints of my performers about 'getting cold'. Now we do a brief warm-up in view of the audience. Those of us with dance training.

When I first began teaching *Trio A* to anyone who wanted to learn it — skilled, unskilled, professional, fat, old, sick, amateur — and gave tacit permission to anyone who wanted to teach it to teach it, I envisioned myself as a post-modern dance evangelist bringing movement to the masses, watching with Will Rogers-like benignity the slow, inevitable evisceration of my elitist creation. Well, I finally met a *Trio A* I didn't like. It was 5th generation, and I couldn't believe my eyes. *40*

38, 104

Trio A at the Anderson was for 3 men doing it simultaneously but not in unison. Behind them was a highly reflective wall of mylar stretching from wing to wing and floor to flies. It was 'flown' halfway thru *Trio B*. This was a hold-over from the Washington "Now Festival" performance (April '66) for which I had had built an accordion-paneled wall of mirrors. Situated at the proper distance — rather close — one could observe simultaneously a performer walking from left to right and his multiple reflections — some of them walking in the same direction and some of them in the opposite direction. Seated two feet beyond this ideal vantage point, however, you saw absolutely nothing in the mirrors. Since the "Now Festival" took place in a roller skating rink, no one sat in the right place to benefit from the mirrors. And, of course, back in NY at the Anderson the stage was elevated, so that particular mirror arrangement was out of the question. My first fiasco.

Trio B was a series of runs and athletic traveling movements performed in unison by three women — Becky, Gay Delanghe, and Barbara. At stage left, running up and down stage, were two three-foot-wide strips of bubble-wrap and half-inch black rubber. This 'decor' derived directly from my having performed in Steve Paxton's *Afternoon* of 1963, an outdoor piece which required us to execute difficult Cunningham-like movement in mushy soil. Though at the time I had been quite outraged by the difficulties posed, I later became fascinated with the idea. At the Anderson the different surfaces made for a change in the sound of the feet as well as a visible change in effort, depending on the particular movement. The bubbles in the bubble-wrap popped delightfully. During the first part of this trio, which was all running, one of the performers counted aloud continuously to indicate the number of steps taken in any given direction. *(page 94)* 23

22 *Lecture* at the Anderson Theater, April, 1968 — Y.R.

23 *Trio B* — Barbara, Gay Delanghe, Becky Arnold

Mat was a continuation of the *Trio A* aesthetic: two people doing the same sequence out of synch. It was a sequence that involved a 4x8-foot foam rubber mat and a 12-pound black dumbbell and incorporated various kinds of rolls, hand- and headstands, and re-positionings of the body and dumbbell in relation to the mat — all executed in the same evenly paced, rhythmically uninflected dynamic. It was one of my favorite dances to do; there was something very satisfying about the constant return to the mat and the subtle adjustments of effort required in handling one's weight with and without the dumbbell. At the Anderson Theater it was performed by Becky and Bill. (*page 96*)

For the record, *Mat* had an earlier debut: Bill and Becky did it on a Choreoconcert at the New School in September 1967. It was preceded by a tape of my voice reading a letter from a Denver doctor to a New York surgeon describing in technical medical terms the details of the gastro-intestinal illness with which I was hospitalized at the time of this performance. It was one of many attempts to deal — via my profession — with the natural catastrophe that had befallen my body. It was using autobiography as a 'found object' without any stylistic transformation. I don't think I could do that today, at least in an instance where the biographical details belonged so exclusively to my experience, as in the case of that particular letter.

24 Becky finishes *Mat* as *Stairs* begins

25

26

27 *Stairs*

Stairs (*page 100*) had a strange origin: I had gotten out of the hospital weak as a 25, 26, 27 fly after the above-mentioned illness. Partly to keep busy I worked with Becky and Bill, having them 'learn' my watery-legged movement as I shakily negotiated running, crawling, getting from a chair to a high stool and back down again. After the first session I got the idea of a staircase with two stairs the exact height of the chair and stool and wide enough to accomodate two people climbing at the same time. The next day a friend, June Ekman, told me about a dream she had in which she couldn't figure out why Becky, Bill, and I were having so much diffi-culty climbing a staircase with tiny steps. As a result I added two 'tiny steps' at the top of my staircase, then later carpeted it and put it on wheels so that it could be moved around. This section had funny sexual references in it: David, Steve, and I took turns pulling or assisting each other up, down, and off the stairs by means of passing one hand through the other's legs and holding the crotch, or — in my case — they each placed a hand on a breast and so supported my torso as I jumped from the top step. I couldn't decide whether to perform this 'fly-in-the-ointment' (in an otherwise formal and 'dignified' sequence of manoeuvers) in a nonchalant manner or underscore its eccentricity still further by some kind of facial response on the part of the person whose privates were touched. We tried various 'responses' — from subtle to exaggerated — and finally we each did what seemed most comfortable: David and I responded less and less, while Steve con- 28 tinued to show a startled expression whenever it happened to him.

28

29

30 *Act* – Harry De Dio on the left

82

About *Act*: I had originally wanted a gymnast to offset the low-keyed imagery of 29, 30, 31 our tableaux on the other side of the stage. I had actually auditioned an acrobat. It just didn't seem right. For one thing the duration of most gymnastic or acrobatic routines was much shorter than I required. Again I was involved with a kind of imagery — static and slow to change — that I felt required a certain amount of time to 'register' on an audience. Harry De Dio and his magic act proved to be just the ticket as far as time went, and his facile manipulation of small objects was an unexpected foil for our careful repositioning of bodies, foam rubber mat, and two swings. My notes read: "Something is always happening — separated by momentary stillness — but only one thing at a time. It is like *Carriage Discreteness*. In the latter the hand of God changed the hugely dispersed configuration into a slightly different configuration. In *Act* the participants themselves re-arrange the configuration, always returning to positions of neutrality, i.e., quietly observing a central focal point while at ease, but perfectly still, in a standing, sitting, or lying down posture, from which they can observe the rest of the configuration. Instructions are given improvisationally by each in a pre-set order to the rest of the group while the 'instructor' remains perfectly immobile. Eye movements are essential in order to maintain a look of attentiveness rather than self-absorption. This section is about changes in a configuration rather than about movement. The changes are made with quiet efficiency." Hand signals were given to the stage manager when an 'instructor' wanted the level of the swings changed, to the stage manager when an 'instructor' wanted the level of the swings changed. It took awhile to figure out in rehearsal what this section was about, which — in view of my then premeditative working methods — was somewhat unusual for me. After repeated and disagreeable vetoing of the groups' efforts at fulfilling my instructions, it finally dawned on me that I did not want intermittent movement 'invention' but changes in static relationships of objects and people, which brought it into the realm of 'tableau' and 'task' rather than 'dance'.

31 *Act*

Interlude No. 7

Conversation (continued)

He   . . . part of that conversation she said "You should have treated me." . . .

She   Oh Oh.

He   . . . you shouldn't have sent me away.

She   She was — I see.

He   So I thought that reinforced it even more . . .

She   Oh, I thought that was her lover, I thought . . .

He   . . . that she was an idle . . .

She   I see — yeh, yeh.

He   . . . rich girl. Yeh.

She   I thought it was her married lover.

He   I took it as her psychiatrist.

She   Yeh. (pause)

He   When did it start to get erotic?

She   Oh, they . . . he's helped her with shopping and they come home and her beads break . . .

He   Yeh.

She   . . . and . . . and then they go to bed, and you think they go, they've gone to bed together, and then you realize they're in separate beds . . .

He	Yeh.
She	. . . and she's feeling herself up . . .
He	Yeh.
She	. . . and then you see him and he's, his fingers are in his mouth — and then all of a sudden he's bending over her. There's . . .
He	Yeh.
She	. . . a shot of her and then he's there . . . and — then that first kiss . . . Oh — and they're dancing — that's not the first one . . . yeh, the first time you see them kiss — the next day she's propped in a chair and talking about how all they do is — in Parma — is . . . Is that the name of the place? . . .
He	M-hm.
She	. . . eat and then talk about eating — it makes a double job of it — and then she puts on a record and they dance — and — uh — . . . All those close-ups — that's very erotic.
He	Yeh.
She	All those close-ups — just . . .
He	You can see the face — yeh.
She	. . . flesh touching flesh — I mean, they — there's no other way to — really to get that sensuality, I guess . . . and then their mouths together — you know — they hardly moved, but it's all there — you know . . .
He	M-hm.
She	. . . you just get swallowed up in that kiss. (pause) I don't know why it — I mean, why talk — think of the — more it seems like Antonioni in that kind of ennui. But then it was different because it . . . in Antonioni you're caught in some episode in people's lives where nothing happens . . .
He	M-hm
She	. . . really — like they don't resolve anything or — or learn anything. They don't know anything more at the end than at the beginning, do they? . . .
He	mmm
She	. . . like in Eclipse and in L'Aventura. — Or if they do know something, they may . . . he doesn't tell you. But this had just the right amount of — for me . . . some kind of — like the fact they changed or did something different from what . . .
He	Yeh.
She	. . . the beginning of the picture indicated . . . not like the . . . seems to me . . . . . that shift is important to me. (long pause) And its so true about radicalism or revolutionary ideology being for many people a sort of holiday — like Gina was a . . .
He	Yeh.
She	. . . an interlude for him.
He	Everything was. I mean — uh — also I guess it's a story of some-body failing. He failed his friend — he felt. He . . .
She	Yeh
He	. . . killed himself. He failed in the Party; the ideology failed him, or he couldn't somehow accept it.

She	Yeh.
He	He failed with this woman and he went back to something he said in the beginning he was leaving.
She	Yeh . . . yeh . . yeh, it's not a happy ending, it's . . . What is the last shot?
He	Of her kissing the . . .
She	Oh, she's kissing the younger brother, yeh.
He	. . . younger brother.
She	That's very strange . . . . Did you find her erotic?
He	As a person, no, not so much, but some of her behaviour was.
She	Yeh . . . and her body?
He	No, she — she was erotic, but she wasn't very sensual.
She	She wasn't?
He	I didn't think so.
She	Gee, I thought she was . . . Her hair, God that . . .
He	Yes, her hair was nice.
She	. . . marvelous hair — so soft — and the way she used it. (pause) That's a real movie woman. I mean, it's a whole thing about the way women are in the . . . . and that kind of des — erotic desperation . . . and it all, it all zeroes in on sex . . . all, the whole, the anxiety, everything about the person, they become — uh — isn't that so — uh — I mean, don't you feel the sexuality of the woman is — is the most and strongest part of her?
He	No, I don't think so.
She	No? I always feel that, that what — what movies do to these women — like Antonioni women too, Monica Vitti. Their bodies are so important . . .
He	Well, this woman didn't have much of a body.
She	. . . the way the camera focuses. Well, what she did with it was . . . mm . . . . .
He	No, I don't think that she was terribly sensual, or that — that was the main — main part of her. It seemed like she was someone who didn't have any particular focus . . . But — uh — I don't know, it didn't seem like she was focused on sex. (pause)
She	mm . . . All that tossing around of that hair and the recl — everytime she was still she was in some kind of sensual — uh, uh — erotic attitude — you know — like slung across a chair or . . .
He	Yeh, but she had a kind of nervousness that . . .
She	Yeh, but that's . . .
He	that made you kind of discount that.
She	. . . that's . . . that's like a mare trying to get away from a horse — or something, isn't it? I mean, animals have that too when they're being courted. (pause) He said he wanted to fill her with vitality, and left her only with anxiety. (long long pause) . . . I liked seeing it . . . Why did you want to see it again? For what . . .
He	Well . . .

She	. . . Was there something about the guy that . . .
He	I guess when I saw it the first time I didn't get r . . there right at the beginning . . .
She	Uh-huh
He	. . . So I didn't really realize his involvement politically until the end . . .
She	Uh-huh
He	. . . So that it seemed as though there were — the story was much more disjointed than it was.
She	I see . . . I didn't understand his friend, I mean, that really was very fragmentary.
He	M-hm, but it was even more fragmentary when I saw it . . .
She	Yeh.
He	. . . not from the beginning.
She	But he was trying to get his friend to join the party, and why — why should the guy be so shaken up by that? Well not, evidently not by that.
He	No.
She	There were other things. Yeh. Oh, those washes of light. Yeh — the photography.
He	Yeh.
She	It looked like an old scratchy film; I think it was a bad print, all those scr — you know, those — that rain-like effect and scratches — but then these washed-out . . . misty . . . images . . . (long pause) Do you want another drink? You still have some.
He	You want some.
She	No . . . mm.
He	Yes
She	No . . . mm . . . You liked seeing it again.
He	M-hm
She	Mm . . . Guess I was just in a mood for something like that.
He	m-hm
She	I mean — well, sometimes I'm in — like I feel very . . . responsive to things — I mean, I'm either quite dead, or I feel like my pores are open. That's what I was saying this morning — like it takes just a little bit of a certain kind of thinking to feel that it's all so dreadful and grim — one's life . . .
He	M-hm
She	. . . and then suddenly somehow it — maybe it just has to do with . . . it takes just a little bit of another kind of thinking to feel that it's quite all right — and even more than that. So, when you start thinking that way, then — I mean everything starts feeding in and — and supporting that way of thinking and confirming it. I mean, something in the NY Times, a subway ride, and the wind on one's face, and . . . a movie — that . . it seems like those things are . . . Do you ever feel that way?
He	M-hm.
She	Kind of . . . pregnant — mm?

He	I guess I haven't for awhile.
She	I felt that way today — like I was . . . I guess I sort of have this passive thing — I feel like a receptacle a lot of the time. Sometimes the top's on (laughter) and then when the lid is off then all kinds of things come in.
He	It's hard for me to know how you feel all the time.
She	A lot of the time?
He	M-hmm.
She	Well, I — a lot of the time I feel I . . . Why, what have you been thinking I'm feeling?
He	Like — I don't know, maybe I haven't been very attuned to you lately.
She	M-hm. Yeh, I knew that. Since we got back. Maybe we've had a vacation from each other.
He	Yeh
She	I enjoyed being with you today.

32 *Trio A*[1] in the short version of *The Mind is a Muscle* at Judson Church, May 5, 1966 — Y.R., David, Bill

33 *M-Walk* in *Horses*

Trio A' (*page 102*) — originally for two men and one woman and later for three   32
men — mainly involved traveling back and forth on a diagonal between two mattresses, also two people getting the third one aloft in various ways, some of them
quite spectacular. I had dreams of flying then, as I had earlier momentarily in the
no. 7 of *Diagonal* of *Terrain,* and later in the *Group Hoist* of *Continuous Project*   52
— *Altered Daily*. It was definitely an extension — or inversion — of the ballerina
fantasy. Later the women would again participate equally in getting the men into
the air. It just took more than one to do it. (*page 134*)

I don't remember much about *Film* except that it was very complicated to learn   34, 35, 36, 37
and made heavy demands on rote memory. It was all about traveling as a herd
— (as was the improvised *Horses* preceding it) with 10- and 20-count halts, always   33
behind a screen on which was projected a movie of legs from the knee down
walking up to a volleyball. The projected image dominated the downstage center
area, and when we were directly behind it our own legs, very small in comparison
and from the hip down, appeared below the screen. Most of the traveling was on
diagonals. (*page 103*)

At a concert prior to the Anderson (Brandeis University, Jan.13, 1968) *The
Mind is a Muscle* was presented in a slightly different order and without *Stairs*.
Toward the end some audience members became quite unruly, almost abusive.
There were others, some of whom later came to study and work with me, who
said that *The Mind is a Muscle* changed their concept of dance. ("When we went
out in the lobby and asked someone where the cafeteria was and he pointed, we
all broke up.") Several even said it changed their lives.

34

35

36 *Film*

Drawings from notebook

37 *Film* – David in Nijinsky pose

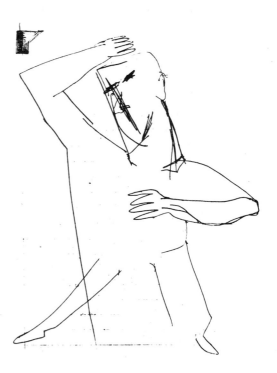

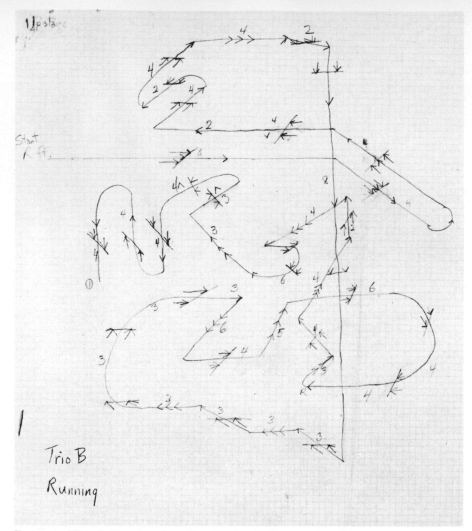

First part of *Trio B*, floorplan of running. Numbers indicate number of steps.

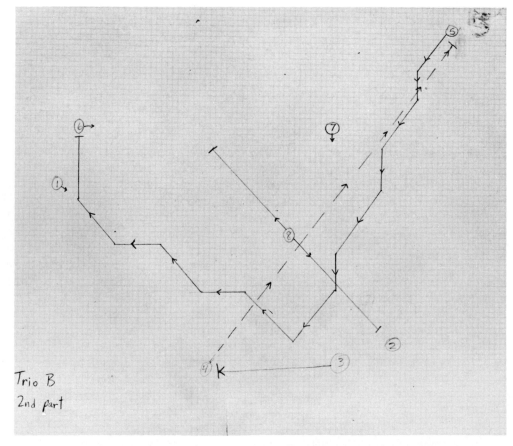

Second part of *Trio B*, floorplan. Numbers correspond to notebook entries on facing page.

2. Trio B

I. Running
   Before 1. (below), run in

II. 1. Walk, walk, run, run, walk combination, moving upst.,
      d.s. r. diag., str. across to left. It goes into
  2. Skip, skip, bent-leg (r.) ronde-de-jambe combo. It
      goes into
  3. Curve back against 1. croisé bent leg, then veers back   23
      as leg straightens, 1st position, 1. leg lunges to
      side and torso drops over to r. bent knee, etc. ends
      in cartwheel.
  4. Walk on heels upst. diag. 1.
  5. Run – 5 steps diag., 3 steps front in V formation
  6. "Sixes"
      a. Ordinary
      b. Step on left to s.r. Continue to turn r. and
         finish s.l.
      c. Step on s.l., pivot backwards in same direc-
         tion.
      d. Step to s.r., pivot forwards and continue
         to s.l.
      e. Step to s.l. on left and right feet, then
         reverse direction on last step, then reverse
         direction to start a. again.
      f. Step backwards to stage r., pivot forwards on
         left foot and finish to stage 1.
  7. 3 kinds of skips going into 1,2,3,4, and 5, and 6 and

  8. ↓ sideways skittering

    ↑ running backwards

    ↓ 2 steps in demi-plié, 2 in parallel ½ – toe

    ↑ sidewards skitter and sidewards leap

    ↓ hip-swivel run with scrunching of torso

3. Mat

5½ minutes

(props: 4' x 8' foam rubber, one 12-lb. dumbbell)

1. Face front. Squat and in even succession:
   a. put hands flat on mat, fingers toward each other
   b. encircle legs with arms
   c. keel over forward, placing hands so that crown of head can touch mat.
2. Sit on l. hip, swing over to right hip bringing bent knees to r. of body. Roll onto r. knee; get up by putting weight on l. foot; walk 3 steps - l., r., l., to face r. with feet together.
3. Stoop, grasp mat both hands, bend it forward (about 1½ feet) while shifting weight in squat to r. foot. Return.
4. Somersault. Legs remain straight and come down slowly. Back comes to rounded sit with palms flat on mat. Torso rolls down to flat recline, r. arm raises overhead and behind head. Stretch arm and roll to l. one complete turn - l. hand flat against hip. As come to rest a) r. arm moves 45° to rest palm down on mat. b) Str. legs raise up perpendicular. c) swing legs directly to r. d) bring l. hand across to exert pressure for e) raise hips by swinging r. hand to proper position off mat on floor and f) straighten body - hips still off floor and body in side relation to floor - as l. arm comes to l. side.
5. Roll onto stomach and walk on all fours backwards - hand hand knee knee hand, etc. Stand. Walk around mat to r.: r.l.r.l., squat at d.s. r. corner with r. foot forward. Bend corner of mat over l. hand. Release. Walk - l., lunge down onto r. foot in order to grasp d.s. l. corner. Roll mat back and shift weight backward onto l. foot with r. leg becoming more straight. Return. Place l. knee on mat, recline on l. side. Register position: legs bent flat to l., l. shoulder and hip on floor, r. hip off, r. shoulder off, arms bent and overhead, hands toward each other, gaze up and to l.
6. Get up: hands to l. of body, weight on bent l. foot, r. foot stretched along edge of mat. Shift direction to r. and walk hands forward in order to shift weight onto r. Just before getting up grasp weight in r. hand.
7. Pivot on r. foot to face s.l. and place l. foot on d.s. side of mat. Swing r. around and place on upst. side of mat. Once more l., once more r.
8. Sit on upper l. corner of mat, placing weight on floor just before sitting. Encircle knees with arms. Roll back - arms str. out along sides of body, palms down - shooting legs str. up - r. leg str. and l. turned - out bent. Roll over

so weight is on l. knee, r. leg stretched behind. Swing
r. leg around so foot rests loosely on floor beside mat,
leg bent, and weight rests on l. heel tucked under buttock.
Pivot on r. foot to reverse direction to face d.s. r. Bring
l. knee forward, put weight on it as l. foot folds up
behind, r. knee tucks to l. of l. knee while r. foot also
tucks up. In other words: the weight is on the crossed knees
while both feet are as high off the floor as possible.

9. Go forward onto r. elbow. Roll to r. to register position:
Face upst. legs crossed - l. over r.; recline on elbows
placed to rear (d.s.) of hips. Uncross legs. Push weight onto
l. bent leg - l. foot on floor upst. of mat - as r. foot
and str. leg swing around - passing thru [squat on l. while
2 arms (face s.r.) parallel to l. of body and str. r. leg
extended upst.] Final position: face s.r. in squat, weight
forward onto r. foot, hands on floor at either side of body.

10. Walk back on arms along edge of mat on floor. Lie flat.
Roll torso onto mat all the way onto chest - arms under
chest - follow thru with head turning to l. to look upst.
Return to lie on back, hands clasped across mid-section.

11. Bring bent knees to chest, shift knees to l. to rest
on mat, straighten legs so that they are at r. angle
to torso, reach r. arm as far as possible so it is parallel
to legs. Keeping head and shoulders as much as possible
on mat, pull weight over onto knees, feet off floor. Rock
back onto tops of feet, push onto bottoms of feet in squat,
stand up, facing upst. l. corner.

12. Plié into squat, place hands in front on mat, shift knees
to l., sit on l. hip. Shift onto both hips so as to face
front (d.s.) with knees bent up and feet off floor.
Straighten legs to rest on mat. Just before or as feet
come to rest, hands rest at either side of hips - palms
down, fingers d.s. Buckle l. elbow, roll back so l. shoulder
touches floor, look to l. over shoulder at floor. Sit,
hands braced on mat to rear of hips. Push weight forward
onto feet while wobbling knees l.r.l.r. On last one
shift onto r. foot and change direction by bringing l. foot
around beside r. foot which is rolled over on inside arch,
focus down at r. foot, direction upst. l. corner. Stand by
wobbling knees - or rotating them once clockwise before
they become straight. Direction is still upst. l. Parallel
arm swing with tight fist: str. out in front elbows shoot
back, fists lead out to front so that arms swing in big arc
out, down and back. Swing back up to forward position and
repeat.

13. Step to end of mat to face l. Place hands for head stand.
Stand up. Take one step (r.) onto mat and do swift somersault, standing up at other end with weight in l. hand.
Face front and plié in quasi - 4th with r. foot forward and
weight on outside of r. foot on mat. Rise. Change direction
to r. - standing at end of mat. Plié placing knees on mat.
Rise. Change direction to r. - standing at end of mat. Plié

placing knees on mat. Rise. Take 2 steps upst. (r.-l.)
across corner of mat. Plié in parallel 4th with l. foot
forward.

Take 2 steps (r.-l.) in small arc to l. to face l. Go down
on l. foot with r. leg stretched str. in front, r. hand on
mat, l. hand releasing weight on floor. Return r. leg so
that position is registered: Facing front, squat - both
feet parallel, hands grasping mat centrally on either side
of hips. Stand - still grasping mat. Turn mat over. Kneel
on it on r. knee. Begin to keel to l. on l. elbow - <u>hands
still in same position grasping mat</u>. Roll over onto back
pulling mat diagonally across body. Release grasp to rest
hands under head. Grasp mat again. Roll onto l. elbow, then
l. hip; get both hips on floor; push feet straight d.s. so
that mat flips over as torso is erect and then rolls down
to back. Raise mat by straightening arms. Lower. Throw mat
up. Immediately roll to r. onto stomach. Get up facing
upst. so that mat slides off back. Face d.s. and adjust
position of mat.

14. Walk to r. end of mat. Pick up, walk forward raising hands
above head; walk backward, lowering mat to floor. Take one
step (r.) onto mat with arms forward and bent ready to do
roll-over and roll - back with rearing up to head - stand
on way back. R. foot lands 1st, step back on l., then r.
Walk forward on left knee, then r. knee, then stand via
l. foot.

15. Stand facing l. at end of mat. Start to sit and at the same
time looking behind - alternating sides. Sit with knees
bent, feet on floor. Straighten legs on floor, recline with
palms outstretched behind, raise knees - feet still on
floor, grasp knees by extending arms to them and draw them
up into a relaxed bicycle position. Do a pumping movement
as legs descend and body rolls to l. Staying in as
compressed a ball as possible place r. knee on mat (to
l. of body, or s.r.), grasp dumbbell, and "walk" forward
- to s.r. - extending body out from r. knee - face down -
by rolling dumbbell with r. hand and walking l. hand.
Dumbbell is released at extreme forward reach of r. arm. As
body comes to rest knees are bent with feet crossed -
l. behind r.

16. Walk back via hands onto knees - feet still crossed. Sit
- in transit on crossed feet; sit on butt with feet crossed
in front. Roll back changing positions of arms and hands
4 times on floor:
1. Arms straight in back palms on floor
2. Palms up
3. Palms down with forearms parallel to sides
4. Palms up with forearms parallel to ears. Start to
   uncross legs - l. foot moves up and over, body rises,
   l. foot is on floor - weight on r. heel is shifted to
   butt with r. leg doubled turned in and flat on mat.
   (Direction is upst.) Roll l. knee to l. side, shift

weight to l. knee, register position: weight on l. knee
and r. foot with r. leg bent and r. foot forward –
direction s.r. – r. hand on floor at side and r. hand
on r. knee with fingers d.s. and elbow up. Stand. Walk
l., r., stoop to pick up dumbbell. Walk to end of mat
and face s.l. Do arm swings with dumbbell in r. hand
Place dumbbell on floor.

17. Walk back – r., l., then forward r., l. Do cartwheel
handstand (to left side). Goal is to briefly register
handstand facing audience. Descend by releasing l. hand,
reversing direction to land in crouch facing d.s. Walk along
edge of mat toward s.r. Reverse direction after one
circumference. Walk in spiral until come to rest facing   24
upst. in center of mat.

3. <u>Stairs</u>

(starts when Becky does handstand.)

I. 1. All 3 walk up and jump off
    2. All 3 walk up and 2 jump off, D descends sitting
    3. All 3 walk up and S jumps off, Y and D descend
        sitting
    4. All 3 walk up and 3 walk down then turn stairs
    5. All 3 walk up and Y and S walk down, D jumps
    6. All 3 walk up and Y walks down, and D and S jump
    7. All 3 walk up and D walks down, Y sits and S jumps
    8. All 3 walk up and D and S walk down, Y sits

II.   (Stairs are moved while D walks up and down)

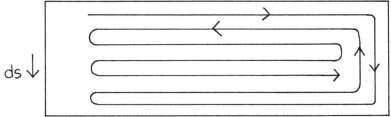

ending with assisted leg boost, stairs facing ↑
and moving from upst. to d.s.
Turn stairs around for III:

III. ds. 1.

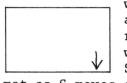

Steve hand stand - David grabs his legs
while Y gets foam, places, rolls down D
and S come front, push mat as D and S
rejoin Y, breast-hold while she alone
walks up and jumps. S and Y replace foam,
S and Y help D somersault up; Y removes
mat as S moves stairs to upst. center (while D does leg
and knee sits).

IV.   Steve ascends, D does his crotch, backs around to 1. side

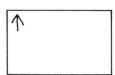

of stairs. Y arrives in time to give S her
r. leg, is lifted onto 1. knee on top of
stairs, facing s.r. Is helped to
standing position; plummets back into
jackknife. David walks up stairs, is
pulled back by buttocks. Steve jump-sits at top does
backward somersault as stairs are moved in counter
clockwise arc

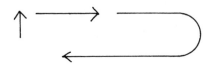

to end facing

V.   as Steve walks up, then down. Steve gets mat as D and Y
            do leg and knee sits.

All 3 walk up holding mat and jump off.   26
Scrabble around - heads toward audience -
throw mat up onto stairs. All 3 climb up
and crawl down on mat. Run with S in
middle - up stairs. He jumps off. D   27
removes mat as Y sits, does backward somersault S and Y
walk up, S vaults off, Y walks down as Steve pulls stairs
to s.r. Both push stairs downstage and turn prepara-
tory to VI.

VI.   S and Y move stairs as D walks up, then down

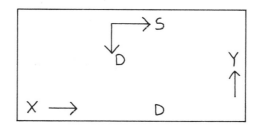

Run up wall - plus - jackknife - D in middle. D somersaults as Y ascends, S catches her crotch,
S ascends, Y crotches him. All 3 walk up,   28
breast holding Y, jump off. Steve
somersaults up, is assisted by Y and D and
lifted off - in ⌐° position. Immediately
Y and D move stairs upst. fast and turn to face ↑   as
Steve sits and does backward roll. D does backward somersault - Y does handstand as S goes around and stands
beside her. D catches her feet. S comes around front.
D and S catch Y on shoulders as she falls from a standing
position. Everyone pushes stairs off.

5. Trio A'

Start

↑   – Roll Bill up in d.s. matt. as D walks away. Bill gets
      up and walks toward D as Y does backward somersault
      and walks backward toward them and does flip over
      their hands. All walk forward. (d.s.)
      Y climbs piggyback once.

↑   Assisted jump and leap – (D) upst. D middle

↓   Turning wheel barrow – 1/2 way run with attempted
      lifts and pushdowns ending with 2 (Y and D) sprawling,
      Bill reversing direction and walking upst.

↑   D and Y follow him. He backs up onto their armchair
      and is carried for a few feet. He gets off. D does
      pig on B. B does pig on Y. Y does pig on B.
      Run D in middle – turns falls on matt.

↓   Run – center person (Y) holding outside hands of
      other two. She stops short just before matt. so that
      she is flung onto it. Stays there.

↑   D and Bill run upst.

↓   D rolls B in mattress. Y starts to walk backward upst.

↓   Jumps beginning with D and B on either side of Y.   32

↑   Walk on heels. 1/2 way reverse and do swivel – hip
      run, D 1st (d.s.)

↑   D does swivel – hip run again while Y and B do
      backward run.

↓   Wheelbarrow – arm chair and belly combo with D.

↑   Run with push-downs.

6. Horses

1. Group slowly converges at a specified point just l. of
center. First person to be aware of the group's arrival at
that point leads the sudden spurt-dash to d.s. r. corner   *(see cover ph*
mattress. Mattress on heads, group moves slowly to upst. l.
and places it on other mattress.

2. Choice of Metropolis Walk   33, *61, 62*
            Snow Tamping
            Herd run with r.-angle changes of direction

Decor: Slide of African gazelles on cyc at stage r.
        1 solitary 8-ft. yellow fluorescent fixture suspended
        at stage left-center.

The sound for this section was a recording of galloping horses.

102

7. <u>Film</u>

<u>designation</u>

kick	1.	Kicking out legs
	2.	Pushing
poses	3.	Nijinsky poses (done with run)
Ball	4.	Lifts - 1 person curling into a ball and being turned over. BALL
walk	5.	Mixture of running and walking
lift	6.	Jumping by pushing off someone else's shoulder
support	7.	2 people alternately (while walking backwards) supporting shoulders and pulling on arms of 3rd person who moves forward with feet traveling in "J" floor pattern with body alternately falling forward - ahead of feet - and backward - to rear of foot direction.
prance	8.	Prance - both feet always on floor - l. bent arm rotates forward while r. fist shoots straight up twice.
head	9.	One person travels by jamming head against some one who is traveling and rotating bent torso so one is alternating bending forward and bending backwards. Help with hands.
leg drag	10.	Overlapping circles (floor pattern) made by plié on one leg while other leg is dragged around. Equal emphasis so both accents are very down.
combo	11.	Travels backward on diag: "Cindy" leap onto r. foot, bring r. way across so weight is into l. hip (facing near diag. corner^2); pivot on r. by bringing l. arm and shoulder around and down (Now facing original corner'); put l. foot down and go back to it while kicking r. backwards, then l. frontwards; walk on l. to face (3), sudden reverse direction with sharp accent into r.= plie, step l. step r. facing (2); step l. facing (1). Repeat whole thing. (Last 2 steps very quick.)

37

34, 35, 36

```
┌─────────┐
│ 3     1 │
│         │
│       2 │
└─────────┘
```

skip	12.	Chassé, skip, skip. Alternates.
run	13.	Very small skip plus 2 running leaping runs. Alternates.
	14.	Pivot to the right bringing l. arm behind and r. arm in front of head. Walk l. foot while l. arm comes forward, wrist bend and r. hand rests on midsection. Pivot to l. on r. foot, swinging l. arm and leg behind.
4 people	15.	L.-shape carrying of a body
	16.	Karate
	17.	Hug - in

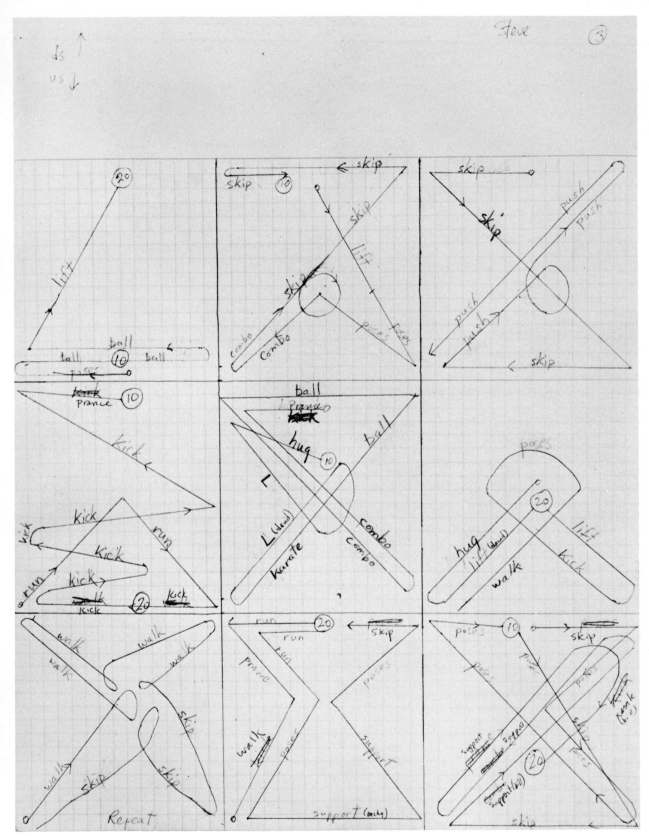

Steve's score for *Film*

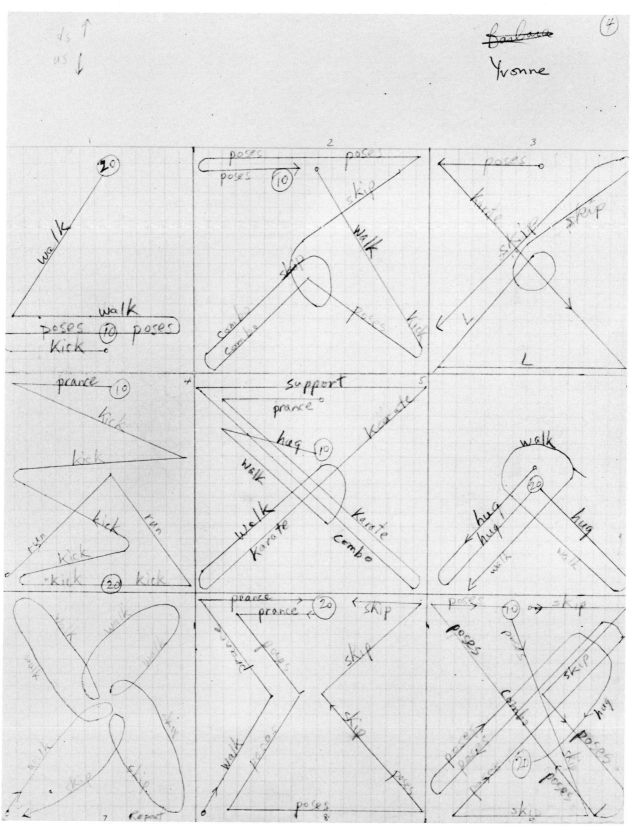

Yvonne's score for *Film*

Miscellaneous notes

1. Objects that in themselves have a "load" of associations
   (e.g., the mattress - sleep, dreams, sickness, unconscious-
   ness, sex) but which can be exploited strictly as neutral
   "objects".
2. Objects which can be used both for their visual and sound
   properties - e.g. the sticks.
3. Sound which can be readily visualized in the mind - e.g.,
   horses galloping.
   #2 is preferred.

Possibility of a light projection that changes the field for a
given portion of the dance, not necessarily to correspond with
movement divisions. A "blended" or "osterized" look is to be
avoided. Each item - be it movement unit (that can include a
whole sequence or "subdivision") or idea, sound unit, or light
unit - retains its discreteness. If of short duration. If of
longer duration, their separation must be indicated.

Example of repetition?: a movement pattern that slowly traverses
a simple space pattern until that space delineation is completely exhausted, e.g., 3 Seascapes diagonal, muscle 2nd trio, "6's",
running dance.

Internal focus vs. extroverted focus. Movement relationships,
people relationships (when they [Trio A'] are "close" together)
belong to the former; accentuated space patterns, sound, simultaneous and separated occurrences, prolonged duration, repetitive rhythm, in fact any kind of repetition, expand the focus
away from the personal psychological confrontation with the
performer. The performer is the residue from an obsolescent
art-form - theater. How to use the performer as a medium rather
than persona? Is a "ballet mechanique" the only solution?

A dance of which parts must be seen at closer range - perhaps
with facial expressions. Demands a situation that can accomodate
a shifting arrangement of audience.

Ideas for decor

mylar cyc descends during Trio A, ascends 1/2 thru Trio B
Rubber floor rolled out during Trio B
Trapezes descend beginning of Act
Screen descends before Film
Fluorescent lights descend before Horses
Grid descends 1/2 way thru Lecture

"When I talk about connections and meaning, I'm talking about the emotional load of a particular event and not about what it signifies. Its signification is always very clear. I don't deal with symbols, I deal with categories of things and they have varying degrees of emotional load. There is often a spectrum of categories in my work. The most elaborate spectrum was an evening called *Rose Fractions* in 1969. Part of the evening dealt with formal groupings of people, and to me that's a category. Using people that way carries a particular weight, not at all psychological. Some other events were more loaded psychologically: a slide of Lenny Bruce lying dead on his bathroom floor, a so-called blue movie, two people dancing nude in another movie, me reciting a Lenny Bruce monologue on snot. All these things were exactly what they were and they weren't connected narratively to what preceded or followed. The decisions I'm talking about have to do with a very subjective set of responses to the impact that certain things have when they appear together in these sequences. That might be hard to talk about, but there is never any doubt about what a given image *is*. It has a specific weight; its intended meaning is clear. Why it is in the piece, and in that particular juxtaposition, is not always so clear. And of course my feelings about these things keep changing."

Performance, a Conversation, edited by Stephen Koch;
Artforum, New York, December 1972.

V 1968-1970

Performance Demonstration

"This piece might be called 'in progress' in that it continues to be rearranged and added to. Nevertheless it is ready for performance. In fact, by the second rehearsal it was ready for performance. The idea of process is not a new idea in art. Duchamp and others thirty years ago revealed aspects of the work process in the presented product. Since rehearsals consume more than 30 times as much time as actual performances, it seems obvious that the rehearsal itself can present a new area of focus: my role of boss-lady to my people-material, the 'people-material' as responding human beings, the tentativeness of decision-making, the revelation or lack of revelation of the boss's thought process. I myself, after many years of making dances and using people, have had to become more sensitive to the peculiar nature of the rehearsal — partly as a result of being somewhat oppressed by guilt, but also as a reaction against the domination of formal dance concerns and the conflict inherent in using people to define these concerns. The weight and ascendancy of my own authority have come to oppress me. As an artist I continue to experience the exhilaration of my own obsessive images which in turn provide their own reasons for realization. It is just that lately I have begun to question the accustomed exclusion in performance of the interactions that lead to that realization. Such interactions are sometimes implied, but are rarely focused on. To do so in a performance situation presents problems that perhaps are insurmountable at the present time; for instance, how much of what is seen would actually take place were the spectators not present? The strain of acting in a so-called 'normal' fashion, i.e., as though the spectators are absent or 'nearly' as though they are absent, continues to be real. It is in this area of realness that the problem seems vital and conducive to renewed efforts toward revelation."
(Taped reading at Pratt Institute, March 1969)

Between 1968 and 1970 my work moved along in overlapping stages. I devised a format variously called *Performance Demonstration*, or *Performance Fractions*, or *Composite*, which would include fragments from old work plus slides, sound and whatever new work I was engaged in. On Sept. 16, 1968, I presented my first *Performance Demonstration* at the Performing Arts Library at Lincoln Center. The cue sheet reads as follows:

1. Tape on. *Mat* starts immediately.   *24*
2. Tape off at leader. (mats have been removed during tape)
3. Lights off for slides.   *39*
4. Lights on for Film and running duo.
5. Film off. Tiomkin tape on.
6. Tape runs into Chambers Brothers ("In the Midnight Hour").
   Steve does *Trio A* once.   *40*
7. Tape runs into lecture on *Trio A*. Frances does *Trio A* once.   *38*
8. Becky does *Trio A* while Yvonne corrects her.
9. Three minutes after Becky starts, buzzer sounds. Group of 20   *41*
   rushes on stage. Two minutes later buzzer sounds again. Group
   rushes off.
10. Lecture tape runs into horses hooves.

Mat from *The Mind is a Muscle* was done by Becky Arnold and me. The tape in   *24*
this instance consisted of my voice reading the following:

"This tape has been made for this particular occasion. It concerns
omissions from this presentation as well as recent reflections about my
work. For another occasion the verbal material would most likely be
different — both in content and placement within the demonstration.
The most flagrant omission today is a film that will be shot in a large
white living room with two large white sofas and two large white nudes
— one male, one female — and one large white balloon about four feet
in diameter. The film is neither pornographic nor racist. The nudes
never touch. They are either separated by the balloon or are apart in
space. They walk with the balloon between them in and out of the
frame. They sit with the balloon between them. They walk on the
sofas. They roll the balloon back and forth between them. They also
roll it out of the frame. Someone rolls it back. They sit side by side as
the balloon is rolled in and out. Many variations on balloon — male-
female relationships within a very narrow format. It is not a symbolic
film, although obviously these descriptions suggest possibilities for
metaphorical reading: e.g., intimacy is obviated by the presence of the
balloon. It is rather a formal exercise on the animate and inanimate
and animated. The balloon at times seems animate in that the source
of its momentum is not seen. The people may become animated in
terms of expressiveness. There are times when all three — the balloon,
male, and female — are completely inanimate.   42, 72

The other omission is a female performer who will be part of a trio
that now appears as a duo. Not the duo you are observing at this
moment with the mats, but one that will occur later in conjunction
with a film about two feet and a white ball. There is also an interlude
during which a mob of people rush out and dominate the stage — even
to the extent of bumping into and interfering with the three performers

who are diligently at work. There is another interlude during which a mob of people, evenly dispersed about the stage — lie on their backs with their legs and hips in the air. They hold this position until individually they get tired; then they leave.

I think of large groups in the same way I think of composed music these days. Both serve as interludes or bridges between similar events. Both are elaborate, richly textured, full of diverse polychromatic effects, the one with its variety of pigmentation, proportions, shapes, and emotional load; the other with its variety of pitches, intervals, and emotional load. Each is complete in itself and effective in small doses. Although I have just begun to appreciate the unenhanced differentiations of beauty in the mob, I still retain my favorite fantasy of being an unabashed music-hater.

That's right: I would like to say that I am a music-hater. The only remaining meaningful role for muzeek in relation to dance is to be totally absent or to mock itself. To use 'serious' muzache simultaneously with dance is to give a glamorous 'high art' aura to what is seen. To use 'program' moosick or pop or rock is to generate excitement or coloration which the dance itself would not otherwise evoke.

Why am I opposed to this kind of enhancement? One reason is that I love dancing and am jealous of encroachment upon it by any other element. I want my dancing to be the superstar and refuse to share the limelight with any form of collaboration or co-existence. Muzak does not accompany paintings in a gallery nor does it encroach on the dialogue in a stage play. True: mussuck is rarely far (in time) from an above-ground film image, but in this case a hybrid beast has emerged which I shall designate as 'movie-moozeek', a form that extends the image and merges with it rather than calling attention to its own quality or lack of quality. A consequence of this kind of subordination is that the closer movie-moozeek approaches cliché and mediocrity the more clarified its function in successfully interacting with the film image.

There have been many minor talents who have attempted to write mediocre moossick for dancing. Louis Horst did this for Martha Graham; Aaron Copland and Wallingford Riegger are two more. John Cage's early oeuvre compares favorably with the most mediocre output of the former. Unfortunately for early modern dance, mediocre moozeek did not reach its zenith until the movies began to exploit the colossal talents of composers such as Dimitri Tiomkin and Henry Mancini. The range and depth of the explorations by these men into the hackneyed nuances of sound stereotype and feeling-form correlations stagger the imagination. Their work makes all previous work in the same genre appear stunted and unambitious.

The early modern dance composers can be classed as more serious. All the worse for them. They just weren't good enough or bad enuf to warrant taking them seriously. These reflections begin to take on the overtones of 'standard Camp'. Nevertheless I am not trying to make a judgement on serious high art muciz as played at the Philharmonic or New School or in Ann Arbor. In that area whatever dialectic has already been mapped out by dedicated composers I here and now pay all due deference to (without having the slightest interest in listening). I simply don't want someone else's high art anywhere near mine. As I said before, I don't collaborate.

Furthermore, I am all for one medium at a time. A simplistic multimedia syntax has always characterized dancing. We see and hear at the same time. When dances are performed in silence — and practically everyone has done one at some point in one's career — they are still considered either dry or revolutionary or both. In Satie's idea of furniture music (altho not in his music itself) I see an alternative that has not been followed thru in theater: Meesik-to-sit-and-wait-by. A juxtaposition in time with visual elements rather than a superimposition. Thereby whatever images the meezake evokes need not be 'applied' to the dance. This is done all the time at the movies during the intermission. No weighty tense exchange of opinions takes place about what one has just seen. On the contrary one sits in a stupor, waiting for the darkness to close down again, one's head enclosed in a sac of candy wrapper crinkling and 'movie-moozeek'."

38 Unfortunately blurred record of first untrained performer doing *Trio A* during rehearsal of *Performance Demonstration* — Francis Brooks

The slides mentioned in the cue sheet were sequential photos of *Stairs* from 39
The Mind is a Muscle. They had been shot by Peter Moore every twenty seconds
and were projected three at a time so that they were 'read' from left to right; each
new set of three wiped out the preceding set. The film was the *Volleyball* film 34 - 37
from *Muscle*. It was projected simultaneously with a running duet by Becky and
me that later became two trios moving at right angles to each other during *Rose
Fractions* of 1969. It was at this demonstration that the first untrained non-pro- 38
fessional performed *Trio A* (Frances Brooks). Her version was preceded by Steve
Paxton's, made splendidly flamboyant by virtue of his bare chest and *In the Midnight Hour* of the Chambers Brothers (ironically conflicting with my priggish 40
music lecture). Teaching Becky *Trio A* right in the performance was probably my
first venture into bringing an aspect of rehearsal into the performance proper.

I had a fantasy, left over from *Dialogues* of 1964, in which a horde of people runs
into the performing area, practically knocks down whoever has been there previously, and just as precipitously leaves. During *Dialogues* three men continually
ran up onto the stage and jostled the female performers. During this performance
demonstration, Becky and I were jostled by an invading horde of 15 people as we 41
went 'bravely' on. The 'horde' walked back and forth and picked up books
and small articles that they had brought with them, then left when the buzzer
sounded.

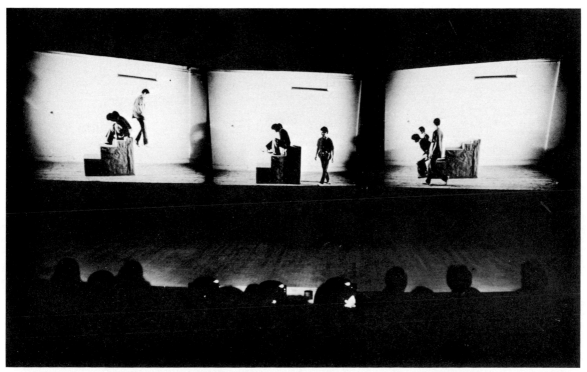

39 Slides of *Stairs* projected during *Performance Demonstration* at the Library of Performing Arts, N.Y.C., Sept. 16, 1968

My concern with large groups and non-professionals was extended in the Billy Rose Theater programs of Feb. 6th and 8th, 1969. Here I presented *Rose Fractions* (*page 116*), a huge sprawling piece incorporating nine non-professionals, five professionals, film, slides, swaths of paper and rubber, books, fluorescent lights, a monologue à la Lenny Bruce (*On Snot*), an aspic fish on an aluminum platter, 'People Walls' and other formal configurations, packages, *Trio A* done by five non-professionals and then by five professionals to *In the Midnight Hour*, the premiere of Deborah Hay's *26 Variations on 8 Activities for 13 People plus Beginning and Ending*, and my own *North East Passing* commissioned by Goddard College in December of the previous year (1968). The difference between this leviathan and *The Mind is a Muscle* lay in the rambling construction of *Fractions* and its constant turning over of the material, in contrast to the thorough and somewhat didactic investigations in each section of *Muscle*. My favorite part of *Rose Fractions* was *North East Passing*, which, alas, not many people remember. 46 - 50 It seemed to have gotten lost in the sprawling shuffle of the whole evening. (Or its subtleties were superceded by the sensationalism attendant on the showing of Steve Paxton's porno film on the second night.)

40 Steve does *Trio A* during *Performance Demonstration*

114

41   Becky learns *Trio A* from Y.R. (not in photo)

115

**Thursday evening, February 6, 1969 and
Saturday evening, February 8, at 8:30 p.m.**

YVONNE RAINER WITH GROUP
ROSE FRACTIONS

Overture: *Rainermusic* (1968) by Gordon Mumma

Lighting: Jennifer Tipton

I*

Elements in this section include the following (not listed in the order in which they appear):

Opening	Oval
Packages	Stairs (slides)
People Walls #1, #2, #3, #4	Mat, Cushioning Material, Tarpaulin, Paper
Two Trios	Proscenium
Contact Trio	Lights
Trio Film	Hard Running
Rhode Island Red Film	Pull, Push
Hand Movie (2-6)	Body and Snot (Lenny Bruce)
Film from Steve Paxton's	Aspic
"Beautiful Lecture" (2-8)	New Slides
Mashes	Layers
Mucis	Dance of Life and Death

Slides by Peter Moore, Trio Film camera: Phill Niblock, RIR Film camera: Roy Levin, Hand Movie camera: William Davis, Aspic: William Davis.

*first performance

Intermission

25

II

Deborah Hay's 26 Variations on 8 Activities for 13 People plus Beginning and Ending*
*first performance

Intermission

III

North East Passing*
(commissioned by Goddard College, November, 1968)

Part 1: Tracks
Part 2: Slides
    Photographer: David Vivian
    Sound track: Bill Braun, Yvonne Rainer, Walter Smith Farm
Part 3: Moving
    Construction: David Bradshaw
    Cover: Ideal Manufacturing Company, Montpelier, Vt.
*pass: To come to or toward, then go beyond.
    Undergo, live during, discharge from the body, convey, transfer,
    undergo transition, take place, occur.
    Come to an end, die, depart, go by, move onward.

IV

Trio A, or The Mind is a Muscle, Part I (1966)
with a tape recording of The Chambers Brothers' *In the Midnight Hour*
(Steve Cropper and Wilson Pickett)

appearing in sections I, III, & IV: Becky Arnold, Frances Barth, Heywood Becker, Frances Brooks, Rosemarie Castoro, Douglas Dunn, David Gordon, Barbara Jarvis, Marilyn Leach, Fredric J. Lehrman, Barbara Lloyd, Susan Marshall, Judy Padow, Steve Paxton, Yvonne Rainer.

appearing in section II: Adele Clarke, Edith Dearborn, Barbara Jarvis, Joan Jonas, Julie Judd, Epp Kotkas, Jean Lawless, Susan Marshall, Pam Mendelsohn, Minda Novek, Kate Rediker, Linda Rubin, Jane Sufian.

27

Rose Fractions Cue Sheet

1. House lights off
2. Overture
3. Curtain opens on empty stage
   Group enters, stands
4. Lights fade out
5. House lights on
6. Stage lights fade up
7. Curtain closes
8. Curtain opens
9. Group walks downstage, stands
10. Curtain closes
11. House lights off
12. Curtain opens on empty stage
13. Curtain closes
14. Curtain opens on group in downstage standing.
    Group moves to shoulder stands
15. 12 minutes after 2 Trios begins,
    Jennifer says "Heads up!"
16. Scrim descends for slides
17. Slides end; scrim ascends
18. (Mats are rolled out, layer quartet, running trios, tarp sandwich,   44
    relocations, oval, mousse quartet, package mash - 3 times) Group
    assembles for People Wall no.1 (with mousse) stage left. Film no.1
    (Hand Movie, Steve's Film) starts stage right; lights turn red
19. 2 minutes after film no.1 starts, film no.2 (Becky and Steve) starts
    stage left. (lights still red)
20. Lenny Bruce story starts. Red light replaced by fluorescents
21. Lenny Bruce story ends. Flourescents ascend
22. People Wall no.3 (passing paper) starts. (Film no.2 ends somewhere   42
    in here)
23. (Proscenium - 3 times with Judy, twice with packages, once with   45
    rubber ending stage left) shoulder slaps start: 2 minutes later Film
    no.3 (chickens) starts stage left
24. People Wall no.4 (kitty litter) starts: lights turn red
25. Film ends
26. Red lights are replaced by fluorescents
27. Curtain closes

Intermission

Deborah's piece

118

Intermission

North East Passing
(Props are placed during intermission)

1. Curtain opens. Group enters for Tracks
2. Group sits down upstage right: scrim descends for slides
3. About 1½ minutes after slides start tape starts (runs thru to end
   and into Trio A)
4. Slides end, scrim goes up, group walks with books, quintet starts 46, 48-50
5. Quintet ends, first group takes place for Trio A
6. As last person from 1st group leaves, 2nd group moves into place
   for Trio A and Chambers Brothers tape starts

42 *People Wall no. 3* and *Trio Film* from *Rose Fractions*. Y.R. is about to deliver the *Snot* monologue (rehearsal)

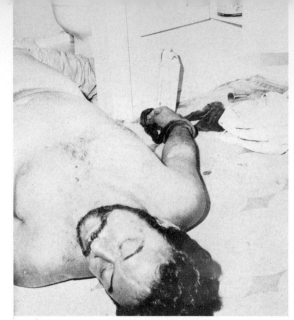

43 Photo used as a slide in *Rose Fractions*

Lenny Bruce *On Snot*, recited during *Rose Fractions*

Alright. I'm going to do something you never thought I'd do on stage. I'm going to do a bit now that I was arrested for. I'm going to tell you the dirtiest word you've ever heard on stage. It is just *disgusting!*

I'm not going to look at you when I say it, cause this way we won't know who said it. I may blame that cat over there. It's a four-letter word, starts with an 's' and ends with a 't' . . . and . . . just don't take me off the stage, just . . . don't embarrass my Mom. I'll go quietly.

The word is — Oh, I'm going to *say* it and just get it *done* with. I'm tired of walking the streets.
> (*Whispers*) "Snot!"
I can't look at you. But that's the word: snot. I know alot of my friends are thinking now,
> "He's so clever, and then, for a cheap laugh, he says 'snot'.
> He don't need that, that disgusting character."
But do you know anything about snot? Except that every time you heard it you go *Phah!* Or *Ich!* or *Keeriste!*? Do you think I would just take snot out of left field and use it for the shock value? *Nada.*

Suppose I tell you something about snot, something that was so unique about snot that you'd go:
> "Is that the *truth* about snot?
> "Look, I'm gonna lie to ya? that's *right*. That's about snot."
> "How do ya like that! I never knew that."
Cause you never listen, that's why. If you'd listen all the time, then you'd learn about snot. I'll tell you something about snot — no. I know, you're smug:
> "We know all we wanna know about snot. We smoked that
> stuff when we were kids."
Well, I've done some research about snot. How about this about snot: *you can't get snot off a suede jacket!* Take any suede jacket straight

120

from Davéga's and throw it in the cleaners and try to run out of the store:

> "*Wait! Stop them!* Alright, block the door. *Get them!* Tell the wife to stand over there . . . . Son, is this your jacket?"
> "Well, . . . yeah."
> "Son, do you know what this is on the sleeve of the jacket?"
> "No."
> *"You wanna go downtown?!"*
> "No."
> "Well, what's on the sleeve?"
> "Well . . ah . . *snot*."
> "Son, you know you can't get snot off suede. It's a killer. Kills velvet too."
> "No. I didn't know that. I didn't know that it was snot."
> *"You knew that was snot,* son. You can't get snot off suede. It's ruined. You can flake it off, but the black mark will always be there."
> "What'll I do?"
> "Just snot all over the whole jacket! That's the only thing you can do."
> "Do you do that work?"
> "No. There's no money in it. Can't get help."

Now, you've seen a lot of snot. You've seen it in back of radiators in Milner hotels. Looks like bas-relief woodglue.

Now, I'm going to show you some snot. Just cause I like you — if I *really* like you, boy! Then it's a show. Would Jack Benny or Bob Hope show you any snot? Fake snot, from the magic store, maybe.

O.K. Snot. Snot that fools old Jewish mothers:

> (*Jewish accent*) "You blew your nose in the *Playboy Magazine* again?"

Here we go (*blows his nose*) I did it! I did it for one reason: to show you how well adjusted I am. Why do I say I'm well adjusted?

Why?

Cause I didn't look later.

Now we see the same man, not well adjusted. See? Slow motion.

A lot of people say to me,

> "Lenny, how come you don't look later?"
A lot of people ask me that:
> "You never look *once*?"
> "Nope! Nope. If you've seen one, you've seen 'em all."
Now I got a handful of snot! That's what I got.
> "Which hand has the M&M? Agh! *Snot!*"

I'm going to take it and put it on the piano. Now, when the pianist comes back for the intermission, she'll think it's a note:

> "Oh, a request! They haven't forgotten the old tunes. Strange envelope . . . . *Foo!* That's *snot!*"

44 *Running Trio* and *Tarp Sandwich* from *Rose Fractions* (rehearsal)

45 Judy Padow being hoisted against the proscenium

Configurations from <u>Tracks</u> *

1. mill
2. press
3. huddle
4. stream
5. perimeter
6. surge (5 times)
7. dash (with somersault)
8. mill
9. scuttle
10. jog
11. bobble (and loiter)
12. shuffle
13. combo (3 times)
14. swarm   47
15. crush
16. side-to-side (twice)
17. lumber
18. mill
19. overtake

46   Detail from *Moving* of *North East Passing* at Goddard College, Vermont, Dec. 6, 1968 – performer unknown

47 *Swarm* from *Tracks* of *North East Passing* at the Billy Rose Theater (rehearsal)

*presented as *Slides* of people doing same configurations in a winter landscape – (see endpapers)

48   Setting up for *Moving* of *North East Passing* (rehearsal) — Heywood Becker, Marilyn Leach, Rosemarie Castoro, Susan Marshall

49   Barbara doing erotic solo during *Moving* (rehearsal)

50   Last part of *Moving* — Barbara, Marilyn, Becky, Douglas Dunn, Fredric Lehrman

Following the Lincoln Center *Performance Demonstration*, teaching during performance was not attempted again until the Pratt Institute *Demonstration* (March, '69) and *Performance Fractions for the West Coast* (April, '69). The cue sheet for Pratt reads:

1. Tape on (muciz)
2. Two minutes later — Stairs slides
3. Lights up. Tiomkin tape on (performers stand upstage)
4. Two Trios (Barbara, Yvonne, Becky and Steve, David, Douglas)
5. Five minutes later tape on (Trio A lecture)
6. Trio Film (shot by Phill Niblock, with Becky and Steve)
7. Rehearsal of "Continuous Project" starts simultaneously with rehearsal tape
8. Trio A — taught to Barbara while others do it
9. Trio A — with the Chambers Brothers

At this performance I worked on *Continuous Project*, a small part of which had already been completed in rehearsal. This is my first large dance not documented by some form of notation. What remains are some elaborate program notes (*page 129*), a list of designated components (*page 132*), a description of the component *Group Hoist* (*page 134*), three letters to the group (*page 146*), and a film of a rehearsal at Connecticut College made by Michael Fajans in 1969.

I kept adding to the list during the summer of 1969 when Becky, Barbara, Douglas, David, and I were in residence — teaching and performing — at Connecticut College* and again that fall for performances at the University of Missouri and Amherst College (November 8, 1969 and December 12, 1969).

By the time of the Whitney performance of March 31, 1970, the accumulated material lasted from ninety minutes to two hours and constituted the definitive version of *Continuous Project — Altered Daily*.**

Basically it was constructed of interchangeable units of material, some very elaborate and requiring the whole group, other units being solos that could be done at any time, or duets and trios. Some units could be done with an indeterminate number of people. The sequence of events — unlike the construction of *The Mind is a Muscle* or *Rose Fractions* — was determined by the participants during the performance itself. It was an expanded version of *Play* from *Terrain*, without the repetition.

---

*Here I presented *Connecticut Composite*, an evening involving 80 students, taking place in five separate performing areas in one building. The audience could move from one to the other at their own discretion or according to a published 'schedule' (*see next page*)

**After that I no longer formally contributed anything new to the performances, but supported and participated in a process of 'erosion' and reconstruction as the group slowly abandoned the definitive "Continuous Project" and substituted their own materials. These continued to evolve and change from performance to performance. Within a short time, with the addition of new members, the group became wholly autonomous and the work almost totally improvisational. It became known as "The Grand Union", under which name it continues to operate.

Connecticut Composite

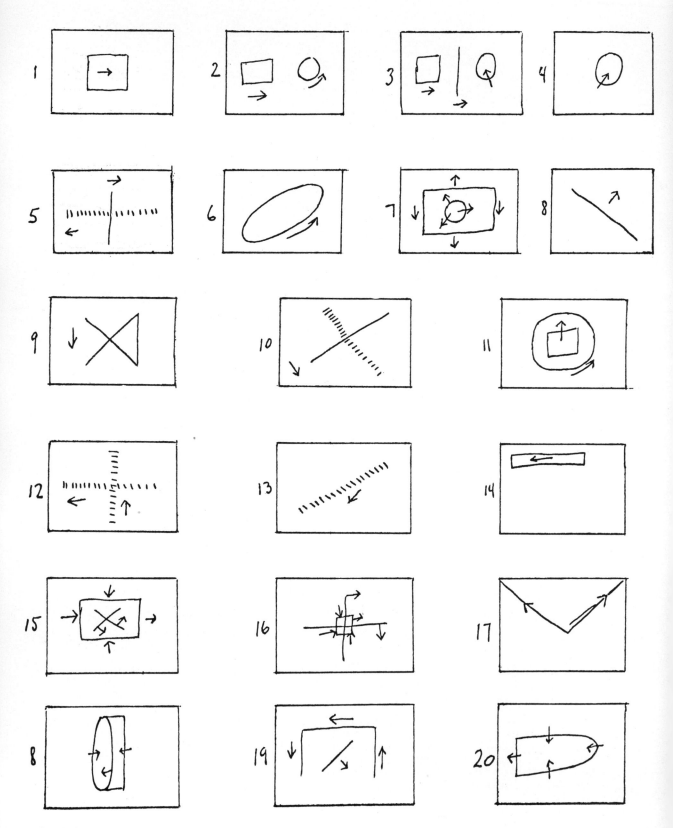

People Plan. Designs represent consecutive static configurations by a group of 20 people. The arrows indicate the direction in which they are to face. An unbroken line means shoulder-to-shoulder alignment. A series of parallel short lines indicates column formation. The performers regroup 20 times.

51 *Audience Piece* (so-called to invite the audience to sit in the vacant chairs) later referred to as *Chair Pillow* (*see page 132*)

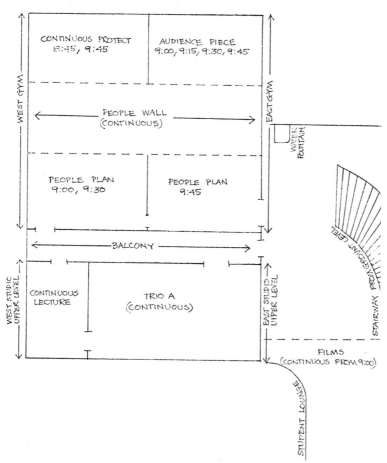

Plan and schedule for *Connecticut Composite*

In retrospect it is hard to account for the euphoria that ensued following those early concerts of *Continuous Project*, especially the one in Kansas City. It was here that the phenomenon of 'spontaneous behavior' really impressed me as a viable mode of performance. And also around this time I returned to my soul-searching and agonizing about controls and authority, as the letters to the group will attest (*page 146*). Now it all seems somewhat overblown. Now there seems to be more clarity in groups as to the role of authority and collaboration, or I would hope so. But at the time it seemed that once one allowed people's spontaneous expression and responses and opinions to affect one's own creative process (in this respect the rehearsals were even more crucial than the performances), then the die was cast; there was no 'turning back' to the old conventions of directorship. It then seemed a moral imperative to form a democratic social structure. What happened was both fascinating and painful, and not only for me, as I vacillated between opening up options and closing them down.

Since that time I have reconnected with my own 'moral imperative' to realize my on-going obsessions, some of which have been decidedly influenced by those earlier brushes with 'real' behavior, i.e., 'rehearsal behavior' transposed to performance. And the role of director has again become appropriate for me.

Continuous Project—Altered Daily utilized the following props:

59 a 6 x 8 foot white screen
2 large cardboard boxes about 2½ feet
    square
5 pillows
54, 55 a large pair of wings
an object that when strapped on the
    back transformed one into a
    hunchback
a lion's tail
a multi-colored striped sombrero
    5 feet in diameter

a stuffed round object with a leg and
    foot attached to it   52
a papier mache hemisphere with the
    eastern hemisphere painted on it
    (Only Becky, who was pregnant,
    wore this over her abdomen.)
2 pieces of 8½ x 11 inch paper
1   5-foot pole   53
1   6-foot pole   56
1 strip of foam rubber 6 x 2 feet   57
6 folding chairs

The performers were Barbara Lloyd, Becky Arnold, Steve Paxton, David Gordon, Douglas Dunn, and myself. Then there were others at the Whitney performances with instructions to step occasionally to a standing microphone and read particular texts. These texts were culled mainly from reminiscences of famous film stars and directors (in "The Parade's Gone By", ed. Kevin Brownlow) and were read by Annette Michelson, Carrie Oyama, George Sugarman, Hollis Frampton, 60 Lucinda Childs, Norma Fire, and Richard Foreman. In two galleries adjacent to the main performing area films were shown: *Connecticut Rehearsal, Line*, and a film starring Barbara Stanwick, which was a last-minute substitute for *The Incredible Shrinking Man* directed by Jack Arnold.

128

Continuous Project-Altered Daily *

It is not necessary to read this program prior to performance.

WHITNEY MUSEUM OF AMERICAN ART
March 31, April 1, April 2, 1970

CONTINUOUS PROJECT-ALTERED DAILY

BY YVONNE RAINER

Performed by

Becky Arnold, Douglas Dunn, David Gordon, Barbara Lloyd, Steve Paxton, Yvonne Rainer and others.

Objects and "body adjuncts" by Deborah Hollingworth
Films by Jack Arnold (The Incredible Shrinking Man)
         Michael Fajans (Connecticut Rehearsal)
         Phill Niblock (Line)
Sound supervision by Gordon Mumma

> THE AUDIENCE IS INVITED TO GO TO ANY OF THE THREE PERFORMANCE AREAS AT ANY TIME. HOWEVER, PLEASE DO NOT WALK ACROSS THE MAIN PERFORMING AREA, BUT PROCEED AROUND THE PERIPHERY OR ALONG THE WALLS TO GET FROM ONE PLACE TO ANOTHER.

Continuous Project-Altered Daily takes its name from a sculptural work by Robert Morris. It has altered and accumulated very gradually since its original presentation as a 30-minute collection of material at Pratt Institute in March 1969. It was there that I first attempted to invent and teach new material during the performance itself. What ensued was an ongoing effort to examine what goes on in the rehearsal - or working-out and refining - process that normally precedes performance, and a growing skepticism about the necessity to make a clear-cut separation between these two phenomena. A curious by-product of this change has been the enrichment of the working interactions in the group and the beginning of a realization on my part that various controls that I have clung to are becoming obsolete: such as determining sequence of events and the precise manner in which to do everything. Most significant is the fact that my decisions have become increasingly influenced by the responses of the individual members. Although it cannot be said that Continuous Project is the result of group decision-making as a whole, it is important to point out that there are details throughout the work too numerous to list that should be credited to individual responses and assertiveness other than my own, or to the manner in which we have come to work together, i.e., freely exchanging opinions and associations about the work as it develops.

I gratefully acknowledge the assistance of the ~~Solomon R~~. John Simon Guggenheim Foundation in the form of a fellowship, which during the past year has permitted me to work unharrassed by the fact that I normally do not make a living at what I do.

*see also p. 125

2

Rudimentary Notes Toward A Changing View of Performance

Levels of Performance Reality:

A. Primary: Performing original material in a personal style.

B. Secondary: Performing someone else's material in a style approximating the original, or working in a known style or "genre".

C. Tertiary: Performing someone else's material in a style completely different from, and/or inappropriate to, the original.

Elements used in Continuous Project (not all of the following occur during any one performance):

1. Rehearsal: Performance of previously learned material that is not in polished condition (i.e., has been insufficiently rehearsed), thereby necessitating verbalizations, repeats, arguments, etc. The material itself may be re-learned (having been performed at an earlier date) or may be having a first performance, in which case all the "kinks" may not have been worked out (cf. "working out").

2. Run-thru: Polished performance of material. May involve verbalizing because of pre-arranged "signals" or actual response during performance. (See "Behavior").

3. Working out: Creation of new material in performance. It may result in intense response-behavior kind of activity. It can resemble "rehearsal" and may involve "teaching".

4. Surprises: Material (objects, activity) introduced without previous knowledge of all the performers.

5. Marking: Performance of previously learned material in the absence of some of the conditions necessary for polished performance, such as adequate space, proper number of performers, proper expenditure of energy, etc.

6. Teaching: A performer teaches previously learned material to one or more performers who do not know it, or choreographer invents   new material.

7. Behavior: a. Actual: individual gestural and verbal activity spontaneously occurring in performance of a predetermined situation. Can occur during any of the above or in "b".

b. Choreographed: behavior that has been observed, then learned, edited, or stylized prior to performance.

*c. Professional: the range of gesture and de-
portment visible in experienced performers.

*d. Amateur: the range of gesture and deportment
visible in inexperienced performers.

*The distinction between these two categories is becoming rapidly
more blurred as seasoned performers begin to relinquish their traditional controls and so called amateurs become more expert in the
new dance modes.

A selection of roles and metamuscular conditions affecting (though not
always visible during) the execution of physical feats.

adolescent	peer
angel	redhead
athlete	Richard Forman
autistic child	sick person
angry child	swimmer
Annette Michelson	short woman
bird	schizophrenic
Barbra Streisand	senile old lady
Buster Keaton	tired person
brother	tall girl
Betty Blythe	12-year old ballerina
black militant	weight lifter
confidante	W. C. Fields
Carrie Oyama	young woman
competitor	young man
energized dancer	anger
Edward Sloman	convalescence
enemy	celibacy
follower	constipation
Fidel Castro	catatonia
friend	drug-induced state
feminist	discipline
George Sugarman	diarrhea
girl with hare lip	exhilaration
head	equanimity
husband	fatigue
hard drinker	fear
Hollis Frampton	gas
hunch back	good muscle tone
leader	in the pink
Louise Brooks	impotency
lover	large bone structure
Lucinda Childs	malnutrition
middle aged fat man	menstruation
male nude	not in the pink
mother	overweight
Martha Graham	puberty
macrobiotic foodist	pleasure
Michael Keith	pregnancy
Norma Fire	pain
old person	power
out-of-shape dancer	relaxation
old teacher	responsibility
playing child	senescence
pregnant woman	sciatica
pompous nobody	terminal cancer

HOISTING DOUG; DAVID'S SOLO; 3-MAN ROLL; BA-DOUG BOX-COAT

P I N K

2nd BECKY SOLO; 1st HEAD-PUSHING; PERIMETER RUNS WI

2nd HEAD-PUSHING; JERKY GROUP; SCREEN DUET-D+D; 4-m
DAV-BA rush with screen; STATIC SCREEN } HERE COM

5-MAN BOX ENDING IN ESTHER WILLIAMS LIFT.

* IKE + TINA - CHAIR - PILLOW ROUTINE: <u>3 people</u> minimum (at the

B L A C K

GROUP HOIST

COUPLES (<u>6</u> people) interrupted by "CONSTANT = GROUP" (<u>4</u> peop

* HERE COMES THE SUN : <u>3 people</u> minimum (except when it occurs

* 1-2-3-4 ($\overset{3 \text{ to } 6}{\cancel{11} \text{ people}}$)

* MARKING ILL.-CONN. CP: ~~was~~ - BA-Y-DAV, S-DOUG

G R E E N

DAV-Y PILLOW DUET

STEVE - BABA PILLOW SOLOS (1 solo, 1 duet each perform

Becky - Yvonne POLE-PILLOW SOLO (ONCE EACH PERFORM

* STEVE - DAV. MAT-POLE ∧(DOUG learning) — *Duet*

BECKY 3-PILLOW BANG (YVONNE LEARNING) - unreheats

INDIVIDUAL THING - ONE CHANCE PER PERSON PER PERFOR

Black - Group
Green - solos + duets
Pink - original CP - now in 4 chunks

* 3 people minimum

TABLES "

EEN; 5-MAN ROLL; FALLING, PITCHING; 1st Becky SOLO

LLOWS

TCHING WITH BOX; DAV-BA DUET WITH BOX; 3-MAN BOX;
E SUN: Dav-Ba; solo circles with box; HCTS with screen. Screen is
removed

g)

imum)

original (CP)

- Trios can operate separately

Steve does not rehearse until performance)- WINGS

y one of us)

52 *Group Hoist*

53 Becky does *Pole-Pillow-Solo* (finally a pregnant performer!)

Group Hoist — for five people — started out as a problem in how to get people 52
into the air and down to the ground in very quick succession. Using pillows, or
utilizing pillows. The pillows functioned literally to cushion landings, but also
worked to mock such a function and to indicate such a function where the function was not actually warranted. Shortly after the Whitney performance of *Continuous Project*, I wrote:

"I love the duality of props, or objects: their usefulness and obstructiveness in
relation to the human body. Also the duality of the body: the body as a moving,
thinking, decision- and action-making entity and the body as an inert entity,
object-like. Active-passive, despairing-motivated, autonomous-dependent. Anal-
ogously, the object can only symbolize these polarities; it cannot be motivated,
only activated. Yet oddly, the body can become object-like; the human being can
be treated as an object, dealt with as an entity without feeling or desire. The body
itself can be handled and manipulated as though lacking in the capacity for self-
propulsion.

134

"The group stands in a tight circle facing inward, five people and four pillows. One pillow is covered with plain muslin and has a leg and foot sticking out of it. Steve falls straight forward holding a pillow and is caught by Becky and Doug and lowered to the ground. Barbara jumps straight up assisted by Doug and David. Becky does handstand, returns to upright position. Doug jumps up and dives forward — arms straight out — into the arms of Steve, David, and Barbara. They lower him to floor. Barbara does handstand over his body, is lifted over and high above the heads of group and placed on her feet on other side of circle. Steve keels over sideways to his right and is caught by Doug. As he rolls onto his back Doug and Becky grab his outstretched hands and armpits and haul him up onto his feet, then into the air assisted by David at his feet so that he is momentarily in a horizontal swan dive. They lower him to floor chest-first onto a pillow that Barbara has meanwhile placed there. Doug, Barbara and David lift Becky straight up so that her knees hug her chest, then lower her to her feet. David keels over sideways right and is caught by Doug and Steve. David hurls pillow he has landed on outside of circle and Barbara runs and places her head on it, then throws it to Steve who throws it to David (still on floor) who throws it up so that it lands in center in time for Barbara to run in and place her head on it. She does headstand, is assisted over onto her feet by Doug and Steve. Becky places head on pillow Barbara has vacated. Steve lowers her hips to ground, then pulls her torso up to a sitting position, then dives across her legs into a headstand on the same pillow, is pulled up to a handstand by Doug, who then lowers Steve's legs sideways to floor. The moment Steve is on his feet (Becky meanwhile has been helped to her feet by David), he initiates a unison movement backwards done by himself, David, and Becky: skip, skip, step, then forwards: step-together-step-clap. On the clap Barbara falls straight backward to be caught by Steve and David, Doug placing a pillow under her head at the last possible moment. Barbara rolls full circle to her left, then does backward somersault ending on her feet. Steve lies down backwards where Barbara was originally and does backwards somersault to other side of circle. Everyone is now standing throwing three pillows around circle. Doug throws pillow onto floor at his left, which is cue for everyone to do unison movement as above, with exception of Becky who does not return forward. At clap Becky runs forward and is hoisted into scissor kick by Doug and Steve, then lowered onto her butt onto pillow that Doug last dropped. Barbara falls forward and clutches David at waist. Steve is assisted to roll down Barbara's back by David and is 'cushioned' at last minute by Doug. Everyone sits — Becky still facing out from circle. Holding hands, everyone stands except Becky. Barbara is lowered to stiff-legged sit on floor, then raised. David is lowered, then Steve. David is raised and in the effort both David and Steve touch soles of feet in center. Steve is raised, Doug is lowered, then raised. Becky falls onto her back with both legs perpendicular. Doug and David hoist her so that her feet rise straight up, followed by hips and arching torso. After making huge upside down arc, she lands forward on her feet."

At the Whitney, because of Becky's pregnancy, I took her part.

54, 55 *Pillow Solo* — Steve and Barbara (Steve is wearing wings)

56, 57 *Pole, Mat* — David and Steve   57

136

55

58 *Couples* – Becky and Y.R.

59

60   Betty Blythe monologue being delivered by Annette Michelson

Monologues:

excerpted from *The Parade's Gone By* by Kevin Brownlow. The Streisand quote is from an unknown source. The Fields quote is from *The Films of W.C. Fields* by Donald Deschner.

"The audience is the best judge of anything. They cannot be lied to. I mean, this is something I discovered . . . not discovered . . . but after almost two years on the stage one learns that. The slightest tinge of falseness, they go back from you, they retreat. The truth brings them closer. A moment that lags, I mean, they're gonna cough. A moment that is held, they're not gonna cough. They don't know why, they can't intellectualize it, but they know it's right or wrong. Individually they may be a bunch of asses but together as a whole they are the . . . wisest thing."
Barbara Streisand

"There has been no advance in technique since the silent days — except for one thing. They're doing away with fades and dissolves. I like this much better than the old technique of lap dissolves, which slowed down the pace. There was a time when we made eight- to ten-foot dissolves. We taught the audience for many years to recognize a time lapse through a lap dissolve. Now they're educating them to direct cuts — a new technique brought about by a new generation of directors who can't afford dissolves or fades. And I think it's very good."
Unidentified director.

"Our farewell scene was tragic drama done in the stillest form of suffering. We were standing way, way down one of the great rooms of the court. As the cameras started to grind, Mr. Edwards called "Action," and we just looked into each other's eyes. Then I walked slowly with

60

138

the little boy right to the very edge of the great doors and then hesitated. I turned around and with my back full upon the audience I just raised an arm and stood there. And he did the same. No blubbering, no weeping, none of that stuff. We just knew the timing because we were emotional people. And finally, I brought the hand down and turned, just looking into the years ahead without him. I put my arm around the child. I didn't look at him. I just looked into the ages I would have to spend without this great love. Mr. Edwards had his handkerchief out. Miss Whistler heard him say as he wiped his eyes, "That can never again be made like that. Cut. Everybody go home."
Betty Blythe

"I was stuck over a scene in which Faust is changed from a ragged old man into a handsome youth, and is transported from a hovel to a glittering palace. Then I had an idea. I got the carpenter to make a platform, with four bicycle wheels. We mounted the camera and the cameraman on this traveling platform and started to photograph old man Faust, in a full-length shot. We moved towards him, refocusing all the time, until we came to a full head close-up. Then we started the dissolve. We marked the head close-up in the camera finder, and sent Mr. Faust to change his make-up to the handsome youth. Meanwhile, the hovel set was changed to the palace. The rejuvenated Faust returned to his former position, the other half of the dissolve was started, and the camera pulled back to the full-length shot — disclosing Faust, impeccably dressed, standing before a huge fireplace. Presto!"
Edward Sloman

"I was a veteran before I went into pictures. I was twenty-one years old by then. I made my first picture when I was twenty-five. Pacing — for fast action, you cut things closer than normal. For a dramatic scene, you lengthen them out a little bit more. Once we've seen the scene on the screen, we know what to do. We get in the cutting room and run down to where the action is. There — as he goes out that door, rip it. That's it. Give him the next shot. Get it down to where he's just coming through the door. Get the two spliced together. We didn't have regular Moviolas. We had machines with little cranks, but they were a nuisance."
Buster Keaton

"I learned to act while watching Martha Graham dance, and I learned to move in film from watching Chaplin . . . . I discovered that everything is built on movement. No matter how well Ronald Colman played a scene, if you saw him lumbering across a room in that hideously heavy way of his, it took all the meaning out of it. Speaking of Chaplin, he said in his book that we must get rid of walks . . . in and out of scenes. What the hell? He built his whole character on a walk. Garbo is all movement. First she gets the emotion, and out of the emotion comes the movement and out of the movement comes the dialogue. She's so

perfect that people say she can't act. People would much rather see someone like Peter Sellers performing than see real acting, which is intangible. People are pretty good judges of dancing, because they've all tried to dance a little. They can recognize a technique. They're judges of singing, because they've tried to sing, and they recognize a technique. So they must have some visible technique in order to judge acting, and there isn't any. Acting is a completely personal reaction. That is why I get so inflamed when people tell me Garbo can't act. She is *so* great. Sarah Bernhardt was always a thousand times more popular than Duse because she gave a "performance." Proust made a brilliant remark: 'The degree of mediocrity produced by contact with mystery is incredible'."
Louise Brooks

"Another key element that is very important to me: clothes. A woman's clothes are not only the key to her personality and her pretensions and aims, they give you an instant image of a period, its morals and manners. History at a glance. I had to go to Berlin and Paris to find directors who understood that costumes and sets were as important as actors and cameras. Maybe that's why people like von Sternberg's old films. They are wonderfully exciting to the eye after looking at westerns, and spies in offices, spies in beer joints, spies rolling broads over beds. Or those goddamned ugly war pictures. This is surely the age of ugliness. Dietrich's clothes in *I Kiss Your Hand, Madame* were fantastic. What she couldn't wear she carried. She was big, strong, and she naturally had the energy of a bull. Sternberg tried turning her into a Garbo. He stopped her dead and posed her. Every time I see her pictures, I ask myself, 'What in hell is she thinking about?' And I remember von Sternberg's story about one scene. He said to her: 'Count to six, then look at that lamp as if you could no longer live without it.' And you can see that she would do these things. In true acting you never think of what you're really doing – it's just like life. Right now, I'm thinking of seven different things and so are you."
Louise Brooks

"I think the auteur theory of *Cahiers du Cinema* is crap; I read the first English issue. It took me two hours and three dictionaries to get through the Bazin auteur article to find out what everybody has known since the beginning of films: that some writers and some directors are jealous of the stars' glory and the auteur theory is just another attempt to wipe the stars off the screen with words. And the silliest yet devised. After a film is finished, words can't help the poor director; and a great director doesn't need them. I was standing with one of the exponents of this sort of stuff in the lobby of the Dryden Theatre at Eastman House, watching a film in the theater through the glass doors. I said, 'Who directed it?' He said 'I don't know.' To me, that was incredible. He himself had selected the film to be shown to a group of people up from New York. The first thing I want to know about a film is who directed it."
Louise Brooks

"Somebody would come up with an idea. 'Here's a good start,' we'd say. We skip the middle. We never paid any attention to the middle. We immediately went to the finish. We worked on the finish and if we get a finish that we're all satisfied with, then we'll go back and work on the middle. For some reason, the middle always took care of itself."
Buster Keaton

"The gag was that I should launch this boat I've built, and it should slide down the launching ramp into the water — and straight to the bottom. It took us three days. We kept running into problems. We put something like sixteen hundred pounds of pig iron and T-rails in it, to give it weight. We cut it loose and watch it slide down the ramp. But then it slows up — so slow we can't use the shot. You don't like to undercrank when you're around water, because you can spot it immediately. The water's jumpy. Well, first thing we do is to build a breakaway stern to the boat, so that when it hits the water it'll just collapse and act as a scoop — to scoop water. That works fine except the nose stays in the air. We've got an air pocket in the nose. We get the boat back up and bore holes all through the nose and everywhere else that might form an air pocket. Try her again. Well, there's a certain buoyancy to wood, no matter how you weigh it down, and this time the boat hesitates before slowly sinking. Our gag's not worth a tinker's dam if she doesn't go smoothly straight to the bottom. So we go out in the Bay of Balboa and drop a sea anchor with a cable to a pulley on the stern, and out to a tug. We get all the air holes out of the boat, we make sure that the rear end would scoop water, and with the tug right out of shot we *pulled* that boat under the water."
Buster Keaton

"I have spent years working out gags to make people laugh. With the patience of an old mariner making a ship in a bottle, I have been able to build situations that have turned out to be funny. But — to show you what a crazy way this is to make a living — the biggest laugh on the stage I ever got was an almost exact reproduction of an occurrence one evening when I was visiting a friend, and it took no thinning-up whatsoever.
At my friend's home it didn't even get a snicker, but in the theater it caused the audience to yell for a full minute.
On the stage I was a pompous nobody. The telephone rang. I told my wife I would answer it, in a manner that showed I doubted she was capable of handling an affair of such importance.
I said, 'Hello, Elmer . . . Yes, Elmer . . . Is that so, Elmer? . . . of course Elmer . . . Good-bye, Elmer.'
I hung up the receiver and said to my wife, as though I were disclosing a state secret, 'That was Elmer.'
It was a roar. It took ten or twelve performances to find that 'Elmer' is the funniest name for a man. I tried them all — Charley, Clarence, Oscar, Archibald, Luke, and dozens of others — but Elmer was tops. That was several years ago. Elmer is still funny — unless your name

happens to be Elmer. In that case you probably will vote for Clarence.

I don't know why the scene turned out to be so terribly funny. The funniest thing about comedy is that you never know why people laugh. I know *what* makes them laugh, but trying to get your hands on the *why* of it is like trying to pick an eel out of a tub of water.

'Charley Bogle,' spoken slowly and solemnly with a very long 'o' is a laugh. 'George Beebe' is not funny, but 'Doctor Beebe' is. The expression 'You big Swede' is not good for a laugh, but 'You big Polak' goes big. But if you say 'You big Polak' in a show you'll be visited by indignant delegations of protesting Poles. The Swedes don't seem to mind. You usually can't get a laugh out of anything valuable. When you kick a silk hat, it must be dilapidated; when you wreck a car, bang it up a little before you bring it on the scene.

It is funnier to bend things than to break them — bend the fenders on a car in a comedy wreck, don't tear them off. In my golf game, which I have been doing for years, at first I swung at the ball and broke the club. Now I bend it at a right angle. If one comedian hits another over the head with a crowbar, the crowbar should bend, not break. In legitimate drama, the hero breaks his sword, and it is dramatic. In comedy, the sword bends, and stays bent.

I know we laugh at the troubles of others, provided those troubles are not too serious. Out of that observation I have reached a conclusion which may be of some comfort to those accused of 'having no sense of humor.' These folks are charming, lovable, philanthropic people, and invariably I like them — as long as they keep out of theaters where I am playing, which they usually do. If they get in by mistake, they leave early.

The reason they don't laugh at most gags is that their first emotional reaction is to feel sorry for people instead of to laugh at them.

I like, in an audience, the fellow who roars continuously at the troubles of the character I am portraying on the stage, but he probably has a mean streak in him and, if I needed ten dollars, he'd be the last person I'd call upon. I'd go first to the old lady and old gentleman back in Row S who keep wondering what there is to laugh at."
W.C. Fields

"Every cameraman in the business went to see that picture more than once, trying to figure out how the hell we did some of that. Oh, there were some great shots in that baby! We built a stage with a big, black cut-out screen. Then we built the front-row seats and orchestra pit and everything else. It was our lighting that did it. We lit the stage so it looked like a motion picture being projected on to a screen. For the location shots, all we needed was the exact distance from the camera to where I was standing. Then the cameraman could judge the height. As we did one shot, we'd throw it in the darkroom and develop it right there and then — and bring it back to the cameraman. He cut out a few frames and put them in the camera gate. When I come to change scenes, he could put me right square where I was. As long as that distance was

correct. On *Seven Chances* I had to use surveyor's instruments. I had an automobile, a Stutz Bearcat roadster. I'm in front of a country club. Now it's a full-figure shot of that automobile and me. I come down into the car, release the emergency brake, and sit back to drive — and I don't move. The scene dissolves and I'm in front of a little cottage. I reach forward, pull on the emergency brake, shut the motor off, and go on into the cottage. Later, I come out of the cottage, get into the automobile, and the scene changes back to the club. I and the automobile never moved. Now the automobile has got to be the same distance, the same height and everything to make the scene work. For that baby, we used surveying instruments so that the front part of the car would be the same distance from the camera — the whole shooting match."
Buster Keaton

. . . . "I went back and shot a couple of dramatic scenes again. One of them was when they'd dragged the girl onto the cannibal island and all those black feet were around her and we went to her close-up, surrounded by feet. He shot it in such a way that it looked like all she was doing was smelling feet. Which would be perfectly natural if we were looking for laughs — but we weren't. Not at this point. So I shot that again so she wasn't half-unconscious and their feet weren't bringing her to, or something. I just had her looking more scared."
Buster Keaton

"I'm in the cage out at Universal, where they had all the animals at that time. It's a big round cage, about sixty to eighty feet in diameter, full of tropical foliage. With a whip and a chair and a gun, the trainer gets the two lions in position, and I go to mine. My cameraman is outside the cage, shooting through one hole. The trainer says, 'Don't run, don't make a fast move, and don't go in a corner!' Well, there *is* no corner in a round cage! I start to walk away from one lion — and lookit, there's another one, there! I got about this far and glanced back and both of them were *that* far behind me, walking with me!" (laughter) "And I don't know these lions personally, see. They're both strangers to me! Then the cameraman says, 'We've got to do the shot again for the foreign negative.' I said, 'Europe ain't gonna see this scene!' Years later, Will Rogers used that gag — 'Europe ain't gonna see this scene' . . . we made a dupe negative out of *that* baby! I've worked with lions since, and some nice ones."
Buster Keaton

"I went to the original location, from Atlanta, Georgia, up to Chattanooga, and the scenery didn't look very good. In fact, it looked terrible. The railroad tracks I couldn't use at all, because the Civil War trains were narrow-gauge. And the railroad beds of that time were pretty crude; they didn't have so much gravel to put between the ties, and you always saw grass growing there. I had to have narrow-gauge railroads, so I went to Oregon. And in Oregon, the whole state is honey-

combed with narrow-gauge railroads for all the lumber mills. So I found trains going through valleys, mountains, by little lakes and mountain streams — anything I wanted. So we got the rolling equipment, wheels and trucks, and three locomotives. Luckily, the engines working on these lumber camps were all so doggone old that it was an easy job. They even had burners. At that period they didn't pay much attention to numbers of engines — they named them all. That's why the main engine was called 'The General' and the one I chased it with was 'Texas.' It was the 'Texas' I threw through the burning bridge. We built that bridge and dammed up water underneath so the stream would look better. I planned the scene with Gabourie and a couple of his right-hand men, one of them a blacksmith. We had a forge and a blacksmith's shop right on the lot. Extras came from miles around to be in the picture. None of them were experienced — we had to train them. And when we did the battle scenes, I got the State Guard of Oregon. That location was around twelve hundred miles from Hollywood. Railroads are a great prop. You can do some awful wild things with railroads."
Buster Keaton

"First of all, we thought we'd use that big tank down at Riverside. If we built it up, we could get five or six feet more water in the deep end. So they went down and built it up, put the water in — and the added weight of water forced the bottom of the swimming pool out. Crumbled it like it was a cracker. So we had to rebuild their swimming pool. Next thing, we tested over at Catalina, and we found there was a milk in the water — the mating season of the fish around the island causes that. The moment you touch the bottom it rises up with the mud, rises up and blacks out your scene on you. Lake Tahoe is the clearest water in the world, and it's always cold because it's up a mile high, and that's an awful big lake. So we went up to Tahoe. I'm actually working in around twenty feet of water in that scene. You imagine: we built this camera box for two cameras, a little bigger than this table square, with a big iron passage up to the top with a ladder on the inside. It holds two cameras and two cameramen. It was built of planks and sealed good so there was no leakage. But it's wood, and there has to be added weight. Well, I added about a thousand pounds to it. Now we find that the inside's got to be kept at the same temperature as the water outside. So we hang a thermometer out there so the cameraman looking through the glass can read it. And one on the inside. First thing in the morning, and the night before, we have to put ice in there, and then add more to make sure to keep the temperature of the camera box the same as the water on the outside, so it won't fog up the glass. Either one side or the other will fog on you, see. The difference was that when two bodies are in there, the body heat means we have to add more ice immediately. So as you put the cameramen in, you roll more ice in. So there's the whole outfit, and me with that deep-sea diving suit down there — and the cameraman says, 'I'm too close. I want to be back further.' I moved that camera box. I moved it. That's how much you can lift when you're

down around fifteen to twenty feet deep. The box must have weighed fourteen hundred pounds, something like that, with two cameras, two cameramen, about three hundred pounds of ice, another thousand pounds of weight — and I picked it up and moved it. I was one month shooting that scene. I could only stay down there about thirty minutes at a time, because the cold water goes through to your kidneys. After about a half hour you begin to go numb. You want to get up and get out of there."
Buster Keaton

Letters to performers

Instructions for Steve and Barbara [mailed to them at the University of Illinois]:

Review all material from *Continuous Project-Altered Daily* that is familiar to Steve: sequence, details, etc., as per the ILLINOIS VERSION; that is, Steve will do his original thing, most of which I did in Connecticut. Example: in the beginning Doug is lifted onto STEVE'S back; Barbara is manipulated by STEVE; STEVE balances on Becky. BARBARA will also do her original thing (as per Connecticut version): paper and sweater routine with Doug, etc. The first tricky place is where Steve/Barbara used to roll along under screen. STEVE will do that in new version; BARBARA do what David does — including my duet with David. (BABA will learn it in performance.)
BARBARA — teach Connecticut stuff to Steve, making sure he understands it. In the group lift STEVE will replace *me* wherever possible; this will probably have to be worked out in performance. Teach BABA'S solo with pillow to Steve only if you have time; however, BABA should be prepared to perform it flawlessly herself.

Performance is beginning to shape up like so:

1. New Material by Dunn, Arnold, Gordon) Simultaneously
   Performance of rehearsal by Lloyd, Paxton) performed
2. Performance-rehearsal by whole group, gabbing, arguing, rehashing where necessary.
3. Films: sometimes simultaneous, sometimes interrupting.
4. YR randomly monologuing, directing, watching, disappearing, participating.

I anticipate an incredible amount of unaccounted-for possibilities. Let me know. Saw Gordon at Debbie's event. I am sorely tempted to fly out this weekend to see your thing, Baba. Your decision to go there now really seems like a good thing. NYC seems very closed down to me now. Everything I see seems like 'Fin de Siecle'. It is beginning to seem not only imperative but possible to think about conducting one's life elsewhere.

Steve don't let them overwork you. I try to imagine what it is like: I teach 6 hours every Tuesday at VA and it takes 3 days to unwind and the next 3 days emotionally preparing for it. After 5 weeks it has dawned on me that the main trouble is that a lot of the kids are simply scared shitless of being looked at; they aren't even at a point where they can think about 'aesthetic problems'. In the light of this that list I sent you is total nonsense. I feel unreal. My God! Can theater finally come down to the irreducible fact that one group of people is looking at another group?!

Miss you both terribly. Look forward to the KCMo Reunion.

Prescript for Steve and Barbara

Originally this letter was meant for Barbara alone. I anticipated communicating with the New York contingent orally, and writing a separate letter to Steve. My concern about writing to Barbara immediately came from wanting to clarify the unresolved friction that put a kind of edge on our communication in KCMo. Her responses affected me with an urgency to deal with them, while Steve, I felt — in the absence of the possibility for extended discussion — was engaged in his own private sorting out of a complex set of feelings about the whole thing. Then as the letter progressed it became apparent that I was elaborating on my own responses to the situation in a way that concerns all of us. So in re-copying the letter I am retaining the mode of addressing myself to Barbara with the expectation that she will show the letter to Steve. I in turn will show it to everyone else.

Monday, November 10, 1969

Dearest Baba: I am lying in Bob's house feeling very chilled. Maybe I am coming down with the cold I have been staving off for the last week. Lots of vitamin C and ginseng going down the hatch.

I have so much to say to you. Talked to your friend and mine D.G. for three solid hours on plane (as I guess you did with S.P. after we left). He with his characteristic sensitivity clued me in to what happened between you and me — which neither of us got to adequately before saying goodbye.

There is something I must tell you about myself that I am sure you will recognize. I do not directly and immediately and spontaneously acknowledge accomplishment. This trait has gotten me into repeated difficulties and evidently I am not yet sufficiently hip to it — or haven't investigated the reason for it. The way it operated in KCMo was like so:

I have this huge trust in you and Steve. In writing out those instructions for the two of you I had absolute faith that however you figured them out I would be pleased and tickled. In other words I am at a point — a dangerous one — where I take certain things for granted. When I saw you rehearsing in the afternoon the 'thing' I am lamenting took place: I saw; then I thought "O yes of course, that looks just like I thought it would; *they couldn't have done it any other way (!)* There is nothing to say (criticize) about that." Blast me! There I stood with my steely gaze brazenly taking credit for what *you* had done. Wow!

Forgive me dear friends. As my affection and esteem for all of you grow I am forced to examine these vestiges of parsimony and control. We cannot take anything for granted anymore — I in relation to your achievement and you with respect to your own. What the two of you did in Illinois was nothing short of phenomenal, and considering that you had to disregard my instructions in order to do it, well — my mouth hangeth open, my mind does boggle, I almost don't believe, but I have seen the glory. That I behaved as though I didn't even have to look at what you did may on the one hand seem thoughtless and disinterested; but it was also an expression of my good faith. I felt free to attend to other matters. However, this is a description and not a justification. You cannot be expected to read my mind *all* the time. In the future I hope that you will be more faithful to your needs and 'call me on it' if you pick up on similar behavior coming from me. I just now realized in remembering something I did in the performance that you could have behaved in similar fashion: I really wanted you both to see what I had wrought in your absence (which is why I was so delighted when Baba came over to me with the chairs to "show Steve"). At one point in the beginning when I saw you both standing there watching 'Becky's solo' but in reality the new stuff, I just about dissolved in my own greasy pleasure and flashed my hugest Rainer grin. Again at the end — Steve lying on the floor — I plunked myself in front of him and 'showed him' myself doing the new stuff. A child strutting her latest achievement. "Hey man dig this." That is probably what you felt in doing your Urbana thing. And the bitch didn't even remark on it. OK so next time make me look — right then and there in performance. I would like to share your pleasure. I would like to acknowledge your feat. I don't want to take anything for granted and I want whatever contact and interaction the situation brings up.

The phenomenal quality of your accomplishment also characterized the whole experience for me. The words I keep thinking of to describe it come perilously close to current psychotherapeutic clichés: reality of encounter, responsible interaction, truthful response. To put it in a more personal way: I got a glimpse of human behavior that my dreams for a better life are based on — real, complex, constantly in flux, rich, concrete, funny, focused, immediate, specific, intense, serious at times to the point of religiosity, light, diaphonous, silly, and many leveled at any particular moment. As David said — the complexity of and differences in the quality of the experience of each one of us in that situation at any given moment balance out and prevent the domination of any one person's involvement. Yet at the same time there is a consistent seriousness of response in the best sense — whether it be giggling, scowling, or reflective — that unifies the whole thing. We are totally and undeniably *there*. We take each other seriously and feel responsible to ourselves and to the whole thing. I think the days of your good-girl-bad-girl syndrome may be coming to an end, Barbara. I suspect that your reason for vetoing your impulse to unbutton Steve's shirt was not that "Yvonne wouldn't like it" but rather that Steve might not like it or *you yourself* might not like it if you had done it. Am I right or wrong or even close?

One of my real problems is being unable to make a 'hierarchy of moments' in remembering those two hours. I mean — when the total and continuous presence

148

of each person is pleasing how can I like one thing they do better than another? But I see a necessity for some form of extrapolation because the strain of performing on such an intense level leaves one at the end with a feeling that nothing happened. Your not remembering those two incidents – with the hump and the chairs – clued me in to this oddity, Barbara. Steve's concentration and presence during the lifting lesson; his lying on the floor at the end; his observation of me doing the pillow-head routine. Doug sitting across the room looking at our shenanigans with a baleful eye. Becky's two solos; her steadiness and fullness of concentration thruout offering recurrent relief from the general busyness. David seriously working on the new stuff by himself; his interrupting me at the microphone to ask for help. As you see, I am talking mostly about behavior rather than execution of movement. It is not because I value one over the other, but because the behavior aspects of this enterprise are so new and startling and miraculous to me. Only on TV does one see live 'behavior'. Never in the theater. I am sure it will all eventually take its proper place for me in relation to the learned material but right now I am luxuriating and marveling and 'wallowing' in these images.

The practical problems that arose (and also the 'social' ones) – like the feeling of being 'shot out of a cannon' and the briefness of contact, the inequality of my role and yours*, the need for new definitions of freedom and limits** – all this must be thought about.

*One of my main functions in KCMo was 'crowd watcher'. I was very conscious of lapses of time and appropriate moments to turn music on or off, talk, etc. in relation to a sensed (or imagined) attention span of the audience.

**Addenda to original letter re 'freedom and limits': I am ready to accept total freedom of 'response'. At this moment I have trepidations about allowing people to 'alter' my material or introduce their own, BUT (concurrent with my trepidations) I give permission to you all to do either of these *at your own risk*: that is, you will risk incurring the veto power of me or other members of the group, *in performance* (I do not want to know about such intentions prior to performance). In short, I reserve the right – and I confer upon all of you the same right – to be true to my/your responses in performance – be they enthusiastic or negative – bearing in mind the *natural precedence and priority of my material*. This last condition is based on the assumption that by the time of performance you are all willing to cooperate in showing the/my material, your initial responses to it having worked themselves out and exerted their influence on *me* during rehearsals. In the case of those who have been absent from preliminary rehearsals (Steve, Barbara, and in the future, Doug), I understand and accept the condition of risk attached to exposing my new material to them in performance. I still wish to establish a sequence of events before each performance. This sequence may be altered or interrupted during the performance at the discretion of anyone.

('Altering' of sequence is not to be confused with the above-mentioned 'altering' of material.) The primary necessity at this point for me is to get the Connecticut version of *Continuous Project* shown.

The above are general considerations that will be revised and/or brought up to date after each performance. If the style is legalistic and impersonal, it is to provide a theoretical base for more personal interchange and discussion. A more specific set of instructions will be distributed before each performance.

Love love love

yr

November 19, 1969

California Dreaming:
news, reflections and reveries from
Vacation Village, Laguna Beach

The typewriter in use is perched on a desk just inside a plate glass door giving out on a 3rd floor 'penthouse' balcony opposite three 4-story eucalyptus trees beyond which is unadulterated (to the eye) Pacific Ocean. Last night we heard hooting in one of the trees and discovered an owl sitting up there, a strange fat feathered raccoon-looking creature hooting plaintively; perhaps he was lost.

In rereading the 'addenda' to the newsletter written after the KCMo performance I find that I basically have little to add other than defining certain 'strictures' that might make that projection more possible and/or operable. My main reservation about the Amherst gig was that we were operating on the assumption that anyone could depart from the basic structure on an individual basis at any time. When you get 6 people exercising this option — well, I kept being reminded of early Judson 'random' activity. Actually all it takes is for one or two out of the six to detach themselves from a group activity and then suddenly the whole thing becomes diffused when the remaining people set about keeping themselves 'busy'. Actually, Amherst was so different from anything I could or would have thought of making that I am still sort of astonished and blown by it. It put into very clear relief the particular nature of my concise and orderly way of arranging things. What I would like to try next time is a system which would produce both the unevenness and diffusion of the Amherst performance *and* the concentration and tight focus of a lot of my imagery. (My memory may not serve me well, but one of the few 'highly focused' moments in the whole performance was the duet of

150

Steve and Barbara doing their Duncan bit.) A dispersed 'look' over a prolonged period becomes a drag, and I am no less dragged at the thought of the tight-ass look of the beginning of *Continuous Project* (where Doug gets hoisted) dominating the evening. I hate to say it, or I almost hate to say it, but I really do seem to be about variety, changes, and multiplicity. Not necessarily contrast, but rather a spectrum of possibilities in terms of spatial density, types of performance (rehearsal, marking, run-thru, teaching, etc.), and perhaps most important of all: durations and sequence. I'm nothing if not a two-bit entertainer.

OK enuf theory. On to a revision of the statute of limitations: I have changed my mind about how much of my stuff can be performed solo; I mean there are either clear-cut solos or unison and group situations. This greatly cuts down on indi vidual options during a break: for instance, the Here Comes the Sun one-legged balance routine must be done with 3 to 6 people (except where Baba and David do it together with the box); also the chair-pillow bit must have a minimum of 4. (Since it was originally conceived for 30 I still consider it a group routine.) What I am trying to get at is a situation where we will exercise more responsibility toward each other. A mechanical way of doing this is to cut down the number of solitary activity possibilities; this will result in one's having to enlist the cooperation of others when initiating a break (more often than previously). At one point I remember making a rule that you could only take a break when you were expendable (when an activity could be handled by less than 6). I guess the Illinois contingent never heard about this, and since I neglected to repeat it, etc. etc. This rule is going to put greater limitations on our freedom of choice as Becky finds it more difficult to participate in everything. All the more reason that the breaks should involve a consideration of other people's situations and desires: If you wish to break for a solitary activity (like talking or doing your own thing) you must ask permission of the group and then set up their time — either by telling them to continue what they're doing or to do something else. In other words, whoever initiates a break must also exercise responsibility for it by choreographing it totally. It seems to me these problems are not at all new to my work. I was dealing with them back in 1963 in *Terrain* when spoken signals initiated changes. The difference lies in the types of material: then it was repetitions and permutations of short dance phrases; today the material is chunkier, consisting of paragraphs rather than sentences, hence more unwieldly in terms of 'mixing and matching'. The New "Quartet" more closely resembles parts of *Terrain (Diagonal)* with its frequency of called signals signifying changes in direction or regrouping. I don't know yet whether I want that kind of flexibility on a larger scale.

VETO POWER: No one exercised it. As Doug said, he looked around and saw everyone having such a good time doing their thing that he didn't have the heart to interfere even when he wanted to make a change. I think I should repeat, or re-emphasize: In the event of a conflict of will concerning duration of elements in the sequence prescribed prior to performance, the wish to continue or repeat (if the material has not been performed to someone's satisfaction) has priority over the wish to break. Similarly, the wish to return to the PRESCRIBED SEQUENCE has priority over prolonging a break. This is beginning to sound a bit doctrinaire, but the Amherst performance introduced a whole new 'wrinkle' that at this point, as far as I am concerned, only muddles the situation. It is hard enuf to perform material that has been, either out of necessity or intention, under-rehearsed and so results in a 'less-than-polished' performance. This I am definitely interested in. It is quite another matter to think you are on top of material and then find that for reasons inherent in the performing situation that you are not. Like the breaks having a disorienting effect and making concentration on familiar material difficult. I think we must begin to make certain distinctions in executing stuff: If something doesn't work that hasn't been rehearsed, then ok, we do it as well as we can do it (like the group up-and-down). But if it doesn't work when it had been ok at a previous run-thru, I think it should be done over (as with the Becky-lift), or someone should call a halt and suggest we concentrate (suggested script!: "OK let's knock it off you guys; pay attention, stop goofing off, enuf fucking around you knuckleheads!). It might appear that these delicate sentiments could be provoked only in the breast of the boss-lady, but I have reason to believe that others of us have similar moments, whether or not you act on them. Given the current scheme of performance "variables" it is important to have certain things done "perfectly", and I don't care how long or repeatedly we have to do the thing (in performance) before arriving at the 'perfect' end of the spectrum. As I remember, the solo and duo involvements at Amherst were all very beautiful. It seemed easier for people to get their teeth into material when they were alone or in couples. It's obvious that we do forfeit something by not being able to rehearse together: The work gains in 'kinky behavior' while losing in unity. It will begin to even out very soon I hope. Right now I love that each time it is so different. At the discussion the next morning a student who had seen both rehearsal and performance asked me "what responsibility (I) felt toward the audience" since the performance looked just like the rehearsal. I was delighted that he had made this observation. Susan Horwitz had also remarked on and been surprised by this fact. We've come a long way since Pratt. I just had this flash that the last performance of *Two Trios* (done with five people, Steve out) has in some respects more resemblance to the current *Continuous Project* than the Pratt CP had to the current CP. All that goofing and gabbing. The basic difference between the two CP's is in the time that I spent in teaching new material in the earlier performance, thinking that 'teaching' was the primary ingredient of a rehearsal. (One result was that the people who were not being taught had 'nothing to do'.) Since then my idea of the rehearsal has become much more elaborate. 'Teaching' is really a very small part of it.

152

I came out here intending to write about where CP-AD is right now, which would involve tracking the various stages from the beginning. Somehow my feelings about it require a more fluid and discursive form — like correspondence and interchange with you guys — and not the kind of nailing down or crystalization that I usually tend to do. I think that ultimately — perhaps May or June — I would like to organize a gab session with all of us present for taping. (By the way, how many of you are available for my May 20 NYU date?)

Some more revisions: re 'doing your own thing' — one chance per person per performance. I'm still fooling around with spoken material. I don't think that a reading of *anything* works. Now I have narrowed it down to commenting directly on the action (instructions, comparison with previous performance) or reciting learned material. I'm going to be sending each of you long quotes by performers and directors — Buster Keaton, Barbara Streisand, Louise Brooks, early movie directors, etc. There are some great bits in Kevin Brownlow's *The Parade's Gone By*. I'd like you to start memorizing these things, and if you get any ideas for other things you'd like to say let me know. The Lenny Bruce idea still lurks in my head. Real performance bits: stand-up comic, reminiscing actress or actor; quotes *about* performance. But it can't be improvisational or 'in the style of'; it must be a performance of someone else's material at a remove from the original or implied performance. There are primary, secondary, and tertiary performances. Primary performance is what we are already doing — original material. Most performance is secondary, i.e., performing someone else's material in a style approximating the original or working in a known style or 'genre' (Dying Swan, Aida, Magician, etc., altho the latter instance can be both primary and secondary, as with Harry de Dio, the juggler). I want our spoken stuff to be tertiary — someone else's material, or material that has actually previously been brought into existence (via media, or live), *as though* it is one's own, but in a style completely different from or inappropriate to the known original. The degree to which it can be established that the material is being quoted rather than imitated will save it from 'bad' performance (cf my hitherto unsuccessful monologues; I (we) have neither the skills nor the familiarity to do 'good' secondary performances, like sportscaster or comic, and at this point I haven't the foggiest notion how to establish that I *want* to do 'bad secondary performance'). This will happen through clues in the material itself — references to actual dates, events, people, etc., obviously not connected to us, the current performers (or 'tertiary performers!'). At one point I really wanted to do a secondary Lenny Bruce — imitate him or find someone who could. I think my ultimate decision was much more interesting. How about a transcript of a Johnny Carson-Ed McMahon bit? Two of us might learn that. Another thought: A lot of things work on tape that won't work live — like Cindy and Bill reading from the transcript of the conversation by Bob and me. But I've gone that route and tape doesn't interest me right now — except to throw

out muciz. The ambiguities and cross-purposes of live presence vs. apparent behavior vs. implied intention conveyed by specific source material vs. unconvincing
performance: It all adds up to a kind of irony that has always fascinated me.
When I say "How am I like Martha Graham" I imagine that my *presence* is
immediately thrust into a new performance 'warp' (in the minds of the spectators). From that moment on people are forced to deal with me as a certain kind
of *performer*, someone who is simultaneously real and fictitious, rather than
taking me for granted as a conveyor of information (simply because I'm talking
half-way rationally). Or do I overestimate the evocative power of that name?
Similarly I feel that the tension that is produced from not knowing whether someone is *reciting* or *saying* something — pushes a performance back and forth, 'in
and out of warp'. The days of thwarted expectations are over. Warping is the
ticket!

Note from notebook: I would like to know what people said at the mikes and
how they felt about what they said. That's all for now folks.

Y.R.
1-28-70

*** The Dance **
By Frances Herridge

The Avant-Garde Is At It Again

Yvonne Rainer is the third rebel this week in Theater 1969's modern-dance series at the Billy Rose. She and her group are also the dullest in their relenting defiance of everything conventional in theater and dance.

Her "Rose Fractions" was performed last night in sloppy street clothes—mostly jeans and sneakers, without benefit of hair brush or make-up, sets, wing curtains or music. And the choreography consisted mainly of walking or running, aimless repetition, without grace, logic, style, sequence virtuosity, or meaning.

They put books down and pick them up and put them down again. They shift a construction cloth about the stage endlessly, or the bodies of prone dancers. They walk and run, in groups of three, or all singly, avoiding each other or not. One trio muzzled each other for a whole number.

The high point in variety was Miss Rainiers reciting from Lenny Bruce while a nude man and woman on the adjacent screen played with a baloon, making no attempt to hide their nudity.

A Bit of Life

In addition to three numbers of Miss Rainer's, there was one by Deborah Hay called "26 Variations on 8 Activities for 13 People." In it 13 girls kept running forward, then walking back, running up a ramp and then walking back. Obvious and simple, but at least a direction!

Only at the end was a rock record played, and the stage exuded a bit of life—but even then nothing you couldn't see from any novice class at play.

Miss Rainer apparently has fans in her work at the Judson Dance Center, but one suspects part of their admiration is for her nerve in taking the audience's money and then ignoring them. She makes no attempt to communicate, and seems quite happy in her private rebellion. A good part of last night's audience took the hint and left in the intermissions.

This program will be repeated

Garden Exec on Talent Hunt

Alvin Cooperman, executive vice president of Madison Square Garden leaves Monday for London and Paris for conferences with producers there on new arena shows for the Garden. In Paris, he will also attend a performance of the Dejart Ballet with a view to ward a Garden engagement.

Saturday night. Seeing it once is something of a curiosity. Seeing it again would be excruciating.

Dance

Blue Movies? Ho Hum

By CLIVE BARNES

IN all probability I have led an extraordinarily sheltered life. I knew, for example, of the existence of stag or blue movies, in which people did things to one another that were perfectly unmentionable in polite society. Yet — believe it or not — I had never seen one. Now I have. And I owe it all to the Ford Foundation. I must, however, tell the Ford Foundation that — perhaps I did not appreciate what was being done for me — I was bored.

My unexpected and unwitting voyeur experience came as a strange bonus to the season of avant-garde dance, sponsored by the dear old Ford Foundation, at the Billy Rose Theater.

Four companies—of extraordinarily varying standards —had appeared during the week. On the last night we had Yvonne Rainer and her company. The first part seemed bland and innocuous enough. Nothing much was happening, but who, I felt, was counting? I sank a little deeper into my comfortable seat, and, probably, my legs strayed too far into the gangway of my aisle. At this point, some flunky of the management came rushing down the aisle to ask me to keep my leg in. About 10 minutes later they started showing movies documenting sexual intercourse. At once I thrust my feet right back in the aisle. I felt that if I and the theater were to be engaged in a dispute about the illegality of our disparate practices, I would at least stand a sporting chance.

On the matter of the Ford Foundation's dirty movies I do, nevertheless, register a very strong complaint. There was no artistic justification for the showing of them, and at the very least it was an offensive lapse of taste. I am not in favor of any form of censorship and believe that if people want to see hard-core pornographic films, they should be allowed to. However, I do not think it fair to show such a film — even as a childish dirty joke — to an audience that did not wish to see it. An audience, in fact, that had come ostensibly to see a dance performance.

*

Miss Rainer used to be a rather interesting dancer. What I saw of her Billy Rose program — I left early as what I had seen was both excruciatingly boring and insulting — leads me to think that she has copped out. I presume she would consider herself a "minimal artist." And that, I suppose, just about sums her up. Minimal.

*

There is no doubt that the Ford Foundation has struck a ghastly blow this week at progressive dance. By giving these dancers its seal of approval and exposing them to public scrutiny, it has damaged the cause of dance in America. People seeing these performances are bound to equate them with the best the American avant-garde can offer, but these hysterical studies in boredom are no such thing.

I do not for a moment believe that the future of either modern-dance or even classic ballet will bear any relationship to our present lunatic fringe. But it is interesting what a vitiating effect on dance development these people are having. It is surely no accident that while the American experimental theater is alive and active, the experimental dance is, except in a few areas, languishing. There is little avant-garde dance as interesting as, say, Richard Schechner's Performance Group, or the Becks and their Living Theater.

In comparison with such theatrical ventures, the dancers seem rank amateurs. Rank amateurs with the support— however limited — of the Ford Foundation.

Dance

Critic's Concern —And Ford's

By CLIVE BARNES

TWO weeks ago I wrote about the so-called avant-garde dance at the Billy Rose Theater and mentioned, in passing, the role of the Ford Foundation in sponsoring some of the performances that took place there. Not unexpectedly, perhaps, the review has aroused a certain public reaction— partly this has been to spring to the defense of Meredith Monk and Yvonne Rainer, the two ladies chiefly under fire, partly to agree with my position.

When I asked one of the organizers why he chose Miss Rainer to participate, he replied endearingly, in a tone surprisingly free of rancor: "Because of you!" It appears —and I do now recall it dimly—that a couple of years ago, when asked by Gian-Carlo Menotti to suggest some avant-garde dancers for the Spoleto Festival, I did indeed suggest that Miss Rainer was among the more talented. Unhappily, that opinion was based on just a couple of her own solos; she has now regressed into non-dance and self-indulgence.

*

The true point is that artists are not worthy of support simply because they are young or because what they are doing is different. Everyone is young at some stage in his life, and anyone can be different.

The giving of money to the arts does involve making choices. This is quite different from censorship—although to the artist unchosen, the difference may seem fine to the point of hair-splitting. But the fact is that public money for the arts cannot be doled out to all and sundry, if only because the subsidy of mediocrity would reduce the sums available to serious artists. Does this mean that only the proven should get money? Yes. Such a policy means not only that the money will go where it will do the most good, but also that it will provide a fine incentive for the unproven artist to prove himself.

Some Like Yvonne Rainer—And Some Don't

To the Editor:

I WRITE in response to Clive Barnes's column in which he expressed dissatisfaction with the choreographic works offered by Twyla Tharp, Meredith Monk and Yvonne Rainer during the recent modern dance season at the Billy Rose Theater. As a critic Mr. Barnes, of course, has the right to like or dislike anything he is called upon to attend, and to state his views about it as forcefully as he wishes.

So here, instead of raging at him, I would simply like to declare that I am a dancegoer whose estimation of these three choreographers is almost diametrically the opposite of that of Mr. Barnes. I consider Twyla Tharp, Meredith Monk and Yvonne Rainer to be three of our most interesting young choreographers and I found their performances decidedly worthwhile. I especially wish to praise the Ford Foundation for having the courage to include them in the modern dance series. Nobody in the modern dance field is rolling in money; every choreographer needs all the assistance he can get. So bravo to the Ford Foundation for supporting mavericks like Misses Tharp, Monk and Rai-

ner as well as such admirable stalwarts as Martha Graham, Merce Cunningham and Paul Taylor. JACK ANDERSON
New York City

To the Editor:

Clive Barnes was quite right to rap the knuckles of the Ford Foundation for supporting that disastrous week of avant-garde dance performances. Now that other very pressing community needs make it more difficult than ever to raise money for the arts, it is especially important that the available funds be spent wisely.

People often forget that nonprofit institutions like the Ford Foundation exist as an indirect government subsidy for the arts. Since a benevolent government has exempted the foundation from paying taxes, they have a great deal more money to spend, and therefore much of that money is, in a sense, public funds.

I also agree with Mr. Barnes's views about Yvonne Rainer's showing of a stag movie, but I almost wish I had seen the Saturday night show he attended I saw Miss Rainer's performance the preceding Thursday, when she did not include that film; it might have enlivened an eve-

ning that was deadly dull.
WILLIAM LIVINGSTONE
Managing Editor
Stereo Review

New York City

To the Editor:

What got Mr. Barnes upset was a very small part of what was going on in Yvonne Rainer's work. He riveted his attention and, by so doing, he missed the dance. It is too bad that his compulsive attentiveness stood in the way of his recognizing Miss Rainer's work as a celebration of human possibilities—as rich, lovely, exciting and direct as any completely charged phenomenon. Also as unassailable to dismissal.
WILLIAM KATZ

New York City

To the Editor:

I agree wholeheartedly with Mr. Barnes's article on the recent season of avant-garde dance at the Billy Rose Theater. It is time that someone said something on the subject, and three cheers for Mr. Barnes.
KATHERINE S. CUNNINGHAM
New York City

To the Editor:

Mr. Barnes deemed to judge the work of Yvonne Rainer even though "I left early, as what I had seen was both excruciatingly boring and in-

sulting," as if his admission of truancy excused this unethical breach. In fact, he missed "Trio A," from "The Mind Is a Muscle," a work destined, I feel, to become a dance classic. "Trio A," besides being a creatively exhilarating work, as aptly demonstrated by the audience's response, ventures into a whole new approach, for Westerners, to human movement. Much like the most ancient of body disciplines, Tai Chi, it is based on the body's relation to gravity—its giving in to and working with this pull in a relaxed, symbiotic manner. This feel is also a key to Rainer's group movements, with their relaxed, subtle play of pressures and pulls—between the group members and with their environment.

What obviously dominated Mr. Barnes's whole response to Rainer's dance, and the entire dance series that week, was his "bored" reaction to the "blue movie." More probably, from the self-righteous tone of the review ("disgrace to the name of dancing," "self-indulgent self-advertisements for people with larger egos than brains," "hysterical studies in boredom," "minimal people," "lunatic fringe"), he was reacting with gut repulsion to un-

abashed human sexuality. The film, however, was used not as a "childish dirty joke" but as one of three simultaneous images of that same relaxed yet exhilarating quality possible in human movement.

Most disturbing was Mr. Barnes's desire to so wield his power to destroy that which disturbed him, to make this kind of dance inaccessible to others. His high-handed dictatorship of cultural taste was aimed not so much at prospective audiences as at the power behind the productions, the sponsor, in this case the Ford Foundation. Indeed, this intimidation by Mr. Barnes has damaged the cause of dance in America more than anything Yvonne Rainer or the Ford Foundation could ever have done.
WILLIAM G. SOMMER, M.D.
New York City

To the Editor:

Mr. Barnes has done a valuable and courageous thing, knocking certain dance "avant-gardistes." While I wasn't at La Rainer's display of ego in New York, I can report the utter boredom of her program last season at the Brandeis University Expressions '68. Bravo, Mr. Barnes.
MARGO MILLER,
Boston, Mass.

FEBRUARY 13 1969
BOX 540 COOPER STA
NYC 10003 NY

DEAREST YVONNE

PLEASE ACCEPT MY THANKS FOR ROSE
FRACTIONS   SUCH EXHILIRATING TIMES ARE
NOT COMMON IN THIS SPEED-SICK AGE
     THE BALANCHINE AGON AND YOUR ROSE
FRACTIONS ARE THE TWO MAJOR DANCE WORKS
WHICH I HAVE SEEN THAT HAVE BOTH PERFECT
INTERNAL BALANCE AND HIGH ARTISTRY OR
RATHER HEROIC ART   AND YOU HAVE REACHED
HIGHER THAN BALANCHINE COULD DREAM OF
     THE RECOLLECTION OF DETAILS IS EXCITING
BUT ONE EXAMPLE PERHAPS   I HAVE ALWAYS
THOUGHT THAT SLIDE AND MOVIE ADJUNCTS IN
DANCE YOURS INCLUDED HAVE FAILED TO
ORGANICALLY JUSTIFY THEMSELVES   BUT
THE COMBINATION BLUE MOVIE LEFT TRIO
STAGE AND BALLOON MOVIE RIGHT WAS PERFECT
MAKING LOVE LOOKS LIKE THE BLUE MOVIE
BUT FEELS LIKE THE BALLOON MOVIE AND IS
DONE BY LIVING LIVE PEOPLE QUA TRIO
OBJECTIVITY LEFT SUBJECTIVITY RIGHT
MEDIATING SHARED REALITIES CENTER PERFECT
GODARD SNOW SLIDES WITH DANCE THE SAME
AND MALE CORPSE RHYMING WITH BOOK-GIRL
I COULD GO ON THANKS MORE THAN YOU KNOW
LOVE Carl Andre

158

Fear, Clarity, Power, Old Age

Fire	Light	stick	box
Smoke	screen	control	hump
Sent away	pencil	height	slow motion
standing still	paper	above	dish towel-knotted
shield	mustache	below	
overcoat		stairs	
lead bra		flag	
hump			
mask			
rope circle			

VI WAR, Judson Flag Show, Indian Journal, Grand Union Dreams

WAR

A huge sprawling non-competitive game-like piece for 31 people who had re-hearsed with me for a month and a half. They were Pamela Cruden, Christine Mullen, Shirley Soffer, Ted Glass, Pat Catterson, Karen Rimmer, David Rimmer, Paula McMahon, John Erdman, Ruth Barnes, Bill Thistlethwaite, Nina Yankowitz, Fernando Torm, Betty Martyn, Joan Olive, Diane Ray, Alfred Kurchin, Abby Cassell, Jim Cobb, Betsy O'Neill, Rick Fite, Epp Kotkas, Susan Hopmans, Lucille Naimer, Nancy Brodsky, Pam Vihel, Tannis Hugill, Deborah Freedman, Jon Hipps, Janice Kovar, James Barth.

The piece was derived from terms of military tactics found in the *Iliad, The Pelo-ponnesian War*, and various accounts of the Chinese revolution and Vietnam war. In performance, a narrator (Norma Fire) read excerpts from the same sources. It was first performed at Douglass College in New Jersey (November 6, 1970) and later at Loeb Student Center, New York University (November 22, 1970), both times simultaneously with the Grand Union in an adjacent space (*page 128*). It had an indeterminate, repetitive form, lasting about an hour.

The 'playing' rules governed things like the limits of particular movement con-figurations and the use of American flag, black overcoat, three-foot square strip of simulated grass, fifty pillows, and an orange, white and green American flag de-signed after a painting by Jasper Johns. I never saw the performances because I was occupied each time in improvisation with the Grand Union. But I heard that neither performance was as good as some of the rehearsals, where more restraint and sensitivity had operated. It occurred to me only later that the existence of so many options might make *WAR* even more demanding on the performers than had I totally pre-choreographed it, especially on those without much performing experience. It required tremendous concentration, a rigorous interpretation of the instructions, and at the same time a playful use of the materials and a serious man-ner of execution. A lot to ask. The rehearsals, however, were a huge amount of fun as we worked out the configurations and I formulated and re-formulated the rules. It was an ass-backwards war, with people willingly relinquishing the flags and opting for capture and death. Physical metaphors for war without motivation.

Read by narrator at one-minute intervals during WAR:

An unscrupulous schemer.

The summer of 1428 was spent in concentrating troops, material, and supplies and awaiting reinforcements from England.

It was not until October 12 that the forces massed beneath the walls of the town.

The surging sweeping strength of a storm.

Led a punitive raid.

The war had exacerbated men's emotions. They relied only on some miracle to rid them of the nightmare.

They attacked the right wing.

Here they came to anchor, laid waste the land, and spent the night on shore.

Strange orders were issued in his name.

Suspicions among his subordinates hardened when some units were ordered in his name to evacuate key positions on the Plain of Jars, to be replaced by others who were in fact Nosavan's men in Long Le uniforms.

They had fallen asleep from sadness.

Each fight against encirclement and annihilation constitutes a campaign which is usually made up of several or even scores of big and small battles.

Therefore we say that our strategic retreat was a continuation of its strategic defensive, and the enemy's strategic pursuit was a continuation of his strategic offensive.

The truce expired.

Contingents led by that formidable captain captured strongholds penetrated with impunity.

In the manner of the time had just struck a hard blow.

So it was that the king of England landed, crossed the district, reached the Seine, thrust forward into the heart.

162

Willy-nilly he had to accept battle.

He had to resort to improvised ruses.

Fences and hedges concealed the despised infantry.

And many another strewed the battlefield with their bodies.

He had shot his bolt and could only go home, full of glory but almost empty-handed.

The elimination of useless officials.

At this time only modest operations were contemplated.

Together they would share the spoils of victory.

At the end of February 1415 the negotiations in Paris were broken off.

Did not restore him to power . . . so he shut himself up in an attitude of hostile neutrality.

They were cut to pieces on October 25th.

Had ceased to over-awe the exasperated people.

The last civil upheavals had no effect on the fate of the war.

But the time had not come to attack him in his lair, though he seemed readily vulnerable there.

On October 16, 1934 the Red Army left Yutu, Kiangsi, by night. The march lasted a year and covered 25,000 li, or some 8,000 miles — more than twice the width of the American continent. The whole journey was covered on foot, across some of the world's most impassable trails, most of them unfit for wheeled traffic, across some of the highest mountains and the greatest rivers of Asia.

And dispersed his inadequate forces in outlying regions.

The mere news of his advance sufficed to make him retreat.

Though her object was simple, her plans had remarkable scope.

Meanwhile his brother was tottering.

Vientiane itself swarmed with CIA agents at their usual work of trying to buy up or eliminate those they considered useful or dangerous.

"Get out of your villages or else . . . " was the threat contained in the air-dropped leaflets — sometimes before the bombs and napalm rained down, more often later — to warn villagers not to try and set up houses elsewhere. In their air-conditioned villas, the American experts could rationalize that it was cheaper to dump surplus U.S. rice and a few cases of condensed milk and soap into the concentration camp villages than to continue the extermination bombing — and more human! In practise they did both and U.S. military spending grew year by year. Cultivation of rice and other food crops was discouraged, or strictly controlled, in the Vientiane-held areas because of the official fear that a portion might be reaching the Pathet Lao. Obviously crops in the Pathet Lao areas were primary targets for toxic defoliants, supplemented by napalm in the harvest season.

Eighty percent of air attacks against North Vietnam were being flown from bases in Thailand across Laotian ait space, guided to their targets by American-manned radar bases in Laos, the bombs actually dropped by electronic signals from these bases. If the U.S. had the right to use Laotian air space to attack North Vietnam, did not the North Vietnamese have the right to cross Laotian ground space to hit back at the bases in Thailand — not to mention the right of entering Laotian territory to wipe out the radar bases? Had Prince Souvanna Phouma cared a fig to preserve Laotian neutrality he would have denied the use of Laotian air space to attack a neighboring country; as it was, he never even raised his voice against it.

61

62 *M-Walk* during *WAR*

<u>WAR</u> manoeuvers

Two groups - individual activities:

milling; standing still; watching (with arms around shoulders); sideways T; sideways T picks up flag, is carried back to group and hoisted.

observing from sidelines: 1. either stand in relaxed position or 2. line up parallel forearms with a group of 3. Buster Keaton hand wringing behind back.

scouting: run or walk with dodging, once around enemy territory; return to one's own group. Scouting-plus capture: run, "flap" around group, which then (must) consolidate into clump with backs out. "Capture" can occur thru clump opening at some point and "absorbing" the scout. (<u>note</u>: the scout <u>chooses</u> to be captured.)

Group manoeuvers:

1. M(etropolis)-Walk with (or without) leaning out and falling 61, 62
   to ground on one's side.
2. Mary Wigman clump. People from behind crawl through legs of
   those in front. People in front slowly advance while
   rotating torsos with raised parallel arms. This formation
   can "nudge thru" a stationary group.
3. Wedges: any number of people (minimum of 3) gathered in
   V-formation, each person grasping the waist of the person
   in front. The one at the apex of the V leans as far forward
   as possible. Can be used for escape.
4. Encirclement. (All 4 can be used for penetration and
   occupation.)

Occupation: One group can occupy the other simply by parking themselves passively among them (via M-walk or Mary Wigman) regardless of what the occupied group is doing.

Prisoners: Once captured, the following options are open to the prisoner:

Stand still and/or raise hand.

"Fall" (called): leader sets up 2 columns. Prisoner falls from one couple to another, progressing down corridor. Corridor extends indefinitely by turning inside out.

"Jump" (called): same as fall, only prisoner is assisted in jumps. Column remains intact; prisoner reverses direction at either end unless a "rescue" is indicated:

Rescue: 1. Two people join hands and run into enemy territory
(providing the enemy is milling), separate to allow prisoner to
come between them; they run out as a trio; 1-2-3-4 and prisoner
squats and takes 2 steps in 4 counts. Repeat until
returned to own territory. 2. comes out of "jump". Leader of
group attempting to rescue simultaneously (a) touches two people
on shoulder while (b) saying "rescue" very loud and stands
where he/she wants a single column to form. The two designated
people go to head of column and prepare to take "jumping"
prisoner and hoist him/her onto hands of people in column who
will then pass the prisoner over their heads to the end of the
column. The prisoner is then "free".

Large flag:

Always in one group or the other. Cannot be laid on the floor.
Can change sides by
    1. Capture (wedge)
    2. Prisoner or infiltrator makes bib, does airplane lift,
        then runs back to own side.
    3. Prisoner says "jump", ties bib; body and flag get
        rescued; or folds flag over arms: only flag gets
        rescued.

Kill and split.
"accelerated pacification" - falls, leans
Buster Keaton whirling house (inside) movement against a clump
of people.
Skinny movement.
Hand-to-hand combat (David-Yvonne ballroon duet)

Athenian-Corinthian battle:

Begins with "hand-to-hand combat" (medium high energy). Right
wing of A pushes right wing of B back to hill. Wait. A withdraws,
B advances. Hand-to-hand deadlock. B reinforcements help drive
A right wing to sea in continuous flow. A drives B back from
hill to original position. B finally is routed and retreats to
hill in disarray. Wild energy.

A ———————   B — — — — —

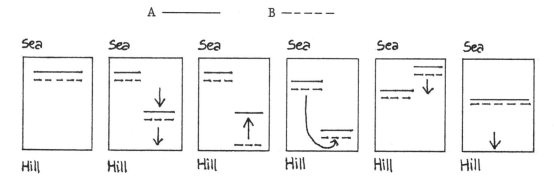

Notes:

Group travel can penetrate milling group.

Wedges - move grass, etc.; escape from occupied zone.

No need to lean out from M-walk, i.e., leaders don't have to stop.

Take every opportunity to quiet group by continuing something for a long time.

Rescue - leader stands and column forms facing leader.

Don't become a prisoner unless you are prepared for the "jump rescue".

Leaders must try to get group back to original territory.

running, squeezing, crawling, falling, catching,
manoeuvering, etc

passing,

push, grab, jerk, hold, press, jam, raise, support

wait

infiltrate

unite (converge)	suppress		formation
subvert	escalate		column
liberate	sweep	operation	line
capture	pursue	skirmish	clump
support (carry, aid)	remove	battle	flank
invade	swell	raid	~~skirmish~~
~~estrange~~	~~liberate~~	seige	battalion
hide ~~obscure~~	occupy	attack	unit
emerge	deploy	treachery	armada
confront (interfere)	intercept	invasion	garrison
overthrow	save	offensive	patrol
challenge	undermine	restraint	skirmish
lead	collapse		
follow	spread	conquer	capitulate
depose	harass	ward off	resist
search	disrupt	call a halt	occupy
~~destroy~~	abandon	advance	~~day~~
withdraw (retreat)	mobilize	withdraw	
close	expand	flee	kill + split
~~flood~~	confine	decimate	(accelerated
pour	surround	founder	pacification)
collapse	outflank	crush	
shatter	escape	overtake	
dissent	raid	slip away	
threaten	penetrate	reinforce	
~~defend~~	pin down		
~~attack~~	confiscate		

List which preceded selection of *WAR* configurations

63 *Trio A* at the Judson Flag Show – David Gordon

Judson Flag Show

64

Early in September of 1970 I was asked by John Hendricks and Jean Toche to participate in a flag show at Judson Church, the purpose of which was to protest recent arrests of people purportedly "desecrating" the American flag. I said I would think about it. In the previous spring — roused by the killings on U.S. campuses and the invasion of Cambodia — I had used *M-Walk* (so-called because it had been inspired by a sequence in Fritz Lang's *Metropolis*) as a protest against these events. Forty people, wearing black armbands, massed in three columns in the middle of Greene Street just below Houston (downtown Manhattan). Swaying in unison from side to side with bowed heads, we snaked our way down Greene, west on Prince (where we were stopped momentarily by a policeman and told to get onto the sidewalk; no one spoke or stopped swaying during this interruption), south on Wooster, east on Spring, then north on Greene back to the original starting point. It lasted an hour; by the end most of the participants had dropped away, and only five of us remained.

During the summer I continued to think about integrating some form of protest against — or at least reference to — the horrors perpetrated by the American government. During a three-week teaching stint at George Washington University in Washington, D.C., I insisted that a huge sign be hung in the gymnasium for that

171

duration, The sign read "Why are we in Vietnam?" On several occasions I conducted classes in the Ellipse opposite the White House. We hung the sign on the fence across the street from a long queue of people waiting to visit the White House. When a guard demanded its removal, we complied. Among other things, I was working with the students on 'war games', material that would eventually be incorporated into *WAR*.

Later, the American flag seemed to be an appropriate prop for use in the piece. (I still have memories of heated childhood games of "Capture the Flag".) In *WAR*, proprieties are at all times observed in dealing with the flag in that the performers try not to let it touch the ground and never deliberately step on it. (It can be walked over only if it is sandwiched between two other props: a black overcoat and three-foot square of simulated grass.) The issue of "desecration" did not seem a relevant one in this particular situation. The flag functioned simply as an object that enhanced the subject and imagery of nationalist conflict. For the *Judson Flag Show*, however, I felt a need for a statement with stronger political overtones. I began to think about the other area in theater that still carries an emotional 'load' in its assault on taboos, viz., public nudity. To combine the flag and nudity seemed a double-barreled attack on repression and censorship.

At 6:30 PM on November 9th, 1970 Barbara Lloyd, David Gordon, Nancy Green, Steve Paxton, Lincoln Scott, and I gathered in the sanctuary of the Church where a large number of paintings and objects and environments dealing with the flag had already been installed. First tying 3x5-foot flags around our necks like bibs, we then undressed totally, dragging non-buttoning upper garments up under our chins, then proceeded to individual spaces to perform *Trio A* twice each.

This particular version was televised by NBC and Global Village. We were not otherwise interfered with, and when we each had completed the task we stopped dancing and put on our clothes. It felt good to do.

Indian Journal

Madras, January 25, 1971

Met David Reck's Tamil teacher today, a man — age hard to determine — very small, head shaved except for tuft in back. Mr. Chellum. Dressed in long white dhoti and orange shawl. I accompanied him to his home in Mylapore from where we were going to observe the evening worship in the Mylapore temple. He knows 7 or 8 languages, including English and German. He pointed out various things to me — the cinema. I asked him if he goes to the movies. Yes, he smiled, sometimes. We got off the bus (The bus was fairly crowded — mostly men. Smell was strong and sweet. Smell in Katmandu was spicy.) and walked down a street lined with vegetables and fruits. He was very curious to know which ones I was and was not familiar with. Do you have that one, etc. We got to his house. Three tiny rooms on ground floor. Stone floor. Old wooden furniture. His wife, Sita, plump and bustling in kitchen chock full of pots and vessels. Huge brass vessels by the door full of water. She knows four languages, Mr. Chellum said proudly, and writes for a journal. Sita served me coffee. Mr. Chellum went into the bedroom and returned sniffing something like snuff and blowing his nose in his shawl. He then took me outside to a small temple immediately adjacent to his house. I am now beginning to see a scheme of things in these temples. Each one is really a temple complex. One very ornate gate with huge doors with row upon row of nipples extruding from them. Then inside 4, 5, 6 shrines varying in size housing images of deities at the end of a corridor. We did not go into any of these. Mr. Chellum explained them all to me outside. Again impressed with the casualness of it all. People of all ages doing all kinds of things in the courtyard: children playing, following us about, people worshiping in various ways — walking round and round a pillar, touching foreheads to ground in front of a shrine while Mr. Chellum is loudly lecturing to me in the middle of which he too touches his two hands devoutly to his forehead, a man following us around pointing to various events for my benefit hoping to horn in on what he thinks is Mr. Chellum's lucrative territory, a cluster of women observing us dispassionately while chanting in unison. They sit huddled at the entrance to a shrine. We stop in front of a place and Mr. Chellum explains that this deity represents the midway point between form and no form. And there inside on a platform is a red shrouded blobby thing. Under another pavillion is a representation of the movement of the planets. People walk round and round it. There is a stable for cattle and a pen for peacocks. There is a gold-plated flag staff 25 feet high with a static representation of a billowing flag with little knobs. Each temple has one of these. Mr. Chellum proudly pointed out the gold.

It all reminds me of Coney Island — gaudy, sleazy, flung about, noisy. Yet it works better. It is not a place that people escape to. It is all part of their daily experience. At dusk the priests came out and blew a long horn and played drums. Then another priest — bare chest, short white dhoti, white stripes across forehead — came out with tray holding fire, flowers, and ashes. He sprinkled ashes in peoples' outstretched palms and they smeared their foreheads with it. Mr. Chellum did likewise. Then suddenly he seemed in a hurry to get away. It was all over. I really like Mr. Chellum. Erudite gentle man living in what first seemed like a hovel. But when I think about it, his house is probably quite luxurious by Indian standards. There seem to be bureaus, but no closets. A clothesline over the bedding on the floor and materials draped over the clothesline.

They worship everything that is close to them. Musicians celebrate composers' birthdays not just by playing their music. We went to a celebration of the 18th century composer, Thayagaraja. After the concert they decked a large portrait of him in garlands of flowers and elevated it on a platform supported at each corner on the shoulders of four men who walked it thru the streets. It was followed by a group of singers who would stop every so often seemingly at the command of an old man with hair style like Mr. Chellum's and teeth all falling out from beetle nut. They sang beautifully, all in unison. Then at a gesture from him they would move on, still singing.

There is singing right now — 10 AM Jan. 26 — next door. Children's voices. I shall go investigate.

Left Katmandu in relief, though would have liked to hear those old men sing again. Missed connection in Benares, spent 7 hours in beautiful pastoral airport. Sat outside with the head administrator drinking tea and watching crows, children. Smelling spicy fragrant flowers. Walked outside down road munching peanuts. Men passed on bicycles. Offered peanuts to a child and was suddenly surrounded by a swarm of begging children. Shrieking, clutching, reaching into my bag. I reversed my direction, shook my head vigorously "No, enough". An older boy held them back. He was very intent looking into my face. Saw my fear perhaps. They gradually dropped away. I walked back to the airport very shaken, crying. Just a pleasant amble in the countryside. Naive rich American. In Katmandu the people who have been traveling for a long time seem completely inured to the poverty. A young guy from Yorkshire cycling around the world, on the last leg of a 2½ year odyssey. Talked about money and food. Yorkshire pudding.

Finally plane came in at 10 PM. I boarded and was invited by steward to join the captain, or rather, he extended the invitation of the captain to watch the takeoff from the cockpit. Of course I was the only woman aboard. Got into Calcutta at midnight. The airport lodging facilities were filled up. A young worker took me in hand. Also several porters were very concerned about me. I notice the superiors and underlings have extended conversations with each other, like consultations. The first young man told me "Don't worry, we'll take care of you. You don't want to sleep in the hotel. Too expensive. You can sleep right in the airport. Everyone does it and it won't cost you anything." Discovered that for all the VIP attention I had gotten in Benares, they hadn't made a reservation for me on the morning plane Calcutta-Madras. On asking if I would get a seat I was told "Yes, yes, you have bad chance." I slept between two chairs that night. Woke up early. The whole place was filled with shrouded recumbent forms. Couldn't tell head from feet. Full of mosquito bites around ankles where my bare feet jutted from clogs. I don't feel afraid here. They are all curious about me, but I feel no menace. I am from Mars and there is nothing I can do about it. In the absence of the possibility of being anonymous, it is a relief to be myself and be acceptable, though alien. It is probably the first time in my life I am experiencing this.

Trichur, January 28

Took an overnight train to Trichur (in the state of Kerala) to see a 3-day theater and dance festival with David and his friend Jim McConagee. Slept on the lowest tier of a three-tier berth. Train clean and spare. Third class, about 24 rupees one way. Am learning to sleep on a hard surface. With no mosquitos I sleep well, wake up every ½ hour to change position. I don't know how the Indians do it, they have so much less flesh to pad their bones. Before leaving Madras I went with an acquaintance of David's to change money on the black market. Gupta, a 24 year old law student. We rode the bus for a distance into a district new to me, then had to walk thru a teeming wholesale market area near the harbor. He is very articulate. Explained that he had expected to take my money here himself and then return with the rupees. My coming with him was causing him some embarrassment. People looked at me and thought "hippie" but "what do they know?" he said. He realized that my way of dressing was for comfort. My Pakistani pants really are, and I think they look OK. In a culture where all the women hide their bodies, I'm not so eager to expose mine. My Accutron watch seems to attract more attention than I do. After changing the money Gupta took me to several eating "hotels." Had a rosewater sweet in one and then on to rice iddlies and a dhosa, a potato filled pancake that is dunked into two kinds of sauce. Gupta is a vegetarian. He eats mainly rice, no eggs, probably a little yoghurt, or curd, and is too poor to buy fruit. He is small but not emaciated like many here. (He asked me if he would be considered "puny" by American standards.) All the waiters gathered around to look at my watch.

On the plane from Calcutta to Madras I had a dream in which an Indian man came to me and said "Your mother is dead."

Trichur, January 29

Saw a folk opera last night. The form is called Chavittu Natakam, and this particular one is about St. George and the dragon. They give absolutely no attention to production finesse. They miss cues, they look around "out of character," the curtain keeps sticking, the two light men run up from the pit where they have been operating the spotlights seemingly at random and carry a banner across the stage, then scamper back down. A photographer walks right onto the stage to take his pictures. Mr. Vasudavan, the PR man for the Kathakali, sat next to me. The only thing that seemed to disturb him was that the lighting guys carried their banners wearing dhotis and Western shirts.

It seems more like European opera than Kathakali. It is done indoors in the auditorium of a music academy. Proscenium stage, but no consideration for the formality of a proscenium situation by either performers or audience. There's lots of talking and going out to tea. All the lines are sung, with occasional brief interludes of dancing — everyone in the scene starts a stamping step from one foot to the other while slightly twisting the upper body. It ends with a slight hesitation, always on the left foot, with the flexed right foot lifted to the side — knee bent — then slammed to the floor. Pow! and the "dancing" is over. This opera usually takes all night, but for this occasion it was cut to about two and a half hours. The scenes are very short with the curtain being drawn at the end of each (cue was a police whistle).

The costumes are elaborate, circuslike renditions of medieval clothing. Lots of spangles. Everyone wore keds or sneakers. The female role was played by a man. The dragon is spectacular — seen frontally — gaping jaws close to the ground, evidently a man on his belly; red lights going on and off operated by a man at a switch fully visible in the wings. It ended quite suddenly with dragon rolling over on his back and St. George leaning his spear against his big white wooden charger on wheels. The chorus and musicians were all out of sight in the wings.

Same evening saw a kind of Bharata Natyam. Beautiful women doing extended solos with very complicated mudras and facial expressions. I kept going to sleep. Had to go out repeatedly for coffee. Finally began to get into it, or so I thought. The Indians follow the story very closely. It is not at all an abstract form to them. I refuse to believe that my enjoyment of it must be dependent on understanding the meaning. But maybe we in the Western avant-garde are really fooling ourselves in our contempt for that question, "What does it mean?" At one point I said to David, "It all looks like hootch dancing to me." Which shows that I am ascribing one meaning to it — sensuous flirtation. The rolling eyes and swimming head and constant smile. When I began to look for the rhythmic changes it made larger sense. The star did a solo that I swear lasted forty-five minutes — with some really vigorous dancing. Musicians — cymbal, drum, male and female voice — all onstage.

January 30

I saw a *Mahadevi* (Kali) dance last night. Usually done only in temples, which in Kerala are barred to Westerners. A group of five or six musicians are lined up at rear of stage: chedra (drums), melan (cymbals), chenei. Single male dancer in the most elaborate costume I've ever seen stamps and wheels and dips for a half-hour. His head and arms are all that are visible. Main impression of red and gold, lots of glitter. Black around eyes like Lone Ranger. He moves eyebrows a lot. The upper section of costume moves with his body when he bends forward, or side to side. He responds to the photographer on the stage by becoming very still, composing his features into a fierce expression, face front to camera. After snap he resumes dancing. His rhythms become more and more interrupted as he begins to grab at the guru — an old man who is responsible for trying to preserve these dying forms. The guru had given a short speech in Malayalam (the language of Kerala) at the beginning and was now standing in wings. The dancer grasped his hands and made him walk out in center of stage. The old man — dressed in white dhoti and shirt — smiled sheepishly, seemed a bit embarrassed. The dancer continued to move and stamp while grasping guru's hands. Finally made everyone stop playing and gave a strange speech facing the audience. He evidently was telling us how glad he was to be here and he thanked the guru for giving him this opportunity. It seemed to me that his speaking was not normal (aside from the fact that it is unheard-of for a dancer to come so completely out of character). He spoke very unevenly, stopping and starting abruptly, sucking in his breath. Perhaps he was out of breath, but I also wonder if he was in another state. I was told that they sometimes go into a trance.

Tonight see Krishnattam. Usually takes seven days to tell all the stories. Two drums (maddalam), cymbals, and gong around pedestal torch. Opener, four *gopis*, or milkmaids, dance behind curtain. Curtain is raised on green-faced Kathakali-like deity and a seated figure with extra pair of arms and mask with three faces at right angles. Change in scene (via small curtain), two green-faced big-skirted guys argue over female character. Change: five women, original one now wearing incredible pink painted plastic nude pregnant "over-body" torso. They do line dance dipping and swaying. She begins to stroke her swollen belly — slight changes in expression — discomfort. Change: four women circle behind curtain, palms together overhead. They all have high red stuffed falsies, veils, gold belts and chains, ordinary makeup. Confettilike stuff thrown from wings. Ma and Pa pay homage to little Krishna — a real child in full green-faced regalia. Demon-Ma cuddles blue doll (boy), then it is replaced by a white doll (girl). Big bully god chases her around and finally snatches doll away. Green-faced sister of mother takes over blue doll. Dances with other women. Mother admires blue doll. Is supposed to suckle infant with poisoned milk. Instead, baby sucks lifeblood from her and she writhes to death clutching doll. Two sisters dance with Krishna and stepbrother. All the women plus Krishna dance in circle after Krishna does solo. Then a line of women move back and forth while Krishna's Ma "complains" about him to sister-in-law. Sister whips him. Long long scene, not much happening — ends with everyone hugging Krishna.

The Krishnattam is much lighter and more condensed than Kathakali. The solo passages are not so extended, and there is more ensemble unison dancing. It also seems more naturalistic, although it has some of the same extremes of stylized violence — as when the demon woman is destroyed by the infant Krishna. I could almost read a lot of the sequences, the facial expressions were so explicit, at the same time subtle. There are fewer masks and semimasks. All of the "women" had heavy stage makeup. The children are beautiful — small movements and changes in head positions carrying extraordinary expressiveness. The whole thing seems much more accessible and charming — the rigor and tension of the Kathakali denotes a zealously preserved tradition. The women here were also very believeable. I forgot at times they were played by men. A lot of contact between children and adults in a folk-dance style. The children are lifted up in the air in one sequence.

Cheruterruthy, January 31

I'm kind of sick. Yesterday took bus with Jim McConegee to Guruvayur, a town on the sea with a famous temple to Krishna. In fact, the Krishnattam comes from this temple. The buses here roar down these 1½ lane roads like demon monsters — playing chicken with oncoming vehicles. Rented bicycles in the town. Rode three miles to the Indian Ocean past thatched roofs and more modern squarish 30's-design bungalows painted yellow, pink, blue with wrought iron gates and filigree woodwork under the roofs. By the ocean was a fishing community — thatched roof huts huddled close together with the usual candy store array of goods in jars: biscuits, plantain chips, sodas in ½ filled bottles. On the shore were their boats — large, round-bottomed, canoe-shaped. The beach stretched for miles. At first we were surrounded by kids who insisted on getting into our photos. Gradually they left. On the way back stopped for a rice meal. Were joined by the owner and several locals. These encounters follow a pattern. We explain where we are from and what we are doing here and how long we will be here and when we came here. And because the English is not that good we say the same things two or three times. Once the ice is broken, it seems they simply like sitting around with us. I was getting very tired, was actually coming down with this thing I have. The owner kept ordering more beer, then some hot salted fried fish — very tasty. He wanted us to stay longer and come visit him, in fact stay at his house and meet his family. We had to decline repeatedly, politely, and firmly. Finally left. Brought bikes back and walked to temple. The streets adjoining the temple are lined with stalls selling sandalwood paste, beads, prints of Krishna, garlands of fake flowers, gimcracks. Bought some beads, a small painting of Krishna for David. Jim was allowed into the temple once he took off his shirt. (All the men must be bare-chested.) He said later it was a very "heavy" experience. Someone prostrated himself at Jim's feet, seeming to worship him. That night I began to get a fever, took some aspirin. It must have been pretty high. As I was dropping off to sleep I suddenly felt it was very important to wake David up (the three of us have been sharing a single room) and tell him that the first night we were there I had dreamed that someone had come in and made me sick. Later I dreamed that someone came in and put garlands of flowers on each bed so that there were 3 mounds of flowers in the room. A death image, but also the Indians use flowers in worship.

The next day went to a local woman doctor. She made me say ah, looked in one eye, listened to my chest with a stethoscope, asked me if I was allergic to any drug, and promptly wrote out a prescription for an antibiotic. The new witch doctor cure. Now the goddam antibiotic is killing me. My gut is a mess. We are in Cheryterruthy where the Kathakali has its school. I begin to panic and then catch myself. Somehow I feel I am not going to get my lethal thing. If I'm sick it will be the way westerners usually get sick here.

Saw the dusk last evening in a very auspicious place. A ghat on the river, a broad sluggish expanse with as wide an expanse of dry shore on one side that probably gets covered over during monsoon. Off to the left is the pedestrian-vehicle bridge. Way to the right a train bridge. As the light changes the sounds and movements become isolated and enhanced — pure sensation. The women slap their wet saris against the wet rocks. A red toy train whistles across the bridge. A bus crossing the bridge is now in silhouette, each passenger clearly outlined against the still-bright evening sky. A cut-out bullock-drawn cart trundles across. Bicycle bells. Slap, slap, soft murmer of women. Flat water changing color, darkening, losing reflection. Automobile lights move across the bridge. Tears come. Slap, slap, slap.

Plantain trees, coconut palms, pepper trees, tamarind trees, bunyon trees (big spreading gnarled with branches radiating out immediately from thick base, rope vines hanging down and bunyon-like spiky tumors bunched on the branches.)

Now on a train moving north from Shoranur to Conanur. From there we will go to a small town — Alikode — to see a two-day festival in which the Kathakali will take part. Have passed countryside that has great aerial views: a huge patch of coconut halves, wash drying by a river — white trousers and dhotis spread flat on the ground.

Four hours on the train 4½ more hours on two buses to Alikode. Then start a climb up a dusty road to the site. Look back at village ringed with mountains. Five of us have met a young American — with beautiful open face and giggle — on the train. We will be the only Westerners. As we start walking with our assorted duffle bags, knapsacks, bedrolls, shopping bags, we laugh at the prospect of an Indian Woodstock. Get picked up by a panel truck loaded with boxes of rubber sandals headed for one of the stalls. The site consists of one long road with stalls on either side: coffee cubicles, bangles, bananas, religious pictures, peanuts and biscuits, rubber sandals, dishes and pots, etc. Then the temple — a rough affair with a kind of corral, then a roofed pavilion, then to one side the inner sanctum housing the deity. *Puja* ("worship") is going on as we arrive. The drums are going and there is a bedizened, caparisoned elephant standing in the corral. A big sloping field stretches down to the stage where the performance will take place.

The stage is entirely bamboo. Thick bamboo poles support it and criss-crossed matting forms the walls. We were incredibly dirty and were told about a "tank" where we could bathe. The only trouble with bathing in India is that women have to be pretty well covered. So I went in in my clothes, figuring I'd wash clothes and body at the same time. Water very green and silty. Changed into a sari I had bought in Shoranur. A group of local ladies and children gathered about staring as an American friend tried to instruct me in proper draping of my first sari. She finally asked one of them to help me. Lots of fussing and pulling, giggling. I was finally in it, very uncomfortable and self-conscious. The women and children thought the whole operation hilarious. Had dinner in a large hutch halfway up the hill from the tank. It was a delicious rice meal provided free for the performers and entourage by a local maharajah who sponsored the whole festival. For two days we ate here.

The Kathakali began about 9:30. Before that there was singing, I think by children, but I didn't pay too much attention. I felt that I should save my attention for the all-night marathon to come. Went backstage. The performers lie two at a time on bamboo mats. Specially trained makeup men apply the paint upside down, i.e., sitting with legs spread and the head of the "patient" between, performers on back. The beards are very carefully built up in ridges with strips of paper, gauze, and a white pastelike substance. Since the performance goes on for so long, the ones who appear later get madeup after it has started. They didn't seem to mind our coming and going backstage. Very relaxed, informal. They don't do any special preparation or warm-up.

They do three stories a night. The stories are mostly episodes from the long epics of Indian mythology — the *Ramayana*, the *Mahabharata*. Someone said that there are one hundred and fifty stories in the *Ramayana* and it would take as many days to do them all. The first story was about Nala, a once great king doomed to exist as an ordinary man after a serpent sent by a jealous god bites him. While in service to another king a messenger comes and tells the king (in Nala's presence) that Nala's wife is in the market for a husband. (This is the wife's way of letting Nala know that he had better come home.) Anyway, the old performer playing Nala — Kunjan Nayar — does a one-hour solo recapitulating his story. The drums and cymbals become very fast rhythmically. I got so involved that I began to mimic Nala's hand gestures. Felt very powerful and quick as though I could actually do it. Now I see what great performance really is in this form. The younger ones wiggle their eyebrows, turn up the corners of their mouths and do a few more things and that's about it. But this guy actually projects *emotion*. His cheeks vibrate, he seems about to cry, he looks startled, he looks afraid, he looks puzzled, he looks proud. But all through extremely small changes in particular parts of his face. Watching his face is like watching a map while on LSD. A chart of human feeling. You notice a change and then register the reading. Perhaps it is a lesson. I don't watch most people's faces that closely, but it must all be there. His hands I couldn't read. I simply responded kinetically. I haven't experienced kinetic empathy for years.

The second night the musicians in their "overture" really went wild. Someone was taping it, and I sensed something was afoot. The maddalam player seemed very fidgety and nervous as they were getting started. Then bam! they were into something — chendra and maddalam facing off, pushing each other to cathartic heights of pure rhythmic energy, sometimes the gong guy giving a cue for a fresh "rush", sometimes one of the drummers. Bam! they were off again. Then it would die down a bit and I would be afraid it would stop. Then pow! the big maddalam guy (with a sixty-pound drum strapped around his hips) would be flailing away, his bare torso pulsing, arms straining from the shoulders, right hand fingers sheathed in plaster sleeves rattling against one end, and open left hand making another sound on the other side — sounding like two drums. And chendra man giving up one of his sticks and pounding with one hand and one stick, his head vibrating so fast it is a blur. Relax a little slow down no no no don't stop now. Rattle rattle rattle plaster cast fingers rattle rattle BAM! flail. One of the cymbal players dropping the heavy brass instruments together and just letting the top one lie around on the underneath one so that it clangs and vibrates deliciously. They must have gone on for twenty minutes. I hated it to end. Went to bed early that night. Really couldn't keep my head up.

Oh yes — another beautiful strange thing that first night. The performer doing the serpent goes offstage over to one side where they have built a big bonfire and whadya know there's this eerie creature dancing around the fire for the next half-hour while the action proceeds on the stage. The flames lick up and create a chiaroscuro effect on his mask. Later when we had gone up the hill a way to sleep, we were nearly trampled by a character-performer and a horde of audience which had followed him as he ran around with two torches chasing another performer. He had to dodge around us.

The energy in that audience is unbelievable. I doubt if anyone leaves before the end. You may see someone nodding out now and then, but they stay. Young and old An old toothless man sat next to us both nights, head bundled against the chill, blanket around his shoulders, gaze riveted on the stage, mumbling and chanting to himself. He was really in there. It means more to him than a moment's entertainment and escape from his life. And something other than what opera is to westerners.

February 7

Julie and I now on a train from Conanur to Shoranur — the "Mangalore Mail" — in a ladies' compartment. A very intellectual matron is giving Julie a lesson in Malayalam. A ragged woman sits with her idiot son. He is playing with garbage. He occasionally bites himself or hits himself under the chin. Most of the young women look as if they're going to a fancy ball in their gorgeous saris and golden jewelry.

I am going to hang around Cheruterruthy for awhile and watch classes. There is another performance on the 9th, then 12th. I have only 2 weeks left. I don't want to leave.

I must write down what David told me awhile back about Calcutta. He and Carol were lost in a slum, a very narrow street. He looked up and about 10 feet up was chicken wire stretched across the street filled with garbage. Over the garbage rats were scampering and feeding. The garbage from all over the city is dumped once a day in the worst slums. The people climb over it and salvage what they can. The next day it is removed and a fresh batch brought in.

February 8

Saw a class in Ottantullal today. One female solo lasting forty minutes — teacher beating out tala with stick on a wooden table, two maddalam players, one girl singing and playing harmonium. The dancer also occasionally sings. It is not only very frontally oriented, but she seems to favor a particular diagonal. Not as narcissistic and flirtatious as Bharata Natyam. Realized something about the male and female dancing I've seen: the women's focus seems to be close to their own bodies, thus the narcissism. Kathakali focus is farther out, in fact often covers great distance.

Cheruterruthy, February 9

Getting a little hung up here. Feel run down, so small things are bugging me — my pen is running out of ink, difficulty of getting another one in Cheruterruthy. This one comes from Shoranur. (Kesri Pen — made in India.) Tonight we go 20 miles from here to see all night Kathakali. Then I think I'll head back to Madras. Julie and I have been banished to a rustic little house next to the rest house, which has been taken over by some cinema people. It has running water and that's all. No toilet or shower. One really can get along without toilet and shower here. The real hassle is that there are windows on each side, i.e. wooden shutters that must be left open for air and light, and they are right off the ground, so we are in a fish bowl again.

Last night Mr. Vasudavan took us to an American couple who are living about 5 miles from here. She is a sociologist doing research on comparative customs in Kerala and Madras, and he is a linguist. She told us about the Theyam, the untouchables whose rituals involve drinking chicken blood, sitting on hot coals, also dancing. Afterwards we went to Vasudavan's house. Met his old mother, wife, two daughters, and brother. Sat on the porch. The old lady was doing something to dry red peppers, squatting way down on her haunches, legs doubled up like a hinged yardstick, laughing toothlessly. I really loved them all. I like Vasudavan very much. One of those people who can live comfortably in two worlds. Very well informed and worldly in western terms, also tied to his roots, his family, his village, his Nambuteri caste and customs. Julie and I did a version of Kathakali that made everyone roar with laughter.

Full moon last night over this ancient countryside.

February 11

Now on train to Madras. Family with small children, grandma, mother, aunt. Smallest baby has huge eyes, big black dot on forehead, black eye makeup, gold bangles and earrings. Went to a wedding reception this afternoon, which takes place 8 days after the marriage. More opulent house than those I've been in. Julie and I were ushered immediately into a rear enclosure that had a lot of tables and benches, also a deep well about 12 feet across out of which climbed ivy and ferns. We sat down to a "tiffen" of bananas, biscuits, a kind of "doodle-peanut" mixture, and a very sweet ball of dal, sugar, raisins, and cashews — all served on a banana leaf. I thought it strange that the place was full of men and boys; the women seemed concentrated in a small adjoining room, and Julie and I were ostracized to our own table. Occasionally a student from the Kalamandalum would come over and laugh with Julie.

Saw another all-night Kathakali performance. Very difficult to focus on it — crushed like sardines sitting on ground, and they keep coming in, threading their way in order to sit beside mother or sister, etc. You start out with legs crossed and end with knees tucked under chin. Excruciating for back, hips, buttocks after twenty minutes. Can't think of anything except my aching ass. The performance site really out in the sticks. We walked half-mile from the road around dusk — full moon already up. Then — since it wasn't to begin until 10 P.M. — we walked about a mile to Ramancutti's house, one of the great old actor-*ashans* ("teachers") with the troupe. Along the earth mounds that separate the rice paddies we picked our way through the gathering night. The tall palms became more and more silhouetted. The moon brightened. Fantastic evening. Came to the house. No electricity. They carry kerosene lamps from room to room. Ate a rice meal. Very charming hospitable people. I wasn't sure who they all were, but obviously all related — loads of children. Three or four statuesque women in elegant saris (several spoke very good English), a man of fifty who stayed close the rest of the night with a flashlight, and an old toothless grandmother who went back with us and sat next to me for much of the night resting an arm on my leg or shoulder. Returned to this house at daybreak. Same people "hanging out" — laughing, talking, drinking tea, eating rice iddlies, cooking, wandering in and out of the house. No one going to bed, neither the old or very young — after staying up all night. I was really pooped.

Again in the performance I was struck by the differences in acting quality. Ramancutti very good as Rowenan — the arrogant king who is tricked and flattered by the crafty sadhu. The younger performers for the most part are less interesting. It looks like classwork once you get past the garish get-up. The sequence of events is extremely ritualized and codified, but it seems that there are sections that can be improvised and elaborated spontaneously. The great actors can re-create their characters in this way. Whether these embellishments get passed down, or how, I don't know.

February 12

I didn't come to India on a spiritual quest. I came because of the opportunity — a passive reason. Now that I am here, and after four weeks, I question why I am here. If I am a tourist then I should see a few more things and then go back. I don't feel good about being a tourist here. That is why I couldn't stay in Cheruterruthy any longer. To live in that proximity with a village and maintain the distance of a tourist seemed indecent. I admire Julie's perserverence with the language and in making contacts, however limited. "I am going, you are laughing. It is good" etc. I stood back and let her work. I am not at this point committed to any greater degree of involvement. Yet not being involved also drains energy, makes me feel self-conscious, even guilty. I am here for my own enrichment. In some indirect way the tourist-voyeur lives at others' expense. One way to deal with this Marxist-Puritan discomfort is to keep moving.

February 13

Have come down to Mahabilapurum, going on to Kanchipuram today. Vishnu, a young guide, attached himself to me. We rented bicycles and went out to the "Tiger Cave", a big boulder out of which is carved a shrine and huge bas-relief heads of tigers. On the shore. This morning got up at 5 AM. Had gone to bed at 9. Around 12 there was a commotion in the corridor. Lots of people bedding down hakking and kaffing like a T.B. ward. When I stumbled out of my room, I had to step over bodies. The same downstairs on the front stoop. I wonder if the proprietor charges them rent. A lot of people live that way here. Bathe in the ocean, sleep anywhere. How do they eat. Vishnu is one of the more affluent. He says he is paid by the government, although he is obviously going to hit me for something. (8 Rupees)

The moon roars eastward thru the paling night
Seeking its peaceful just end
As the sun advances a cloudy dawn
Before thrusting up from the floor of the Bay of Bengal.

A temple to Siva right on the sea shore. I keep being reminded of Stonehenge and those sight lines. A portal, a tank, a gate, a shrine. A vertical opening, a watery opening, a cleft opening, a doorway. Lots of preliminaries before you get there. Inner sanctum, outer rectangles, tank, portal, rectangular mound in the middle of tank. None of these remains in use or completely intact. The different kinds of architecture existing side by side are astonishing.

How much more interlocking, overlapping are history, everyday life, fact, myth, superstition, daily worship in this country than anything I know about. In India the earthly and divine are all mixed up together. Dung in the cathedral; idols at eye level, the temporal and eternal, peeling paint and granite elephants that will last thousands of years; unsaintly deities; hurdy-gurdy temples; monkeys and peacocks and the midway point between form and no form. Could I shave my head, smash coconuts on the Shiva Lingam, get ashes smeared on my brow, walk in circles around the deity? Went into the temple used for worship here. 50 NP. Monkeys playing in the tower, red-faced unafraid monkeys. Mama, Papa, Auntie, Baby. Shaven-headed devotees offer both monkeys and deity bananas, coconut. A woman sweeps. I weep.

New Delhi, February 20

Jasma Odan from Gujarat at Sangeet Natak Academy. Music — two long horns (sometimes four feet, sometimes six feet), two tabla, cymbals. Opening — priest's monologue — singsong with an attendant making small steps back and forth while holding a brass tray before his face. Then charming toothless old guy comes on and buffoons for a while, sidles up and down, wagging elbows. He wears a white dhoti, over which is wrapped a gold cloth and on top a seedy green wool sweater. He talks and chants and seems to compete for a while with one of the musicians. He does a windmill with arms and lots of gestures. He comes back later with red turban and pencil sticking out of it. Fake white mustache. He also carries a "shield" — a flesh-colored piece of papier-maché or leather — and occasionally brandishes sword. Singing alternates with talking. The old guy does a great bit sideling on his ass without use of his hands, covering about ten feet in this fashion. Female characters played by men. Very graceful and forceful at the same time. They sing and dance. Lots of turning.

Fire dancing. Then fantastic female solo: brass pot on head, clay pot in that, smaller brass pot in that. Flaming torch attached to front of it, two more in each hand. She finally removes torches. They lay a blanket on the floor with a brass pan on its edge. She starts to lie down while balancing pots, gets ring of pan in her teeth. Then something goes wrong. Whole thing falls off, including wig — revealing his shaven head. Audience roars with laughter. Directrice comes out and exhorts audience not to make performer nervous. Performer looks extremely discomfited. Doesn't try that one again. Does a complicated routine with two smoking braziers that are taken apart, belayed out on rope as she turns. Character enters: long curly wig, beard, silver dunce cap, long silk midi coat, long white skirt, carrying a white flag, the end of which is a torch.

He tussles with female character. They dance together, holding hands — go apart. She holds two small torches when alone. With him she holds both in one hand. He has a sword, and bells on his ankles. At once elegant and seedy, a lot of the costumes are tattered. Others look like they were just purchased in the bazaar.

185

The performers are not self-conscious, nor do they try to conceal their intensity of concern about what they are doing. There is much fussing with costumes, wrinkling of noses, looking over at musicians — "getting ready" for next action.

New one: white body paint, white bodice to midsection, suddenly turns into woman. I didn't see how — under cloak. My old guy comes back — now a sadhu, gold dhoti and pink shawl, bare chest, ratty wig. The characters frequently appeal to the audience and members of the audience laugh, talk back, clap, etc.

The ladies dance with the sadhu, whirl around him, let him go; he falls to ground (laughter). He gradually eliminates three ladies, leaving one, whom he proceeds to chase. Spiral funny duet. She evidently persuades him to remove his sadhu outfit. He takes off his wig, wraps shawl around waist, dusts the ashes off his arms. She seems to complain and he chews her out.

Performer is led in under gold cloth — flapping his hands. When revealed he is in black face — white lips, white stripe down nose, horizontal white bands under eyes. Something to do with a curse and a female character giving birth to a deformed person. Or so a Brazilian girl in the audience explained to me. If this is so, then they must have a thing about skin color, i.e., black is bad.

February 21

Delhi has been an interesting nightmare. Last night's drama was the only real enjoyment I've had since I'm here. I'm ready to go back to NY. There are too many westerners here. Delhi is a huge hustle. I didn't feel it right away. What first hit me was the incredible din in the heart of the city, far worse than NY, and the effort of crossing the streets. You *jump* — or else! and the squalor of the YWCA where I'm staying (a cross between Oliver Twist and Bellevue.) I met two pinched girls at this Y, one from New Zealand, on her way to London to work, the other from London headed for Australia. Both of them were traveling by bus — 18 days across Asia Minor and Europe! All they talk about is penny-pinching and avoiding getting gypped. Constant complaining about the service, the difficulties, the Indians. I didn't mind the "Indian way" until I decided to come home. Funny how I fell right back into my American compulsion for expediency, efficiency, quick results following a decision. When I came here I adjusted very quickly to the different sense of time and energy-output. It was all very curious, and I was in no hurry. Now the pressure of only three days in which to "see Delhi", buy gifts, gather information, see cultural events — plus dealing with a queasy gut — is too much. I can hardly wait to get on the plane. I can't stand the westerners I see: drifting hippies, palm beach tourists,

Wandered thru Old Delhi today (Sunday). The men (can't tell whether they are Muslim or Hindu) really jostle hard. They have a trick of holding arms at full length by their sides. Then as they jostle you they can get an extra feel on the thigh or — if they're skillful — the crotch.

Went to Maya Rao's studio. The "new" choreography put me to sleep with its literalness, but their skills are incredible. They all are competent in Bharata Natyam, Cuttack, singing, drum, and several know Yakshegana. Satya Narayan showed me some Cuttack. Have never seen such fast footwork. The atmosphere of the place was very nice. When they asked me to show them something I did *Trio A*. Afterwards they applauded. Sonar Chand (who looks Malaysian) said it seemed to be about "human frustration." He explained what he meant, but I didn't get it. His kinetic memory is unbelievable. In talking about *Trio A* he all but danced the whole thing out. Strange how I am no longer making work that can be demonstrated at the drop of a hat. Would anyone ask a film director to "perform" an example of his work? Not a good comparison, but I'd better hang on to *Trio A* for awhile, at least for travel purposes. There I was in my black pants outfit, vitamin pills falling out of the vest pocket, legs wobbly from *la turista,* churning out *Trio A* in a space 10x8 feet. It still comes off OK. Human frustration. I'll have to think about that.

Have vivid impressions of certain kinds of spaces here. A big temple in Kanchipuram and the Jima Masjid mosque in Delhi. Huge structures beside huge open spaces making it possible to take in the totality of the structure at a distance from it. The space next to the mosque holds 10,000 praying Muslims. What an incredible sight that must be! It is like a concrete football field. At the far edge one looks down on the Muslim quarter, an insane jumble of shacks, rags, used goods, bedraggled squatters, a row of men pissing against a wall. It was too much for me; I had to turn my eyes back to the vast empty space. On this day I was sightseeing with a Sikh who picked me up at BOAC. Prem Singh, 27 year old architect who wishes to exchange sight-seeing services. He is coming to America in March. Good enuf. He very patiently took me around to Lakshmi temple — a recent Walt Disney-like array of different styles of architecture, including caves for the kiddies, a pagoda for the Buddhists, pink stone elephants, bulls. Then the Red Fort mosque. Then his family's house, then a Japanese restaurant because I said I like Japanese food, then a discoteque. Then I had it. A funny thing happened: We were in a taxi on the way to my YWCA. I had the pint of brandy he had secreted in my bag to defray the expense of the cabaret. I remembered that I should give it back to him, then remembered it had originally been in the pocket of his jacket, then noticed he wasn't wearing his jacket and remarked on it. He had left it in the discoteque. We went back. He kept berating himself for his stupidity: "I never do things like that." When the taxi got to the place he asked *me* to go in and get the jacket. I asked him why he couldn't do it himself. He seemed very agitated, said, "No, no, I don't want them to see me walking around here," or something like that. I got the jacket. I couldn't figure him out. Very westernized, alienated from his origins, refusing twice to marry girls his parents had arranged for him. He feels he doesn't belong in his country, yet talks down the hippies for escaping from the problems of their country. Doesn't seem to see a similarity.

He wears the traditional Punjabi long hair wrapped in a turban, and bracelet. He told me there are five "K's" the Punjabi Sikh must adhere to all his life: Never to cut his hair, to wear underwear, bracelet, and turban, and to carry a knife. He is not religious, although he recounted a story from the Ramayana with great feeling. He does not like his father.

February 22

Want to write more about Jasma Odan. The performers do not try to hide their unabashed glee. I don't know how this performance style can survive for long in the MOMA-ish atmosphere of the Sangeet Natak Academy. It was a jolt whenever a break occurred and the directrice came out and offered explanations — how this part went on much longer, but . . . etc. Then they would start a new episode. The setting is quite opulent: The audience sat on colorful rugs within a richly draped pavillion. Beautiful, elegantly saried women, western garbed men with sideburns and horn-rimmed glasses. Leicos for illumination. A sizeable portion of the audience seems knowledgeable about the form and responds to cues or provocation or whatever that periodically come from the performers. On both evenings that I attended — the drama and music — the duration-tolerance of the audience had definite limitations. After three hours only a handful of people remained (from a total of 300 or so). Quite different from the music concert I attended in Madras that lasted 5 hours and where no one left before the end. During the concert in Delhi I was delighted to recognize several ragas that I had heard in Madras. The singer was from Mysore.

Grand Union Dreams

In January — February, 1971, I traveled in India for six weeks under a fellowship from Experiments in Art and Technology (EAT). Through the guidance of David and Carol Reck, the American composer and photographer then living in Madras, I attended some ten or twelve events — mostly music and theater — in Madras, New Delhi, and the state of Kerala.

As it has had on so many Westerners, India had a profound effect on me. Immediately on returning I went into a deep funk, was flooded with contemptuous feelings toward my culture and my place therein, entertained fantasies of giving up my profession because I had no longer anything meaningful to say and going back to school to learn something more useful. (Nursing, marine biology?) During the long trek out of it (the funk) and while compulsively eating my way through countless jars of peanut butter (and gaining 15 pounds), I was poring over three books: Jung's *Memories, Dreams, Reflections**; Miguel Serrano's *Jung, Hesse: A Record of Two Friendships***; and Colin Turnbull's beautiful book about the Pygmies, *The Forest People****. And out of this reading I began to gather the sentences and paragraphs that would form the backbone of *Grand Union Dreams*; the substance of *Numerous Frames*; and the background of *In the College, Performance,* and *Lives of Performers.*

Grand Union Dreams was so called for two reasons: 1. The piece in its original conception was to incorporate objects and images that had appeared in Grand Union, or related, performances. As it turned out there were only three of these images used: the hats and "dying" (sliding down the wall) from David Gordon's *Sleepwalking,* and Steve Paxton's bolt of pink tubular jersey. (There were, however, a number of references to my own previous work: the stairs and bubble-wrap from *The Mind is a Muscle,* the red ball from *Terrain,* the wings and screen from *Continuous Project,* the "people wall" from *Rose Fractions.*) 2. The Grand Union itself (with the exception of Steve) constituted the characters known as "Gods" in the piece. The two other groups, the "Mortals" and "Heroes" — and their actions — could be construed as the dreams of the Gods, hence *Grand Union Dreams.*

---

*Carl Gustav Jung, *Memories, Dreams, Reflections,* recorded by Aniela Jaffe, Pantheon Books, New York, 1963.

**Miguel Serrano, *C.G. Jung & Herman Hesse: A Record of Two Friendships,* Schocken Books, New York, 1966.

***Colin M. Turnbull, *The Forest People,* Chatto and Windus, London, 1961.

Grand Union Dreams
directed by Yvonne Rainer
Emanul Midtown YMHA   May 16, 1971

Since I know nothing at all, I shall
simply do whatever occurs to me.
Prologue.
The Heroes Reveal Themselves.
Mortals Meetings.
The Plot Thickens.
I abandoned all further attempts
to understand.

Mortals: Jeanne Nathan, Cynthia Hedstrom, Shirley Soffer, John Erdman,
Pat Catterson, Carrie Oyama, Tannis Hugill, Janice Kovar,
Jim Cobb, Lois Barrow.

Heroes: James Barth, Epp Kotkas, Valda Setterfield, Fernando Torm.

Gods: Nancy Green, David Gordon, Barbara Lloyd, Dong, Trisha Brown,
Yvonne Rainer, Douglas Dunn, Becky Arnold.

190

In an Interview published in *Avalanche* (Summer, 1972) Liza Bear asked me "What made you decide on Gods, Mortals, and Heroes for *Grand Union Dreams*?" I quote myself: "That came after seeing a lot of theater in India. Mainly I was impressed with mythology being such a fruitful source and so accessible to a large cross-section of the population. And when I came back, I was reading Jung and the Indian myths, and got this idea for Gods and Mortals. In the past, everyone who's performed in any piece of mine has had identical, or equal, things to do; in large group pieces no one person stars or dominates over anyone else. So I decided as a test for myself to make totally different roles for three different groups of people. And it fell in very naturally, because the Gods were played by the Grand Union, which reflected my relation to them and their star status. The Mortals were represented by and equivalent to the groups of dancers I'd been involved with, using individuals in a mass. And the Heroes represented . . . well, led directly into what I'm now pursuing. They were the most differentiated and had very specific things to do individually; they were the only ones treated as individuals, and that was the beginning of my involvement with plot and this fictional kind of thing."

Script

Arrangement of objects and people in the space at beginning.

(heroes) screen blue medicine ball, grass, rope, towel, clock, notebook, book, pencil, suitcase, cleaver, suitcase, overcoats, hat, ball	wood box	pole, brown medicine ball
	long plexiglass box	
	(mortals) hats, food, thin rope, red sun, felt signs with crocheted relationships ("sister mother" etc.), wings (worn by Tannis thru- out)	
		(gods) stairs tape re- corder

Audience

The speeches in the following text are either 'said' or 'read' from 3x5-inch cards.

> "Since I know nothing at all, I shall simply do
> whatever occurs to me."   (C.G. Jung)

PROLOGUE:

The Gods stand and sit on stairs (downstage left). Mortals sit center with pot of food, hats, rope, felt signs. Heroes gather props upstage right, stand in a row facing audience, walk toward audience, stop, bow — leaving arms in same position so that all the props fall to floor. They step over debris, turning their backs on audience, pick it all up as before and walk upstage, turn around to face audience again in a row, bow. The blue medicine ball, fake grass, thick rope, towel, clock, notebook, book, pencil, suitcase, cleaver, flag, two overcoats, one hat, and red ball — all tumble to floor once more.

THE HEROES REVEAL THEMSELVES:

1. Valda and Epp walk to mortals, Valda carrying suitcase in one hand, her right arm around Epp's shoulders. They stand looking at swaying faces of mortals. Valda passes suitcase (which is passed over heads by the mortals and received by Yvonne who then places it beside stairs). They then turn and walk back.

2. Jim walks slowly toward Gods. He wears hat. Barbara is helped down from stairs. She goes to Jim and says:
    "If you come back another time, you may no longer find me here."
    She returns and walks up stairs. Jim returns. Halfway back he turns and doffs hat, then proceeds.

3. Before Jim gets back Fernando walks toward him. Jim places his hands on Fernando's shoulders and says:
    "Somewhere there once was a Flower, a Stone, a Crystal, a Queen, a King, a Palace, a Lover and his Beloved, and this was long ago, on an Island somewhere in the ocean 5,000 years ago . . . ." (Jung)
    Long pause; he looks and says:
    "No one understands what I mean."
    Jim returns.

[Mortals' Meetings begin, operating simultaneously from here on. *See page 194*]

4. Fernando proceeds forward with Epp, who walks abreast of him downstage of mortals. They start to meet on other side. Doug walks between them just before they embrace. Doug says:

    "I am sorry, but you have arrived at an awkward moment. We were supposed to have gone on vacation yesterday, but my wife was stung by a bee, and we have had to postpone our trip. Everything is topsy-turvy here." (Miguel Serrano)

    Doug returns to stairs and is helped up. Long silence before Epp and Fernando return.

5. Jim passes them wearing overcoat and hat on his way to upstage left corner. He stands, looking into corner.

6. Valda makes big loop — upstage to downstage — around mortals. She wails inconsolably during whole transit. Gods shuffle on staircase. (They are disturbed.)

7. Jim returns (after her return). Mortals knock on floor during his journey.

8. Fernando and Valda carry big rope to stairs. Valda slowly lowers Fernando (who holds himself very stiffly against her back) to a 45° angle. Nancy says:

    "They are very familiar with my rope. They understand and appreciate it."

    Valda and Fernando return via downstage.

9. Epp and Jim pass them in overcoats and hats, walking in unison looking down with hands clasped behind backs. They go as far to stage left as they can, then stop. Epp looks 'off in distance', Jim looks 'at sky' and says:

    "How beautiful it is here. I should like to live here forever." (Serrano)

10. Jim starts to return. Halfway he turns and waves to Epp. They walk toward each other. David goes between them, faces downstage and says:

    "What is your favorite word?"

    They each reply. David walks between them and back to stairs. Jim starts back. Almost back, he turns and waves again, then again walks toward Epp.

11. Valda starts to overtake Jim. Epp (still standing where she originally stopped) says:

    "It was late when I left his house, and as I walked down towards the lake, I thought of our conversation and tried to put my feelings in order." (Serrano)

    Jim comes to a halt about three feet from Epp. Valda, carrying red ball, passes between them. She hands ball to Doug on the stairs.

12. Valda returns via downstage. Jim, whose focus has followed Valda since she passed between himself and Epp, follows her at a distance. When she has arrived extreme downstage right she turns and waits for him. He stops two feet from her. She says:

> "The dream urged upon me the necessity of clarifying this situation." (Jung)

(Epp's gaze has followed Jim.) They all return.

MORTALS' MEETINGS [begins after no. 3 of *The Heroes Reveal Themselves*]

1. Janis (friend) and Shirley sit crosslegged at right angles downstage right.

2. Jim (brother) lies in front of plastic box; Jeanne walks up to him and nudges with foot. Jim looks up, then departs. Jeanne squats.

3. Cynthia (sister) stands behind Jeanne, who is squatting. Both return.

4. Pat walks to right. Carrie (daughter) follows. Pat turns sharply. Carrie runs back and gives her sign to Lois, who beckons to Pat. Both return.

5. Shirley sits leaning on arms facing right. John (enemy) follows when she is still and sits downstage behind her in same position. Shirley looks back over downstage shoulder. Both return.

6. Lois goes to upstage left and squats facing diagonally downstage left. Carrie (enemy) goes and stands behind her. Lois looks up. Both return.

7. Cynthia (lover) sits same as no. 6. John squats beside her, looks out. Cynthia looks at him. Both return.

8. Jim (leader) starts out to same place; Janis starts out. Jim squats, Janis squats (both facing left), Jim returns.

9. Pat (wife) lies on back downstage of Janis. Jains looks at her. Both return.

10. Cynthia and Shirley (friend) walk in opposite circles, pass each other downstage center, stop, look back, smile, embrace, come apart. Shirley says:

> "Yesterday when you visited me, it was my son's birthday. He was 50 years old." (Serrano)

Both return.

11. Tannis (daughter) throws out "pebble" hats. She is followed by John, who brings her back by manipulating her feet over the "pebbles."

12. Jim (father) and Pat walk to right. Both return. Jim jumping from foot to foot as though 'looking down at the earth.'

13. John walks all the way left, turns. Jeanne (disciple) goes to him. He says:

> "I understand you have just come from India." (Serrano)

Both return.

194

14. Lois goes to downstage center, sits leaning back on arms with face up. Carrie stands by Lois' hands facing right. Jim (other man) stands with 'sun' over Lois' face and right hand on Carrie's left shoulder. He says:

> "I dreamed of my mother last night, and of my wife. My mother was crying for me." (Serrano)

Carrie leaves, making Jim's arm drop. Jim and Lois return.

15. Janice (wife) sits in chair looking to left. Pat stands to her left, leaning over on chair and Shirley to her right, both looking at Janice. Shirley (other woman) turns away to her right with great hauteur and returns. Long pause. Pat and Janice return.

16. Janice (leader) walks to left. Cynthia (sister) and Lois go to her as she starts back. They both grasp her bent arms, slightly supporting her on way back.

17. Jeanne (husband) shakes Tannis (wife).

18. Janice and John stand in place. Janice says:

> "I have come a long way, I began, but of course you are very well known in my country."

She sits. John remains standing.

19. Shirley (mother) sniffs Pat (daughter). John remains standing.

20. Jim (other man) stands and faces John. Both turn completely around while focusing on each other as long as possible. Both sit.

THE PLOT THICKENS:

At beginning of Mortals' Meetings no. 20 Doug throws ball to Jim's outstretched hand. Jim and Epp begin duet with grass and ball (*page 206*). As they lie down on grass David and Yvonne cross space (Yvonne carries suitcase) in time to pull them in an arc on the grass. They help them up; Yvonne stays on side lines until end of duet; David starts to return. As he reaches mortals they stand up — now completely connected by rope around each one's middle. He takes food (he already has red ball retrieved from Jim and Epp) back to stairs (Olympus).

Mortals start to 'walk backwards in circles, at the same time obstructing the way of Jim, who tries to 'get through". Simultaneously (J. carries suitcase) Epp, Fernando, Valda do trio with Yvonne, screen, cleaver, rope loops, blue medicine ball, clock. (*page 206*)

After about two minutes of 'getting thru', mortals do 'balancing act' with suitcase and Jim. Four or five minutes later he starts to go away (to right) then turns and tries to get through again. This time the mortals obstruct his way with the 'hand-wringing step'. Jim gets discouraged, goes away a few steps, then tries again.

65

Fernando, **carrying** book, comes up behind him, places hand on his shoulder, and turns to quietly face downstage right. James sees him and also turns to look where he is looking. (Mortals dissolve quietly to sit upstage of stairs.) Fernando and James stand quietly as Barbara reads:

> "As he turned around to look behind, I turned with him, and even I was overcome with the•beauty of what we saw. It was one of those rarest of moments, which come perhaps once or twice a year and may last only a few seconds, when a violent storm has cleared the air completely and the whole mighty range of the mountains is exposed in a wild and glorious harmony of rock and snow. The lower slopes green with the dense forest, the upper slopes rose in steep, jagged cliffs, and above them the great snow-capped peaks rose proudly into the clearest possible sky. There was not a cloud to match the pure whiteness of the snow." (Colin Turnbull)

Mortals have been untying themselves during the preceding speech. When Barbara finishes speech they start 'brain-fever' song: the chromatic scale minus the eighth note using vowel-sounds, syllables, words, parts of sentences, etc. This shortly dissolves into animal concert: howling, yelping, screeching, etc. Becomes very cacaphonous.

196

66

After Barbara's speech James has gone downstage to 'sleep' on his suitcase. His head is toward stage right and he removes his glasses. Fernando goes to center to sleep. He lies on his side, duplicating James' position. The brain-fever song is their common dream, sung by both mortals and gods.

Mortals finish concert and become advancing herd with 'bobbing heads', Tannis takes end of rope and crawls thru plastic box. Valda and Epp have run to front of herd (just to right of box). They receive end of rope from Tannis. They 'pass through' herd (stand still while herd passes by on all sides of them). The herd then proceeds slowly to the sleeping Fernando, who takes the other end of the rope. (At this point Yvonne goes to wake up Jim and takes his glasses.) Epp and Valda turn the box. James stands extreme right center and passes through herd, which then sits at extreme right.

Valda and Epp support Fernando under the shoulder blades as they all run, he with flailing arms (still holding book), until they come to the standing James. Fernando places book against face of James. 'Book battle/caress' ensues: Alternating actions of pushing other's face against open book and down to floor and caressing body with open book. Epp stands center right with ball that David has given her (rolled) in the 'squeeze' position. Valda has gone away. After about one minute of book battle Yvonne reads:

67

"In the old days the medicine men had dreams and knew whether there is war or sickness or whether rain comes and where the herds should be driven. But since the whites came, no one had dreams anymore. Dreams were no longer needed because now the White Man knew everything." (Jung)

Valda and James go to Epp and begin 'squeeze'. Mortals form 'house of cards' around them. Fernando proceeds with suitcase to meet Trisha (wearing mustache), who has poled from upstage left on big medicine ball. As Fernando passes her, Doug reads:

"Here was a man who obviously possessed no pocket watch, let alone a wrist watch; for he was obviously and unselfconsciously the person he had always been." (Jung)

Epp says:

"She is my very dear friend and I don't like seeing her caught in the middle."

Trisha threads her way in among mortals and says to Epp: 67, 68

"You will soon see things of which you have never heard, and which you have never seen. Then you will understand things that I can never tell you. But you must stay awake — you may see them only once." (Turnbull)

68

Fernando has proceeded (after his encounter with Trisha) to wooden box to do 'plastique' poses in box with suitcase.

Mortals do unison walk to get upstage left (led by Nancy). Barbara says:
> "They were in the habit of walking abroad and showing themselves."
> (Jung)

Trio between Valda, Epp, and James with red ball (*page 206*). When mortals arrive upstage they do David's "dying" against wall. Fernando rushes out of box and tries to sleep. John and Jim Cobb and Tannis pursue him. Four or five times they place box about 4 feet from his sleeping form. Tannis pushes it over. Fernando rolls over just in time to avoid it crashing down on him, jumps up and dashes to another place to try to 'sleep'.

At end of box crashing, Barbara (wearing 'contempt' shirt) and Doug come down from stairs and walk with Fernando, making the box retreat to its original position. They enter box and do very slow plastique. Trio — James, Valda, Epp — does spirals (passing ball) until Valda faces audience holding ball. Epp and James do "pupil-pointing" ending seated in audience. (Holding her index finger close to his eyes, she leads him — at a run — to look at a point on the floor.)

69

Valda does her solo. During this time the gods have descended from Olympus to place Kleenex boxes on the feet of the corpses. The "Danse Plastique" in the box goes on simultaneously. *81*
89

After Valda's solo is over, mortals line up facing stage right. A god gives one of them the pot of food. During the next manoeuver the pot travels up and down the line, stopping when anyone wants to eat.

Doug goes behind Valda, who stands center. He puts cardboard mask in front of her face and holds it there. Doug and Nancy carry tape recorder and microphone as PA for the next five speeches. Fernando stands before line of mortals, appraising them, ready to back up as they advance. 69

Line starts to shuffle forward in Kleenex boxes. Pat, who is furthest upstage, keeps abreast while crawling through plexiglass box. When she has emerged and stood up, the line stops. David walks around in space behind the mortals — in great agitation in very squeaky shoes. After about one minute line moves forward again. David continues to walk about. Doug reads:

> "A man who has not passed through the inferno of his passions has
> never overcome them. They then dwell in the house next door, and at
> any moment a flame may dart out and set fire to his own house. When-
> ever we give up, leave behind, and forget too much, there is always the

70

danger that the things we have neglected will return with added force."
(Jung)

Mortals stop. David continues his agitated walk. One minute later mortals resume their inexorable forward shuffle.

Fernando retreats before them. He says:

"See how cruel they look. Their lips are thin, their noses sharp, their faces furrowed and distorted by folds. Their eyes have a staring expression, they are always seeking something. What are they seeking? They always want something: they are always uneasy and restless. I do not know what they want. I do not understand them. I think that they are mad." (Jung)

Line reaches end of space. Mortals proceed to unroll bubble wrap. They walk around on it; their steps produce popping sounds. Yvonne has brought suitcase to James. He and Epp run around periphery twice. Nancy reads:

"With lightened baggage he continues his journey, with steadily increasing velocity, toward nebulous goals. He compensates for the loss of gravity by the illusion of his triumph, such as steamships, railroads, airplanes, and rockets, that rob him of his duration and transport him into another reality of speeds and explosive accelerations." (Jung)

201

James and Epp arrive downstage right and lie down, heads resting on suitcase, feet pointing upstage. Mortals continue walking on bubble wrap. Doug and Valda are now in a prone position on their sides, having been "toppled" by mortals in the line as the line shuffled past them. Doug still holds the grey cardboard mask in front of Valda's face. Doug reads:

> "How long they have lived in the forest we do not know, though it is considered opinion that they are among the oldest inhabitants of Africa. They may well be the original inhabitants of the great tropical rain forest which stretches nearly from coast to coast. They were certainly well established there at the very beginning of historic times." (Turnbull)

Mortals stop walking and prepare the pink cloth. Valda reads (on card stapled behind mask):

> "I only wish I could somehow convey the sound of his voice — soft and musical, so quiet that I could hardly hear it. I have seen many of the forest people talk like this when they are feeling deeply. Even the movement of his mouth and his eyes and gestures of his hands conveyed what he was saying. As if singing to himself, he said, 'I was wrong. This is a good place, though I don't like it; it must be good, because there are so many animals. There is no noise of fighting. It is good because the sky is clear and the ground is clean. It is good because I feel good; I feel as though I and the whole world were sleeping and dreaming. Why do people always make so much noise?' And then he added, with infinite wistfulness, 'If only there were more trees . . .' "
> (Turnbull)

Epp and James do their second duet (with towel and notebook, *page 207*). Afterwards, Doug leaves Valda, who rolls over onto her back. Gods roll the stairs into position at stage left. James adjusts pink fabric around his forehead at stage right. Fernando takes his place about 7 feet behind him, ready to counterbalance James' forward lean by gripping the two clumps of fabric streaming past. Epp stands ready to take up the slack behind Fernando. (The fabric is a bolt of pink jersey about 80 feet long.) Tannis (who has worn wings thruout the performance: meta-mortal, bird-woman, harpy, now perhaps about to be 'avenging angel') takes her place behind James and in front of Fernando.

The 'ascent and fall' begins: In torturous fashion James leans forward almost at 45°, walks with faltering steps toward Valda on the floor who is also in a direct line with the stairs surrounded by the waiting gods. He continually speaks directions to Fernando: "Let me out, take it in" etc. When he reaches Valda he continues walking — his feet on either side of her. Tannis follows suit. When they have both passed, Valda sits, grasps both sides of fabric and lets the tension produced by James' forward movement pull her to her feet. Mistake and correction:

90

202

She does this after Fernando has passed over her. So the final order in the column
is James, Tannis, Fernando, Valda, Epp.

Just as James reaches stairs David and Doug help Tannis jump onto his back. In
this terrifying state he assays Olympus. Mortals go to upstage center and begin
'yearning' formation: a long line that gradually snakes downstage, always one
person at each end leaning outward in a 'yearning' pose — supported by the rest
of the line. Yvonne reads:

> "At the beginning of the illness I had the feeling that there was some-
> thing wrong with my attitude, and that I was to some extent respon-
> sible for the mishap. But when one affirms things as they are, without
> subjective protests, accepts the conditions of existence as one sees
> them, accepts one's own nature, as one happens to be, when one lives
> one's own life — then one must take mistakes into the bargain; life
> would not be complete without them. There is no guarantee — not for a
> single moment — that we will not fall into error or stumble into deadly
> peril. We may think there is a sure road. But that would be the road
> of death. Then nothing happens any longer — at any rate, not the right
> things. Anyone who takes the sure road is as good as dead." (Jung)

The preceding speech is read just after James and Tannis have finished leaning
way out over the top of the stairs (which he has succeeded in clambering up) and
they begin to crumple in a misshapen heap into the waiting arms of the gods, who
then lower them onto the floor. They remain there as Epp, Valda, Fernando, and
the gods join the 'yearners'. A good five to ten minutes later when the yearning
has moved completely downstage, James and Tannis move the stairs to center.
Mortals and heroes assemble stage right, gods move to stage left. The mortals and
heroes very slowly and simply start the sun on its ascent. (It is a red paper circle
about 10 inches in diameter, rather tattered from rehearsals.) It changes hands
frequently. The only instructions are that its motion must be smooth and even
and that everyone must constantly be in a position where he or she can focus the
gaze upon it. James assists it up the stairs to its zenith. Carrie — held high in the
arms of big Jim Cobb — receives it to begin the descent to its setting. As it begins
to set, Doug reads:

> "What we do, we do not only for ourselves, but for the whole world.
> Everyone benefits by it. If we did not do it what would become of the
> world? After all, we are a people who live on the roof of the world. We
> are the children of Father Sun, and with our religion we daily help our
> father to go across the sky. If we were to cease practicing our religion,
> in 10 years the sun would no longer rise. Then it would be night for-
> ever." (Jung)

The sun sets.

> "I abandoned all further attempts
> to understand."   (Jung)

Devices   animal concert

kilometer stones   △

speech

signs – Pain., Power, sex, knowledge, contempt

life-size drawings

~~the~~ relics & remains, shards

up-ended sandbox

gates, doors – squeeze past – boxes

stairs – plummet down, steep descent, get to the bottom

suitcase: "With lightened baggage he continues his journey,
with steadily increasing velocity, toward nebulous
goals. He compensates for the loss of gravity by the illusion
of his ~~triumphs~~, such as

bubble wrap – Kleenex boxes

soft sticky mass, pulpy mass

red sun | red ball | red rope | red paper steamships,
railroads, airplanes, and rockets, that rob him of his duration & transport him into another reality of speeds & explosive
accelerations.

keys, locks)   lock up   key to the puzzle
– keyed up   key in   locksmith
locked out   under lock + key   keys to the kingdom

clocks: time of day (won't give you), all the time,
watch out, wrist watch, watchful

knapsack   cleaver   photo figures

towel, pencil & notebook

pole, medicine ball

204

Props:

Mortals: hats, food, thin rope, felt signs, red paper sun.

Heroes: Blue medicine ball, grass, thick rope, towel, clock,
         notebook, book, pencil, suitcase, cleaver, flag, two
         overcoats, one hat, red ball.

Red sun and screen are placed upstage right. Brown medicine ball
and pole are placed upstage left.

1. Duet - Epp and James (red ball, grass)   65

(Doug throws red ball to James just as mortals meet; Epp places
grass.) 1. Walk backward and forward sweeping ball down to graze
grass. 2. Facing each other (profiles to audience) they do side
to side bending while exchanging ball, slowly shifting their
placement to right side of grass. 3. Lie on grass facing each
other with ball hand doing big arcs; ball is exchanged. David
and Yvonne drag them on grass in a circle, then help them up and
give them grass as they do side to side bending - this time,
however, standing next to each other, first facing right, then
shifting to face audience - slowly traveling to right and off.

2. Trio - Epp, Valda, Fernando (screen, clock, cleaver, blue
    ball, rope loops)
         1. Chain with rope loops, turning screen around.
         2. F sits, with woman standing over him.
         3. Props are revealed as screen moves downstage; F on
             left, V on right.
         4. V and E fight over clock; F throws out rope loop,
             falls.
         5. Cleaver is handed over screen; E and F play catch.
         6. Valda on ball. (left to right)
         7. Epp runs away, is caught by Fernando.
         8. Epp is 'plopped'. (left to right)
         9. Fernando on ball. (right to left)
        10. Spirals with rope loops.

3. Trio - Epp, James, Valda (following 'squeeze' of Epp)

Epp 'hypnotizes' J and V, who are still leaning against her.
When mortals have cleared away they pass ball around. Anyone who
wishes does tortured squeeze pose, at which other 2 press each
side of 'squeezed one.' Ends in triangle circles with ball. When
Valda takes her place for solo, E does "pupil-pointing" with J,
ending in sitting in audience.

4. Duet - Epp and James (notebook, towel)

Improvise with: elbow wiggle, spitting on palms, slapping palms with turns, bump bellies, lindy step, lassoing with towel, slapping ass with notebook, etc.

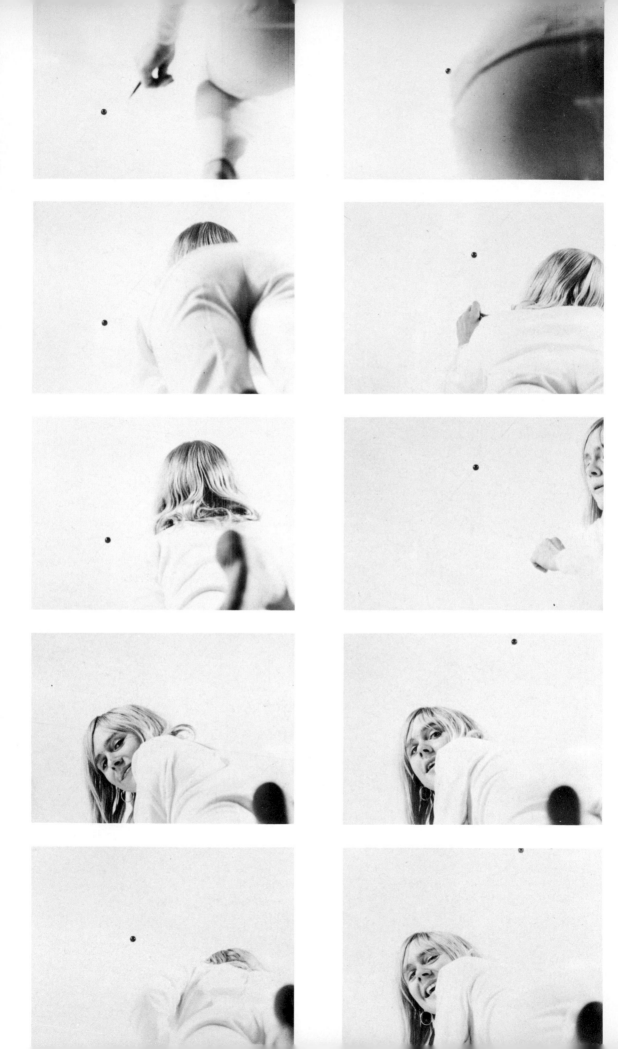

VII 1972

Films

In the summer of 1971, while conducting a workshop with Barbara Lloyd at the Vancouver Art Gallery, I was reconsidering my relation to film-making and wrote the following (previously unpublished) essay:

I'm no longer interested in mixed media. You either make a movie or you don't make a movie. I didn't make movies: I made filmed choreographic exercises that were meant to be viewed with one's peripheral vision. When I recently viewed several of my films head-on after not seeing them for awhile, they seemed a boring hybrid, too obvious and simplistic to work as either film or dance. The not-moving movie camera cannot have too 'interesting' a subject. 'Interest' must be wrestled out of the subject — as in Warhol's portraits — by the viewer. Otherwise the camera must participate, become a collaborator rather than voyeur. I am sick of voyeurism. The closest my movies came to an active rather than passive participation of the camera eye was in the very first film, shot by Bud Wirtschafter (*Volleyball*). (Why is the language of cinematography so bellicose?) 34 – 37 The camera chased a volleyball that was rolled into the frame and came to rest when it (the volleyball) came to rest.

My movies were an extension of my concern with the body and the body in motion: legs, a hand, later a whole body clad in white (a female) dominating the frame. Blow it all up. (More bellicosity!) One of my favorites was a ten-minute voyeurism of the perpetual-motion interior of a chicken-house in Vermont. During the last thirty seconds you see very faintly the almost transparent image of a man gathering eggs way back in a sunlit corner of the huge building. Somehow a very bitter, funny film.

I guess at the time of making these movies I was not very concerned about their quality as independent works. Which is no reason not to make more movies. I must simply keep reminding myself not to take them too seriously, or else take them seriously enough to think through a bit more deeply some of the possibilities of the camera. Maybe the kind of film I have made might be classified as amateur movies. Not home movies. The term 'home movie' very quickly moved into 'underground' or non-commercial movie. My movies are not to be taken that seriously.

Opposite page: 71 Stills from *Line*, 1969 — Susan Marshall

Trio Film is a kind of documentation of what might be a proscenium stage event. It takes place in a room with white walls, white carpet, white sofa, and two white club chairs. You almost expect the walls to shake a little, the way the fake walls of a stage set do. Two nude people and a 2½ foot white balloon interact in a very decorous manner for fifteen minutes. The two people roll the balloon back and forth, walk around with it, somersault in unison over sofa and chairs, sit on the sofa and chat. There was some camera movement and editing on this film. The pace is very measured and slow. It was my version of "Dinner at Eight" and "Dejeuner sur L'herbe." Phill Niblock, the cinematographer, persuaded me to end the film on a whimsical note: Becky Arnold sits on couch facing camera. Steve Paxton stands on couch holding balloon. He is seen from the balloon down (it is held just above his crotch). Becky is seen from the waist up. Steve jumps up and down on sofa. His testicles and penis bounce. Becky's breasts bobble. Her expression slowly changes from professional detachment to a bemused smirk to unabashed glee. End of blue movie.

72

72   *Trio Film* screened during performance of early version of *Two Trios*, Oct. 19, 1968 — Barbara and Becky (see page 116)

Then there was the *Hand Movie*. A five-minute blow-up of a hand, seen vertically. The fingers rub each other, move around. Two or three times the hand turns over and the camera follows it. Otherwise the camera is still. Very erotic film.

The fifth and last was the most curious of all. It was first called *Bead*; later I changed the title to *Line* when I realized that *Bead* let the cat out of the bag and destroyed the mystery of the image . . . Phill Niblock constructed a device that allowed a motor-driven bead to ride slowly up a diagonal taut string. (Actually the bead was stationary on the string and the string itself moved.) Directly behind this device is white paper that fills the entire frame. When the bead appears in the lower left corner of the frame you can't tell how big it is as there is no point of

71

210

reference to indicate its size. It slowly moves upward. When it is about half way, these huge white-trousered legs walk in from the side, and a blond girl (Susan Marshall) squats down and lies on her belly, feet toward the camera, body very foreshortened. To my surprise what I thought would necessarily happen, doesn't. That is, her body does not indicate a key to the size of the still-traveling round object, because the white background does not give a clue as to the distance of the object from her body. So it might be any size — from a small object very close to her to a large object very far from her. In fact one can fantasize that it is a large object in the sky. *But then* (the plot thickens!) she whips out a pen and starts writing something illegible on the paper, so you know that the whiteness is a vertical surface very close to her. Somehow the bead remains mysterious. Then she does some irrelevant things like look over her shoulder and smile a classic toothpaste-ad smile. She rolls over again, backs up onto her heels so her rump looms into the camera, leans on an elbow talking out at the spectators (it is silent, as all my films have been) and, smiling, finally rolls out of the frame, and the bead dissappears out of the upper right hand corner. Very strange — the combination of the automated inanimate object and the blond vacuousness of the female image. I don't usually combine objects and bodies in this manner. People may become object-like in the way they are manipulated in dances like *Continuous Project — Altered Daily*, but rarely take on a 'characterization' that so dominated this film.

I'm also tired of ambiguity.

OK, what do I have to say about this woman writing on the wall? If I revealed what she was writing — maybe she was writing "At 4 o'clock this afternoon your name will be placed on the danger list" — would that be any less ambiguous? How about "The only feeling I am certain of these days is a complete loathing for myself."

My next movie will be about human relationships:

Camera follows Taki thru glass door down narrow hallway past Glen in bed. Taki says "Good morning". Glen raises head, blinks. Cut to close-up of Glen's head. Cut to Taki's back still walking. Camera stops. Taki goes off left thru doorway. Scene thru window: backyard (very lush), bay in background. Camera slowly pans 180 showing sleazy kitchen, pots, pans, food, sink, etc. Stops on Shuzo showing large shell to Grin, the dog. Grin is wagging tail, sniffing shell. Shuzo leaves. Close-up of Glen's head in bed watching Shuzo leave. Cut to Grin, Benjy emerges from far room in wheelchair. Someone calls Grin, who runs away. Brakhage-like flashing around of camera, coming to rest on group of people in empty white room wringing their hands in silence. Cut to close-up of old-fashioned wringer. Camera dollies back, revealing a large photo-poster of wringer with "ROSIE" stencilled below it. Photo is on wall. Camera dollies up close. Cut to scene with photo laid on snow bank. Cut to photo on Glen's bed. Glen gets up, takes long look at poster. He then examines his right shoulder. Gets out of bed. Camera now focuses on his head while he takes a wad of string, tacks one end to his desk and walks backward until it is stretched across room. He sits, holding string between his knees (camera still on his head), breaks some hashish into a stone pipe, inhales deeply on it. Grin comes into frame, licks Glen's face. Cut to Yvonne entering room. Cut to floor level view of Yvonne approaching string and getting stopped by it. Slow dissolve into garden scene — Taki, Shuzo, Roy sitting around a table.

There will be 100 in the cast. Speech will start maybe halfway thru. Sounds like something between "Chant D'Amour" and "Orpheus".

(Comment: The preceding was written in a year when I was smoking a lot of grass.)

List of Films

	Title	Cinematographer	
1967	Volleyball (Foot Film)	Bud Wirtschafter	16mm, b/w, 10 min.
1968	Hand Movie	William Davis	8mm, b/w, 5 min.
	Rhode Island Red	Roy Levin	16mm, b/w, 10 min.
	Trio Film	Phill Niblock	16mm, b/w, 13 min.
1969	Line	Phill Niblock	16mm, b/w, 10 min.
1972	Lives of Performers	Babette Mangolte	16mm, b/w, sound, 90 min.

Lives of Performers

Lives of Performers, the 16mm film I directed in the Spring of 1972 (Cinematographer — Babette Mangolte), unfolds in roughly fourteen episodes, each having a different cinematic approach toward integrating real and fictional aspects of my roles of director and choreographer and the performers' real and fictional roles during the making of previous work and the film itself. The first section (and a later one) is edited footage of an actual rehearsal of *Walk, She Said* (*page 274*) for a live performance (*Performance* at the Whitney Museum). The second shows photographs of *Grand Union Dreams* while the voice-over narration describes the content of the photos and the changing intimacies of these same performers — fictional in this instance (*see below*). In other sections the narrative zigzags along as the performers talk and move about in a barren studio setting containing a couch and several chairs. A simultaneous voice-over commentary by the performers themselves — sometimes read, sometimes improvised from the scenario — alternating with inter-titles, constantly interprets the enigmatic sequences of unheard (seen) discussion and implied emotional complexities. The narration is further complicated by the fact that part of it was recorded during an actual performance, so that the laughter of the then-present audience is heard at various times. Valda Setterfield performs a solo dance at one point (which I had originally choreographed for *Grand Union Dreams*). It is not very well appreciated by Fernando Torm, her (presumed) lover. ("He has seen it a hundred times.")

The film ends with a 'real performance', a series of imitations of stills from G. W. Pabst's *Pandora's Box* or *Lulu*. The other performers are John Erdman, Shirley Soffer, Epp Kotkas, James Barth, Sarah Soffer, and myself as director.

Script for Soundtrack of the Second Sequence

The passages enclosed in brackets [] were read only in *Performance* (*page 241*), and omitted in the film for the sake of greater brevity. In this section, consisting of six shots, the camera is stationary and frames each photograph against a background of assorted technical memos and notations concerning the film itself.

photo no. 1

Yvonne This is the first of eight photos from *Grand Union Dreams*. Shirley was a mortal, Fernando and Valda were heroes. I was one of the gods. It was done about a year ago. [I just got an idea. There were lots of props in *Grand Union Dreams*. In most cases they were used with consideration for their actual physical properties; for instance, the suitcase was

213

photo no. 1

photo no. 2

photo no. 3

214

carried, the two people lay on the fake grass, the hats and wings were worn, the long plexiglass box was crawled through. Yet in all cases the objects worked as symbols if for no other reason than that the meaning of their function was unspecified and disconnected in time. The sequential coherence of the work was entirely physical and spatial. The only consistent narrative cohesiveness lay in the division of people that was established at the very beginning — the division into gods, heroes, and mortals. I draw closer to my forbears.]

In this first photo Epp and James are engaged in a duet. David and Yvonne have just finished dragging them on the fake grass in a small arc. When they stand they undulate their upper bodies in unison while passing the red ball back and forth. They are about to pick up the grass and involve it in their undulations. Valda waits. My question is: "What does it mean?" Are they celebrating something? Yes, that sounds good: Epp and James are doing a dance of pleasure at the advent of spring.

Shirley   It actually was spring when we began working on this piece and I first met you, Fernando. I think some people went over to your house after that first rehearsal.

Fernando You asked if we had any booze. That was where I first had a hint of your humor — the look on your face when you asked.

Shirley   Yes, I remember the look you gave me. I thought "Oh, I'm discovered in my discomfort, but he's sympathetic."

photo no. 2

Yvonne   Ah, there's the suitcase, and there's Trisha. Trisha has come down from Olympus and has laboriously poled her way toward the group of mortals who are putting the 'squeeze' on the heroes, especially on Epp, who is squeezing the red ball. In this photo she has said "She is my very dear friend and I don't like seeing her caught in the middle." Trisha threads her way in and says to Epp, "You will soon see things of which you have never heard, and which you have never seen. Then you will understand things that I can never tell you. But you must stay awake. You may see them only once."

Shirley   And there's Fernando in the box . . .

Yvonne   . . . with suitcase. Why does Fernando have the suitcase? Is he going away or has he just arrived? Why is he in the box with the suitcase? Is he trying it out as a body-supporting device? And what is in the suitcase? Dirty sox?

photo no. 3

Fernando The complete works of Aristotle in Greek. (Long pause) On the stairs. I was going up the stairs and I heard my name. I didn't even know who was calling me, but I felt it in my spine. Something about your voice, and I turned around and it was you.

Shirley   Uh-huh. I didn't know there was anything special about my voice at that time, but I distinctly remember seeing you on the stairs and realizing for the first time that you really were going to be taking this thing seriously and I felt a strong surge of liking for you, and that must have shown in my voice.

Valda   I was always aware of your presence. It was equivocal, sometimes sinister in that it didn't declare itself — especially on that ride we took into the Menonite country with Shirley and Lena. I didn't know what you were about or who you were attracted to . . . .

Fernando Actually, I hadn't intended to ask you to go, but somehow — meeting you by accident like that, passing through the doorway — I did it on the spur of the moment.

Valda   Yes, and I immediately asked if Shirley and Lena would come, because I didn't want to be alone with you.

Shirley   Then he kept coming to the house with those messages for you.

Valda   That really confused me — not that I thought much about it in a personal way — but rather, you know, in that way that one does when you are trying to figure out someone else's intentions, whether or not they are directed at you. So I didn't really think anything about him personally until you told me about those talks you had with him about me. I think then I began to look at you differently. Maybe with more curiosity. When we went to the theater that night I was very aware that you were sitting next to me. I don't know how aware I was that you had *manoeuvered* to sit next to me. Do you remember — when the whole audience stood up so enthusiastically — I turned and looked at you as if to say "O Christ, do we have to do this too?" and we stood up.

Fernando Yes, I remember. Then later I sat next to you in the pancake house and at one point I took out a pencil and was writing something which you noticed in a certain way. I was embarrassed.

(Long pause)

photo no. 4

[Yvonne This one is out of proper order. All this actually took place before the 'squeeze'. The mortals — and Fernando — have just finished the "brain fever song", which is the common dream of both mortals and gods. They sing it together. Maybe we should demonstrate. (Y,F,S,V sing.) Here the mortals have become an advancing herd with bobbing heads.

216

Valda and Epp are standing still, waiting for the herd to pass. Epp and Valda will then pull him through the plexiglass box, which isn't really visible here.]

Valda   The night of our last performance you said after it was over that you'd be coming to New York and that you'd like to look me up. I told you my address and said that information had my phone number. Then later at that small party I was aware of you — for no particular reason. You were across the room talking to Donald. I made that gesture with the bottle of brandy — offering the last drop to anyone who wanted it before I wolfed it down — and finally you sprang laughing up and accepted the bottle. Then later you were lying down. As I started to leave, on impulse I went over and lay down on top of you, saying "Goodbye, Fernando" thinking it was the last time I was going to see you there. Almost instantaneously — as though you were expecting me to come to you — you grasped the back of my head and drew me down to your chest. You caressed my hair and sighed deeply. (pause) Then there was all that confusion about who would drive us to the airport. We didn't expect you.

Shirley   Yes, I didn't know what to think either, although I sort of knew. I guess I was just a little uncomfortable, because you had already showed me that piece he had written for you.

Valda   I regretted that later. It seemed too intimate to show anyone, even to Shirley, but I was still not ready to acknowledge your intentions toward me, so for the moment I had to pretend it was not as intimate or private as it later seemed to me. By the time you arrived to drive us to the airport I knew what was going on and I was getting excited.

Yvonne   What made you excited?

Valda   It was like the excitement of performance, experiencing my beauty and value when all those eyes are focused on me. I am at my best as a performer.

Yvonne   Why did you have to wait before getting excited? Don't you ever experience attraction to someone before you are sure whether or not they are attracted to you?

Valda   Yeh, sure. But I really wasn't in that frame of mind a year ago. You know what I had just come out of; I was very depressed, so I wasn't able to use my eyes too well. Besides, I really do enjoy performing.

Yvonne   OK.

Fernando When we went back . . .

photo no. 4

photo no. 6

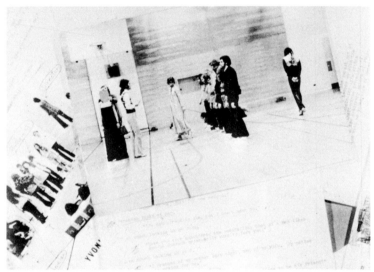

photo no. 8

218

Valda   Wait. Yvonne, were you reading that?

Yvonne   What?

Valda   Those questions.

Yvonne   Yes. Why'd you want to know?

Valda   I just wondered. Sorry, Fernando

Fernando We went back to find your eyeshade, went upstairs, looked through
          the rooms. There was hardly any light.

Valda   I wondered why you didn't touch me, wondered why I didn't touch
          you.

Fernando I stood on the landing beside the doorway as we were going back down-
          stairs. I thought you'd have to squeeze through.

Valda   O God! You gave me so much room.

Yvonne   What else happened while we were rehearsing that piece?

Shirley   The hotel

Fernando The hotel . . . that's where I first got a sense of certain aspects of your
          mind that made you seem very different to me. I was lying on the bed
          and you were sitting on it . . . I can't remember now exactly what led
          to talking about Henry Miller.

Shirley   Somehow we got into who influenced him and I said Blaise Cendrars
          influenced him and we started to argue, only it wasn't an argument
          because I simply repeated my opinion while you repeated yours.

Fernando Yes, I was trying to remember the name of someone else. I still think
          it was someone else — his name starts with a K.

Shirley   No, it was Blaise Cendrars.

Yvonne   So how the hell did that give you a sense of her mind? Did that seem
          like obscure information or something?

Fernando It just had to do with that moment and yes, I guess her access to that
          particular information.

Yvonne   This is where Epp and Valda propel Fernando across the space supporting his upper back while his arms flail. One hand is holding a book. Trisha has started her journey on the medicine ball. Oh, for God's sake, this one should have come way back there too. You can see the plexiglass box here. I wonder what Fernando was reading? Balzac, maybe. Père Goriot.]

photo no. 6

Yvonne   Here the mortals have become an inexorable wall, shuffling forward on Kleenex box-shod feet. On the right one of the gods — David — is walking about in great agitation in very squeaky shoes. Doug stands behind Valda, obscuring her face with a grey cardboard disc. Dong stands behind Doug with a microphone. Doug reads a speech from Jung about how if you don't pass through the inferno of your passions, you'll never overcome them. "Whenever we give up, leave behind, and forget too much, there is always the danger that the things we have neglected will return with added force." Somehow I transposed that into David's squeaky agitated walk. Understated passion. Fernando walks backwards before the greedy wall. (They are eating from a big pot, as you can see.) Fernando says:

Fernando   "See how cruel they look. Their lips are thin, their noses sharp, their faces furrowed and distorted by folds. Their eyes have a staring expression, they are always seeking something. What are they seeking? They always want something; they are always uneasy and restless. I do not know what they want. I do not understand them. I think that they are mad."

Yvonne   That's also from Jung. He quotes a Pueblo Indian about the white man. The mortals have become cruel white men.

Valda   I want to finish about the airport. I have to tell you this. When you kissed me goodbye, or rather, you were leaning against that rail with your feet crossed — the way you do — and I moved in to kiss you goodbye because people had begun to board the plane. You reached for the back of my neck with your left hand and drew me toward you. Your right arm was bent so your forearm was against your chest. As you pressed me against you and kissed me, my breast momentarily rested against your hand, which didn't move.

Fernando Yes. Is that what made you think of those lines "all day he sits before you face to face, like a cardplayer. Your elbow brushes his elbow; if you should speak, he hears?"

Shirley   "The touched heart madly stirs."

220

Yvonne   Bullshit!

Valda   Oh for Christ sake, Yvonne. Get with it.

Yvonne   Ok, Ok, go on. I'm really enjoying all this.

Valda   Then I watched very carefully while you kissed Lena and I saw that it wasn't the same at all. You see, I was still not clear.

Shirley   It was so obvious.

Valda   As I said before, I wasn't in a state of mind to think of such things.

Fernando When I got to New York I tossed a coin about whether to call you.

Valda   What would you have done if it had come out tails?

Fernando I would have called anyway, but I would have felt it was all wrong.

Valda   You're funny.

[photo no. 7

Yvonne   This one is my favorite picture. I always like the backs of people. Epp and James are resting on the suitcase. The mortals on the left are walking in their Kleenex boxes on a sheet of bubble wrap that makes popping sounds under the pressure of their feet. Valda and Doug have been laid prone by the inexorable wall. Doug is reading about the pygmies from Colin Turnbull's book *The Forest People*: "How long they have lived in the forest we do not know, though it is a considered opinion that they are among the oldest inhabitants of Africa. They may well be the original inhabitants of the great tropical rain forest which stretches nearly from coast to coast. They were certainly well established there at the very beginning of historic times." The mortals on the bubble wrap are transformed into pygmies by this reading, I hope. The mortals lend themselves to various anthropological interpretations. Why is Valda's face covered? Maybe she is the Medusa, from whose granite gaze Doug protects the mortals.]

photo no. 8

Yvonne   Now the hero James is reaching the climax of his brief odyssey. Tannis in the wings — harpy or avenging angel — waits to mount his back at the most difficult stage of his journey. Fernando and Valda aid and impede him at the same time, supplying resistance and support to his forward lean. The gods wait expectantly on Mt. Olympus. This episode resolves itself as James — with Tannis riding piggyback — clambers up the stairs. On reaching the top they crumple into the waiting arms of the gods, who then lower them to the floor on the other side of Olympus. As they are lowered, Yvonne reads from Jung: "At the beginning of the illness I had the feeling that there was something wrong with my attitude, and that I was to some extent responsible for the mishap. But when one affirms things as they are, without subjective protests, accepts the conditions of existence as one sees them, accepts one's own nature, as one happens to be, when one lives one's own life — then one must take mistakes into the bargain; life would not be complete without them. There is no guarantee — not for a single moment — that we will not fall into error or stumble into deadly peril. We may think there is a sure road. But that would be the road of death. Then nothing happens any longer — at any rate, not the right things. Anyone who takes the sure road is as good as dead."

Shirley   Such righteous sentiments. Now at this remove from that piece it seems terribly burdened with a kind of relentless truth-mongering.

Yvonne   What do you mean? In this last speech Jung seems anything but righteous. Righteousness implies a certainty that he is arguing *against*.

Shirley   It's the tone of self-congratulation or complacency of someone who has had a revelation and is laying it out. "Anyone who takes the sure road is as good as dead." Really! Maybe it's simply the fact of isolating such things from a longer text that bugs me. I just don't like the sound of it.

Yvonne   Well, you know, Shirley, that I have always had a weakness for the sweeping revelations of great men. That's why I'm going at this concert so differently. The line "Oh god, you gave me so much room" is really very much more moving to me than anything I used last year, even though on an aesthetic level I'm simply doing another form of story-telling — more intimate, less epic.

Shirley   What do you mean "Oh god, you gave me so much room?"

Yvonne   (Explains)

Valda   Were you saying that or reading it?

Yvonne   Saying it.

Shirley   I get it. Let's go on. I'm tired of all this.

Shooting script — Lives of Performers (beginning with third sequence).
Inter-titles are in **bold**, soundtrack is in *italics*.

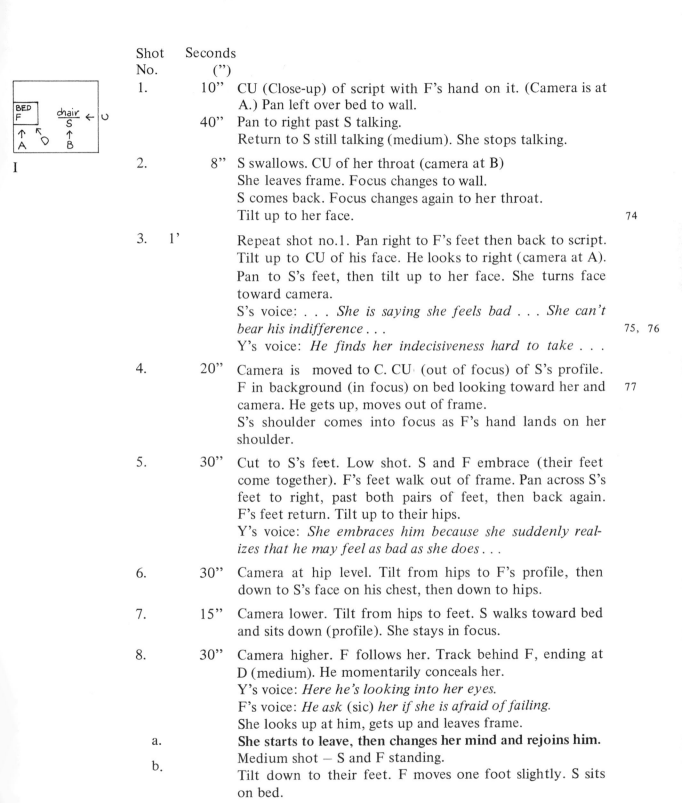

Shot No.	Seconds (")

1.   10"   CU (Close-up) of script with F's hand on it. (Camera is at A.) Pan left over bed to wall.

            40"   Pan to right past S talking.
Return to S still talking (medium). She stops talking.

2.   8"   S swallows. CU of her throat (camera at B)
She leaves frame. Focus changes to wall.
S comes back. Focus changes again to her throat.
Tilt up to her face.   74

3.   1'   Repeat shot no.1. Pan right to F's feet then back to script. Tilt up to CU of his face. He looks to right (camera at A). Pan to S's feet, then tilt up to her face. She turns face toward camera.
S's voice: *. . . She is saying she feels bad . . . She can't bear his indifference . . .*   75, 76
Y's voice: *He finds her indecisiveness hard to take . . .*

4.   20"   Camera is moved to C. CU (out of focus) of S's profile. F in background (in focus) on bed looking toward her and   77 camera. He gets up, moves out of frame.
S's shoulder comes into focus as F's hand lands on her shoulder.

5.   30"   Cut to S's feet. Low shot. S and F embrace (their feet come together). F's feet walk out of frame. Pan across S's feet to right, past both pairs of feet, then back again. F's feet return. Tilt up to their hips.
Y's voice: *She embraces him because she suddenly realizes that he may feel as bad as she does . . .*

6.   30"   Camera at hip level. Tilt from hips to F's profile, then down to S's face on his chest, then down to hips.

7.   15"   Camera lower. Tilt from hips to feet. S walks toward bed and sits down (profile). She stays in focus.

8.   30"   Camera higher. F follows her. Track behind F, ending at D (medium). He momentarily conceals her.
Y's voice: *Here he's looking into her eyes.*
F's voice: *He ask (sic) her if she is afraid of failing.*
She looks up at him, gets up and leaves frame.

   a.   **She starts to leave, then changes her mind and rejoins him.**

   b.   Medium shot — S and F standing.
Tilt down to their feet. F moves one foot slightly. S sits on bed.

S's voice: *She doesn't feel like talking about it anymore..*
F leaves frame and starts walking around room.
Camera pans randomly, sometimes catching him.
F's voice: *But Fernando doesn't know, he is confused...*
All the time he lose the track of the issues... He ask her
to go away with him, but all she say is 'Do you have any
money?'
Camera comes to rest on F and S sitting on bed and look-
ing to left.
Pan to Valda in opening at extreme right. V leaves frame
at left.
Track back, revealing only right-hand chair. F sits in chair.
Track continues back to reveal S on other chair. V on end
of bed.
V's voice: *Valda is disconsolate...*

9. CU of V's face. She continually moves her head out of
    frame. Each time the camera makes small adjustment to
    keep her head in center.
    V's voice: *She tells about a visit to John's house; it was so*
    beautiful she would like to live there forever... a movie..
    The old woman had moved her deeply...
    Pan to CU of S looking toward V.

a. **"I remember that movie. It's about all these small betray-**
    als, isn't it?"

10. 1' 30" Medium shot of S, J, V facing camera. They perform
    "Story", continually changing their facing in choreo-
    graphed sequence. (*page 234*)
    V's voice: *You might describe it that way. It's also a story*
    about a man who loves a woman and can't leave her when
    he falls in love with another woman. I mean, he can't
    seem to make up his mind. Or I could tell it from the
    point of view of the first woman: she loves him and en-
    dures his cruelties (yes, cruelties. You see, from her van-
    tage point his weaknesses become — yes, become — cruel-
    ties) yes, endures his cruelties because he always returns
    to her, and although she won't acknowledge it, she really
    does think — no, feel — that she can't live without him.
    (How did she ever get into such a fix?) She also thinks that
    he loves her best and that that love will finally conquer all.
    After all, he always returns to her, doesn't he? Or I could
    tell it through the eyes of no. 2 woman: She loves him and
    wants him to leave no. 1. She even gets pregnant. Then her
    own husband demands a divorce; he's had enough. (How
    did she ever get herself into such a fix?) But I don't care to
    dwell on no. 2. (How can such things continue to happen?)
    As I said before, he can't make up his mind. Then no. 1
    gets sick, so he stays with her but doesn't give up no. 2.

Or rather, no. 2 doesn't leave him. I don't want to make it sound as though he holds the controls, even though the two women sometimes act as though he does.

11.   3"   CU of S's face.
S (lip-synch): *Which woman is the director most sympathetic to?*

12.   4"   CU of V's face.
V (lip-synch): *I think no. 1.*

a.   **Valda replies.**
b.   CU of V's face
V (lip-synch): *maybe simply because she appears first.*

13.   30"   Medium shot — V in J's lap.   87
Y's voice: *Now John is remembering a particular event . . . outside of their house when he was mugged . . .*
Pan to bed. (suitcase is against wall)
Pan back to chair. S and F have replaced J and V.
Track forward to frame heads in CU. S looks to right, gets off F's lap.
Pan right to meet V walking left.
Pan left to meet S walking right.
Repeat until women meet. (They actually walk backwards when not on camera so as to extend the time.)
S's voice: *. . . Shirley tells Valda she was really impressed with some of the things she said, like 'Asia is not clay in the hands of the West.'*
Pan to right past V. V enters frame from left, turns.
F's voice: *She says 'Wait a minute' . . .* V exits.
F comes into frame, leans against pillar.
F's voice: *They don't know where she go.*

14.   10"   Medium long shot — F on bed, S on chair — legs crossed.
Y's voice: *Here they're waiting for her to come back. She doesn't come back.*

15.   10"   CU of S's legs (still crossed).

16.   1"   CU of S's left shoulder.
John enters, pauses behind chair.
During the ensuing action, camera dollies slowly back until scene is in extreme long shot with light standard exposed.
F's voice: *Here come Johns to pick up Fernando . . . They are going to take the train to Chile. [laughter of performers]*
F, holding suitcase, joins J. They both exit to right.
V enters from right, lies on couch with her face in her hands. S sits beside her.
Camera is now still. V and S alternately change positions   78
on the bed.

Their voices alternate in a conversation about a difficult situation. E.g. *"Shirley tells Valda that she is her very dear friend and she doesn't like seeing her caught in the middle . . ."*
S's voice: *Shirley tells Valda about a dream she had.*

17.   1'   30"   Medium CU of Sarah bouncing ball in slow-motion.
S's voice: *I had a dream about a wall. The wall is not concrete or metal; it is steel mesh like the fence in a schoolyard. There are no doors; rather, it's the kind of a wall that I would like to climb rather than walk through a ready-made door. I do climb the wall, and it feels terrific. I'm stretching my body as I climb, feeling the pull on my legs and arms as I reach the top and climb over. I enjoy going down the other side. What I like about this wall is that I have no fear of being locked out or locked in. I can always get in or out by climbing, by my own physical nimbleness and agility.*
On the other side I find that I am in a schoolyard, which is, in fact, the schoolyard of the school across the street from the house where I was born. There are no children in the schoolyard on this day although it is a beautiful spring day. I run around freely, the wind blowing in my hair. I am happy, bouncing a large volleyball. I bounce it up and down and against a brick side wall. It feels good just to run around and be free and have all that space to myself. I feel my body stretching and I am running around the yard very fast, but I am full of energy, not at all tired. I have an enormous sense of great physical well-being, of a stretching and toning up of all my limbs and the back of my neck. When I wake up I am really happy. I remember that I have caught a glimpse of something alive and free within me.

18.   30"   Long shot as in end of shot no. 16.
V and S embrace. V's voice: *Valda thanks Shirley. She's made her feel better.*
S walks across frame to right.

19.   15"   Medium shot. S walks from center-frame to right.

20.   5"   Medium CU. S's legs walking from center-frame to right.
V's voice: *It's not easy for her to go.*

21.   30"   Medium shot — V sitting on bed jiggling foot. Camera at A.
V leaves frame to left.

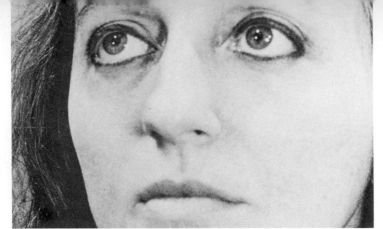

74

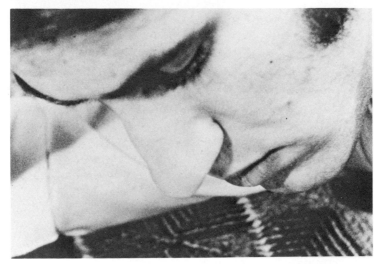

75

76

77

22.   Medium shot of chair.

V enters with package and sits on chair. Starts to unwrap it, pauses, continues, takes out eyeshade, stands up.

V's voice: *When Valda first received this package in the mail, she wondered whether to open it . . . she isn't sure she wants to accept gifts from him.*

Tilt to upper half of her body.

V primps as though before a mirror, then sits in chair.

Y's voice: *The face of this character is a fixed mask. We shall have her wear an eyeshade to reveal her inner and outer appearance. The eyeshade hides the movement of the upper half of her face, but the lower half where the*

a.   one week later

b.   V sitting as before.

tongue works, stays visible. She must function with a face of stone and at the same time reveal her characteristic dissembling.

F walks in from left with suitcase in left hand and letter in right.   79

F's voice: *Now Fernando has come back from Chile. He has that funny letter he doesn't know where it comes from. She asks him if he meess her, and of course he meess her a lot.*

V and F embrace behind chair (she has put letter on chair and he has removed her eyeshade) as

Camera dollies back to medium long shot of embrace.

V's voice: *She asks him if he received her letter and where he was when he read it.*

c.   Simultaneous with F's voice reading: **"I was in the living room talking to Nina, when Theresa came in with the mail and handed me a letter. I looked at it, saw that it was from you and stuck it in my shirt pocket. I had to finish my business with Nina. Later I took it out of my pocket on the way upstairs; I paused half-way up the stairs to open the envelope, read the letter hurriedly, then continued on up to the bedroom to sit and pore over it."**

d.   **He asks her what she meant by "ebb tide." She tells him.**

23.   Medium shot of V and F lying on bed, heads toward camera (B in diagram III). Chair is out-of-focus in foreground. Letter is on chair.

V disengages herself from F (who sleeps). Pan follows her to right as she picks up letter and walks to pillar against which she leans as she reads the letter to herself.

S's voice (reading): *I am sorry about the whole thing, mostly for myself, of course . . .*

Pan as V walks to left, puts letter back on chair, lies down beside F.

F props himself up on elbow. Lip-synch:

F: *Do you think I should say that?*
V: *What?*
F: *I mean about admitting that I feel superior?*
Slow fade.

24.

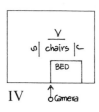

IV

Medium long shot — S, V, J in three chairs, V in middle, bed in front. S and J are talking.

Y's voice: *Here they're talking about the performance. John is telling Shirley . . . that he was in such a bad mood he couldn't applaud, he couldn't go backstage . . . Shirley says 'It's too bad you can't take pleasure in a friend's success' (audience laughter) . . . Shirley asks Valda 'How did you feel about the performance?*

V's voice: *Oh, I didn't know what I was doing. There was so little time for adequate preparation, and I didn't always know what was expected of me. I mean, if I come in a door and see you two here, what am I supposed to register — fear, surprise, nothing?*

25.

Medium long shot — same as above, except that V's chair is empty.

V enters frame from right, sees J and S, then leaves at right.

Jump-cuts as follows:

a. V enters, sees them, turns back to camera.

b. V enters with F; both are laughing. V sees them, goes toward S.

c. V enters followed by F. He grabs her wrist, turns her around, looks into her eyes.

d. V enters, sits in chair. F enters, sits on floor with head in her lap. She strokes his hair.

e. V enters, stops. F enters, puts arm around her waist, and looks over her shoulder. She starts to break up. They both laugh and carry on, look out at camera.

f. same as above without the breaking up.

g. V enters, followed by F. He kisses her head to toe.

h. V enters, goes to couch, sleeps. F enters, goes to couch, tries to waken her, can't, runs out. He then does a series of "double-takes" — starts to re-enter, looks at camera, exits. J and S also look toward and away from camera. F re-enters, goes to V on bed, backs up onto chair, talks to J and S, smiles.

26.

Medium long shot — V enters, walks to left. F enters, leans against pillar.

Pan follows V to far left wall, which she leans against.

a. Cut to F against pillar as above. Pan left to V against wall.

b. F against pillar as above. Pan as he walks toward V.

c. **"I need to talk to you, to see you before me."**

80

230

27 a.   CU — V and F embracing. F fidgets.
    b.   "You're never still, are you?"

28 a.   CU — midsections of J and S embracing.
    b.   "I woke up this morning feeling anticipation and excitement at the prospect of seeing you."

29 a.   CU — midsection. J holds S's hands at her side.
    b.   "I have behaved as though I am exempt from the conditions that I constantly impose on others."

30 a.   CU — hip level. V and J embrace.
    b.   "I have such strong feeling for you."
        "I know."

31 a.   CU — V's and F's feet against wall.
        F's voice starts: *I don't know what*
    b.   Fernando stands sobbing against the wall. Valda lays consoling hands on his shoulders.
        F's voice continues: *to do next. I feel like a shell. I am so afraid.*

32 a.   CU — V's crossed legs, S from waist down.
    b.   "What he did to my children I shall never forgive him for."

33 a.   CU — midsection of S in chair; V stands.
    b.   "I am living a loneliness I never expected. I feel so vulnerable, so inferior, so unsure of myself."

34 a.   CU — Fernando in chair reading, V bending over him. F is framed from nose to book.
    b.   "The dream urged upon me the necessity of clarifying this situation."

35 a.   CU — John's head (he sits); F's midsection (his fingers caress each other mid-frame).
    b.   "The only feeling I am sure about these days is a complete loathing for myself."

36 a.   CU — F's face center-frame. V's profile on edge of frame
        Her hand touches F's face.
    b.   "Look at me, just for one second."
        Fernando looks at her.
        "I'm not afraid to die, but I don't want to."

37 a.   Medium shot — F and J sitting on bed. F leaning against wall, looking at J.
    b.   "Have you ever considered the possibility that if a man likes you he doesn't necessarily want to fuck you?"

38 a.   same as above, F and J have exchanged positions.
    b.   "I dreamed of my mother last night, and of my wife. My mother was crying for me."

78

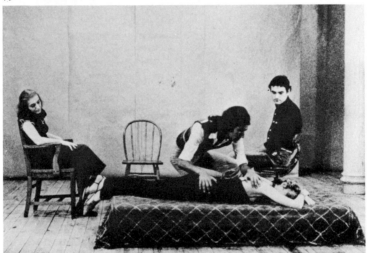

79

80

81

39 a.   same as above, with S and V on bed, S leaning against wall looking at V.

b.   **"All of this being the case, how can I continue to be his friend?"**

40 a.   same as shot no. 24.
b.   **"We're going to be married."**

41 a.   same as shot no. 24.
b.   **"Now that we understood each other, it was a relief to continue our talk on lighter terms."**

42   Medium CU — F leaning against wall.
Pan to right past S, V, in chairs to J (only heads are seen). Pan left to frame V. She looks to left, then gets up so that her midsection is framed.
F's voice: *She tells him they were just discussing the performance. And he asks them if they want something from the delicatessen; he is just going to buy some cigarettes. She tells him not to go because she wants to show him something, and besides, the delicatessen is closed.*
Pan left as V walks toward F.
a.   **Valda shows Fernando her solo**

43.   7"   Long shot of V's solo (filmed at the Whitney Museum).   81

44.   30"   CU — F and V, arguing, F against wall.
F's voice: *Meanwhile back in the studio, he asks her why she shows him that; that he has seen it a hundred times. But she say she does it differently now, but it looks the same to him.*
As camera pans to right, V turns front and makes angry grimace. Pan continues all the way right to frame Y leaning against pillar.
Y's voice: *Uh . . . meanwhile Yvonne has come in, and Epp and James, for the rehearsal.*

45.   Rehearsal of *Walk, She Said.* (*GU Dreams* box stands against wall.) At one point S and F lean against wall and are seen to argue.   79

a.   **Emotional relationships are relationships of desire, tainted by coercion and constraint; something is expected from the other person, and that makes him and ourselves unfree.**
b.   More rehearsal.
V leans against wall while Y, F, J, and E do tableau in box.
c.   **I began to think of him in a particular way.**
d.   Everyone leaves frame; only the box remains.

46.   **Final performance:**
LULU
in 35 shots

47.   Series of "Lulu" stills begins. During the final three minutes *No Expectations* by the Rolling Stones is heard.   84, 86

233

Shot no.10

    <u>Story</u>   (starts with Shirley, John, Valda standing in a row
           facing camera.)

All 3 face forward.
Man & woman #1 embrace.
#1 faces forward.
Man & woman #2 face each other.
#1 faces his back.
He turns to face #1. (#2 faces front.)
She turns her back on him.
He & #2 face, embrace.
He turns & faces #1 (puts hand on her shoulder)
#1 faces him. They embrace.
#2 turns away.
He turns to #2.
#1 turns away.
He turns to #1.
#1 lies down.
He squats & holds her hand.
#2 faces front.
He gets up & faces #2.
#1 gets up & faces him.
He faces #1.
#2 turns away.
#1 turns away.
He faces front.
Both #1 & #2 face him.
He faces #1, then #2.
#1 lies down & does backward somersault.
He & #2 face front.
#1 gets up & takes original position.

Repeat entire sequence once.

82 Production still from G.W. Pabst's *Lulu* (1928) — Louise Brooks

83 *Lulu* in *Performance* at the Whitney, April 21, 1972 (Y.R. in jacket replaces the absent John Erdman)

84 Still from *Lulu* in *Lives of Performers* — John Erdman, Valda Setterfield, Shirley Soffer, Fernando Torm

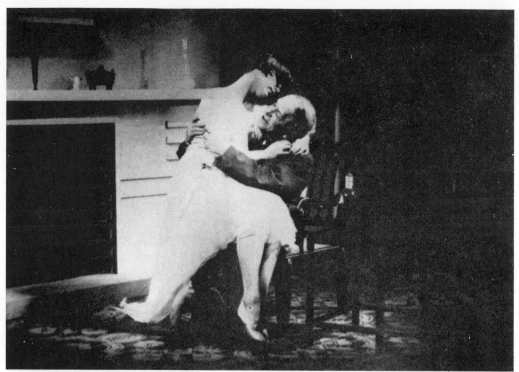

85 Production still from Pabst's *Lulu* – Louise Brooks and Carl Goetz

86 Still from *Lulu* in *Lives of Performers*

87   Shot no. 13

Exchange of letters with Nan Piene following screening of *Lives of Performers* at Millenium Film Workshop, N.Y.C.

January 27, 1973.

Dear Nan,

I thought I recognized you in that audience at Millenium last week. If it wasn't you then you are going to think this letter very strange indeed. I forget the exact wording of your question — something to do with my passage from dance to film. For the next three or four days I was obsessed with what I "could have said" or "should have said". I have not had to ask myself the kinds of questions that were asked that night. I mean, I find myself where I am and if I think of where I've come from at all, it may be with a sense of wonder and gratitude, but I don't have to know *how* I got here in order to proceed. Which may account for some of my slow-witted responses that night.

In any case my "setting-it-right" fantasies since then have produced some additional insights that may be of interest to you. I had started to talk about how as a dancer the unique nature of my body and movement makes a personal statement, but how dancing could no longer encompass or "express" the new content in my work, i.e., the emotions. And you had supplied me with the word "specific": dance was not as specific — meaning-wise — as language. There is another dimension to all this that excited me no end when I thought about it: Dance is ipso facto about *me* (the so-called kinesthetic response of the spectator notwithstanding, it only rarely transcends that narcissistic-voyeuristic duality of doer and looker); whereas the area of the emotions must necessarily directly concern both of us. This is what allowed me permission to start manipulating what at first seemed like blatantly personal and private material. But the more I get into it the more I see how such things as rage, terror, desire, conflict, et al., are not unique to my experience the way my body and its functioning are. I now — as a consequence — feel much more connected to my audience, and that gives me great comfort.

The implications of this change as they concern art and the avant garde must be most complex, something I would like to see a historian cope with. For example, is there some connection and polarity between formalism/ alienation/"humanism"? Or indeterminacy/narrative? Or psychological content/the avant garde? Or am I creating straw men? Obviously I have some ideas on all this myself; it just seems too early to get into it.

. . . .

Best regards,
Yvonne

238

Dear Yvonne,

I was very pleased to get your letter. Re "setting-it-right", I did understand you
more or less correctly at the Millenium, that film has enabled you to accommodate
emotional content in a way you feel dance had not. What produced my question
about from-dance-to-film was that I have been puzzling a lot about the viability
of narrative today; I wanted to know your reasons for risking involving yourself
in it, and you told me clearly and directly. After the screening I asked myself
about just the polarities your letter discusses, particularly indeterminacy/narrative
and psychological content/avant garde. I don't think they are straw men at all
but feel or hope they can be understood beyond their seeming oppositeness. Or
that works of art such as *Lives* will make such understanding possible. ("Avant-
garde", actually, doesn't pester me as an issue the way it did five or six years ago.
I mean it doesn't seem to matter, if the work is good. In fact it seems almost not
to matter, whereas the issue of connecting with the audience does.) I am nowhere
myself with all this yet; until your film I was just clinging to Godard's response
when asked if his films have a beginning, middle and end: "Certainly, but not
necessarily in that order." That doesn't say much really, but clears the air in less
numbing fashion than a Robbe-Grillet novel.

I have only seen you dance once — at Judson, in '65 I think, a piece with falling
wood slats (large "randomly dropped toothpicks"?) — but the experience was so
moving and my memory of the experience, though possibly not of the actuality,
has been so persistent that I don't feel too silly talking with you about your
work.

It appeared to me then that within the apparent neutrality and banality lay a
kind of virtuosity all the more compelling, poignant really, for its surface absence
or cloak. Perhaps what moved me most, in addition to exposure to your unique
stage presence, was the strong feeling of being present at the raw creation or
certainly bold enactment of a Style. Ironically it gave me an emotional commitment to the avant garde I doubt I'd felt before that, emotion for art's sake,
maybe. (I had, admittedly, some personal reasons at the time for opening up to
the state of being a believer.) And there was the minor irony that indeterminacy,
although it shuns romance, has an immediacy that produces drama.

Anyway the style of "formalism" I had seen in the dance ran of course all the
way through *Lives*. I found it extraordinary that this did not seem glued onto the
narrative situations but rather was a part of them, that you used style to present
narrative not exactly discretely but certainly not novelistically. And also that as I
guess artists have always done used style to intensify the psychological content.
This went as far as inversing itself; it seemed at certian moments, for example, as
if your employment of such loaded personal material so baldly was on one level a

sort of far-reaching extension of using 'found' material. Thus while the film raised the formalism/humanism question vividly it seemed to me certainly to overcome any old implication of a necessary polarity. It is too simple to say that your manipulation of style in the film induced and *permitted* access to being moved by the mimetic? For me the emotion 'conflict' was especially acutely conveyed; so was the actuality, which has never reached me via a novel, of the way women at times communicate intensely through the medium of men.

One question at this point would have to do with the organization of the parts of the film. At the Guggenheim I thought I sensed along with the disjunctions and overlappings a kind of crescendo-decrescendo symmetry, but your cut of the last dance makes me realize I'm wrong and must have been anyway.

. . . . . Thanks very much for writing.

Warmly,
Nan

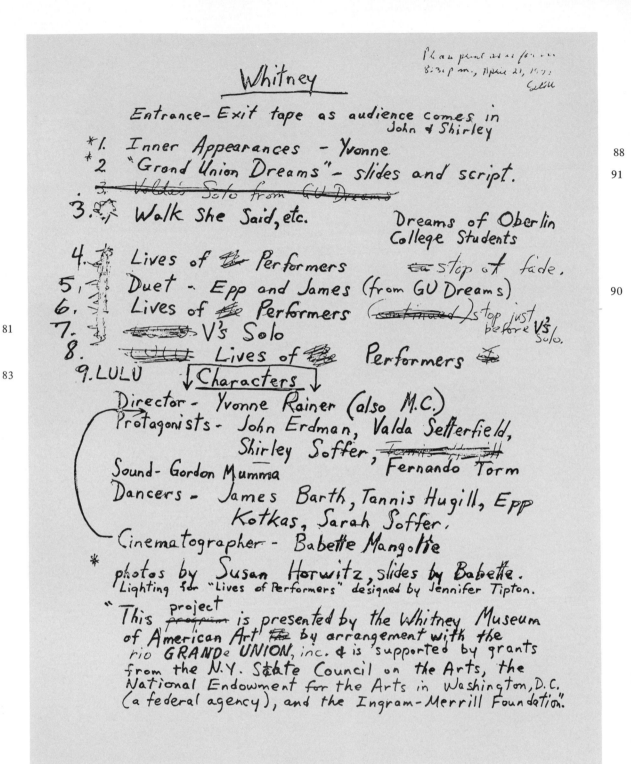

Program for *Performance* at the Whitney Museum, N.Y.C., April 21, 1972

In the College

*In the College** and *Performance* continued the process of accumulation and juxtaposition of old and new components that characterized *Performance Demonstration* and *Rose Fractions*. *In the College*, performed on a large proscenium stage, was assembled from the Oberlin College students' use of various texts that I contributed to the working sessions. In some cases these texts were revealed in performance via slides or speech; in others they were replaced by the activity or event that they had inspired. I, in my role of director, usually made this particular decision, as well as others involving sequence and transition, style of performance, numbers of people in a given event, etc. I also contributed episodes of my own. It was a complicated piece in that two groups, each containing 20 members, were often working simultaneously on the huge stage. Taped readings of the students' dreams were heard intermittently during the performance. (*page 245*) The intertitles of *Lives of Performers* were anticipated here in a fragment of film that showed texts in quick succession for about three minutes. There was also more of the concern with character and melodrama that had begun in *Grand Union Dreams*. A green eyeshade was used to distinguish a female performer, and this device later appeared as a "costume" in *Inner Appearances* and *Lives of Performers*. And it was on this occasion that *Lulu* was first performed.   88, 79

In the College had two commentators, Jani Novak and Mary Overlie, who occasionally read things and at one point spontaneously 'interpreted' a particular sequence for the audience. There was also an episode in which a male and female performed a series of poses with near Mickey-Mouse rapidity. The poses had been inspired by such lines as "Our affair is the talk of the whole town. I'm ruining my career!" and "As agreed, then, you'll come to see me tomorrow." and "I'll dance for the whole world but not in front of that woman!" and "If you would only come with me. Wouldn't you like to come with me?" etc. The lines, in this instance, did not accompany the action, which was a kind of speeded up, arrested-motion soap drama.

It was a work that I could not possibly re-create, having very few notes and no photos, a work belonging very much to that particular time and place, sifted through the memories of those particular participants. At one point a huge corrugated metal door slowly rose at the rear of the stage while a slide was projected on the left side of the proscenium arch. The slide read: "A man who has not passed through the inferno of his passions has never overcome them. They then dwell in the house next door, and at any moment a flame may dart out and set fire to his own house. Whenever we give up, leave behind, and forget too much,

*Oberlin College, Ohio, January 21, 1972.

there is always the danger that the things we have neglected will return with added force." Behind the door was the cluttered workshop of the theater department. The text, of course (from Jung), had been used in *Grand Union Dreams* (*page 201*) as was the other verbal material of *In the College*.

Texts function very much like the objects I have used in that they keep reappearing in a new work (e.g. the red ball, the stairs, the suitcase, etc.) As my interests change, I find that old components have new uses. If formerly I maintained a general attitude about a certain interchangeability of materials, which was appropriate to the formal and repetitive structures I used, more recently I find my reasoning in ordering things is more connected with psychology and autobiography. This makes me interested in 'testing' old materials against my changing basis of selection. Consequently the old objects pop up again and again in new contexts, and the one-liners and paragraphs reappear to form a new syntax. This development is not so clear in the instance of the above-quoted paragraph: Originally that text was accompanied by a performer's squeaky, agitated walk rather than by the opening of the huge corrugated metal door.

A change is more evident when I re-use something like "How beautiful it is here; I should like to live here forever." In *Grand Union Dreams* this line was used as one element in a series of sequential but unrelated short events. By the time of *Lives of Performers*, one year later, it had become part of a larger speech in which a woman tells how she had enjoyed a visit to "John's house". This is followed by a description of a movie she had seen with John, which in turn is followed by a comment by one of her listeners about the movie (*page 225*). Inventories of disconnected story elements are being replaced by more extended passages of cohesive narrative.

Let me say that I am no longer interested in unlimited interchangeability as I labor toward a kind of ordering somewhere between the arbitrary and the open-ended, between the excessive specificity of the story and the emotional unspecificity of object-oriented permutations; a kind of ordering between commitment and ambiguity, between giving the game away and eliminating the familiar rules, between a horizontal and vertical examination of human behavior. Maybe something between the analytical and sentimental. From *Grand Union Dreams* on, all my work has reflected this movement, even the 'unconsummated' transitional piece like *Performance* (unconsummated because it was essentially a preliminary study for *Lives of Performers* and *This is the story of a woman who . . .*). *This is the story . . .* continued this process of syntactical 're-positioning' in a search for connections more appropriate to my current concerns. Perhaps I should end on this note as applicable to everything I have done. "She moves obstinately between her calculation and sentimentality. Sometimes like a pendulum and, less often, like a tuning fork."

244

Dream of an Oberlin College student
from *In the College*

We are driving long a narrow road through a thin forest of birches and young maples. The leaves are pale yellow, as if in spring or fall. Suddenly, groups of small children ran across the road, and we can see small shacks and the ruins of old cars among the trees.

The car moves out of the forest, and we can see across a large field of yellow grass, with trees at one edge. Far in the distance in a path of trees, is an immense figure of a man, made of a brown stone, or rusted metal. It is several hundred feet high, huge and desolate. We are filled with a peculiar feeling of awe and confusion.

Now we notice a burned out building beside the road, overgrown paths leading away from the road, more ruined buildings, and rusted machinery.

The focus of the dream moves inside the figure, and we can see huge masses of decaying mechanisms, great holes in the walls, broken doors, ruin and confusion.

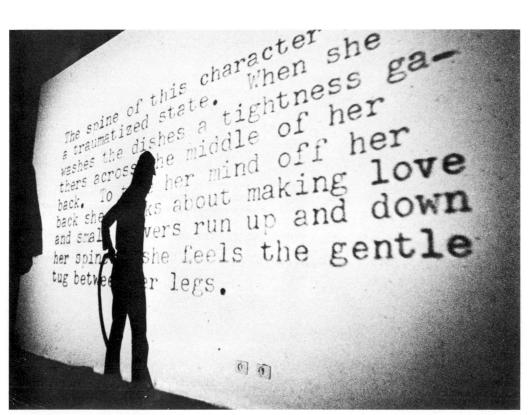

88 *Inner Appearances* at Festival of Music and Dance, L'Attico, Rome, June 14, 1972

89 *Performance* at the Whitney — Shirley, Valda, Epp, Jim

90 *Duet* in *Performance* at the Whitney — Jim and Epp

246

91   *Grand Union Dreams* section of *Performance* at the Whitney Museum. (The projection is the first in a series of six slides. *See page 213*)

This is the story of a woman who . . .

THEATER FOR THE NEW CITY   BARTENIEFF/FIELD
presents

this is the story of a woman who...
by
yvonne rainer

a 2-hour mixed-media theater work for 2 women & 1 man - performed by JOHN ERDMAN,
Yvonne Rainer, & SHIRLEY SOFFER - offering (among other things) Inner Appearances (1972), Three Satie Spoons (1961), Walk, She Said (1971), Trio A (1966).

Photos from the Erdman, Mangolte, & Soffer families.
Lighting: Jennifer Tipton; Camera Work: Babette Mangolte; Satie & Grieg piano:
Philip Corner; Technical Assistance: Charles Atlas & James Barth

MARCH 16, 17, 23, 24, 30, 31

AND

lives of performers

a feature-length film directed by Yvonne Rainer - Cinematographer: BABETTE
MANGOLTE - starring the above performers plus VALDA SETTERFIELD, FERNANDO TORM,
and JAMES BARTH, EPP KOTKAS

MARCH 18, 25, APRIL 1

the
"for it was not so much by knowledge of words that I came to the understanding
of things, as by my experience of things I was enabled to follow the meaning of
words."   Plutarch
8:00 PM   Reservations: 691-2220
Admission: $2.50, students (with ID) $1.50, "Lives of Performers": $2.00
THEATER FOR THE NEW CITY   113 Jane St. (between West & Washington)

A two-hour performance work for 2 women and 1 man, first performed at Theater for the New City, March 16, 1973. Its technical requirements are three 35mm slide projectors, one 16mm film projector, one tape recorder, and one microphone (into which the narrator speaks). The pre-set stage (with white back wall or cyclorama) contains 3 chairs, 1 mattress, 1 small cardboard box (gift), an ashtray, an airmail envelope containing a folded sheet of 8½ x 11 paper, a hard cover book, a cannister vacuum cleaner, and a suitcase, inside which are a sheaf of 8½ x 11 inch papers, red ball, and toy gun.

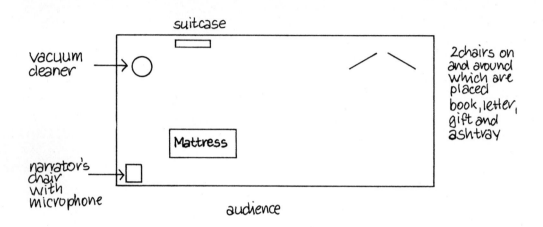

In the script that follows various symbols are used: * denotes a change in image coming from the previously indicated slide projector, or tray. A large bracket (]) denotes simultaneous projection. **Black** stands for "no image". Numbers to the immediate right of the text indicate length of time (number of counts) each slide is held. Descriptions of activities appear in *italics*. Film and slide-projected photos are indicated in **bold**, whereas slides of text appear in regular type.

Script

Before the stage lights come up, as Shirley takes her seat in the narrator's chair, thunder is heard, followed by heavy rain. The rain fades out before "The rain makes him think . . . ."

1. Tray 3   **Shirley on beach**
   *   **Shirley in field**
   *   **Shirley with children and mother**
   *   **Shirley with camel**
   *   **black**

2. Tray 3   Inner Appearances (*Slides are projected in the center of the back wall. The source of light (other than the projection) is dim and not directed at the performing area. John enters, wearing a green eyeshade, black shirt, blue velvet pants, and ochre vest. He turns on the vacuum cleaner and vacuums for 45 to 60 seconds before the first slide appears. During this time he starts to sing a repetitive ditty. It goes: "duh, duh, dee, duh, dum" (C,E,G,E,C). The five-note tune can be started in the middle, started in the beginning and not completed, played with as regarding different durations of each note. It should not be syncopated. The slides stay on for the length of time required for the projectionist to read each one through twice to himself. The duration of black between slides is 30 to 45 seconds. The performer systematically vacuums the entire space, singing or not singing, vacuuming or standing still (with the vacuum cleaner turned on or off), occasionally sitting on a chair or mattress (singing or not singing). Sometimes nothing happens at all, neither slide nor singing nor movement. The time sense of this section is protracted and melancholy. When he is through vacuuming, John rolls up the extension cord and places the vacuum cleaner out of sight. He then sits in one of the upstage chairs. This happens shortly before the appearance of "Cliche is, in a sense, the purest art of intelligibility . . ."*)   88

   * The face of this·character is a fixed mask. We shall have him wear an eyeshade to reveal his inner and outer appearance. The eyeshade hides the movement of the upper half of his face, but the lower half, where the tongue works, stays visible. He must function with a face of stone and at the same time reveal his characteristic dissembling.
   * black
   * This character is now feeling a growing irritation. On the way to the performance he ran into someone he hadn't seen for a year. Some banter was exchanged. Now he is reviewing the conversation in his mind. "She hasn't changed a bit." he muses. His mind works in spirals behind the eyeshade.

Tray 3   The spine of this character is in a traumatized state. When he
vacuums the house a tightness gathers across the middle of his
back. To take his mind off his back he thinks about making
love, and small shivers run up and down his sides as he feels the
gentle throbbing at his groin.
black

* The rain makes him think of when he was 18 years old, spending a summer in Chicago. He was sitting by an open window in
a room with five other people. It had started to rain heavily. A
woman was talking about her baby sitter. She said, "I hope the
stupid boy has sense enough to close the windows." Without
a second thought he reached over and shut the window. A
stunned silence fell on the room.

* **black**

* Now this character is thinking about a friend with great contempt. "Why do men value their work more than their insight?"
he thinks. Now he is laughing inwardly at his cliché — the
inverse of the old female intuition bit. But it seemed true in the
cases where the *women* valued men's work more than men's
insights. The generalization as usual could be discredited.

* Earlier this week he saw them on the other side of the street
and was surprised at his response — mild distaste rather than the
rage he had anticipated. The whole thing now seemed rather
sordid. It was receding. He had ducked into a shop to avoid
them.

* Again he thinks about making love, then about being in love,
then about performing. Then he thinks about her: his very gaze
seems to transform her into a performer, a realized fantasy of
herself. Sometimes it is almost as if she is saying "Look at me,
look at me — a small price to pay for my love in return." He
agrees.

* But only momentarily. It is quite probable that by this time the
character feels very bad. This stage of his life as a captive
audience-for-one seems based in artifice and as such must sooner or later come to a close. He sighs to himself, "such delicious
artifice. Nowhere is captivity less painful or more complete."

* **black**

* This one is complicated. Now he is thinking about his friend's
story about being mugged. How ferociously he had gone at his
assailant and scared him off, how his wife had observed the
incident, how she had later become excited and erotic, how he
had resented this and become disagreeable, how they had made
love without ending their argument. Now he is suffused with
anger toward his friend. He fantasizes kicking him in the balls.
Now he is greatly relieved.

* **black**

* He tries to reconstruct the passage from the novel that had so
impressed him. The best he can do is: "All is finally clarified.

252

It is unspeakable, but clear. The reach of my jealousy, of my certainty of betrayal, engulfs me at every step. It is unthinkable that I live in this condition in intimacy with another person. And the possibility of living a life without intimate connections is equally intolerable. Is it any wonder that the most plausible solution is to remove my existence? I see no way through my dilemma. I am not one to compromise; I wish I were; my life would be easier. The phone is ringing . . . . It's always been all or nothing for me. This statement is for ART, even though at this very moment I don't know where to turn." He can't remember, hard as he tries, the passage that followed. It had suggested that such a dire solution might not be necessary. He is now wracking his brain to remember . . . . What else, what else, what else?

*   **black**

*   Events of the past rose like waves and battering against his mind threw it into a wild commotion of shame, grief, and joy.

*   **black**

*   He thinks about the snow in Vermont, and their last night in the cabin — the four of them lolling about the sleeping-loft warmed by a wood fire. Their talk had ranged over motion and phallic-vaginal body parts and illusion and comfort and back to sex-as-illusion. Again he repeats to himself the remembered phrase, "easy locomotion between comfort and discomfort." Now it all seemed like good social titillation. "Contempt again" he thinks. "But I can't help it. Social interactions seem to be mostly about seduction."

*   **black**

*   His mother's face now appears in his mind's eye. The face is dulled with senility. He tries to remember the face before his father died. All he can remember is the determination around the mouth and the moist softness of the cataract-shrouded eyes. Now the mouth is slack, the family battles abandoned. In the absence of desires, he thinks, the will to fight cannot sustain itself.

*   He thinks about himself in the third person: "He remembers the Sappho poem: 'The moon slides west

> It is midnight
> The time is gone
> I am alone.'

She thinks she can hold him with her romantic detatchment, her dark sense of portent. He stands trembling between fascination and skepticism. He moves obstinately between the two."

*   **black**

*   Cliché is, in a sense, the purest art of intelligibility; it tempts us with the possibility of enclosing life within beautifully inalterable formulas, of obscuring the arbitrary nature of imagination with an appearance of necessity.

Tray 1   **Tray 2**

93

3.	Tray 1	Wedding group (remains during	*(4 counts)*
4.	Tray 2	3 women and baby	*(8 counts)*
5.	Tray 1 ⎤ Tray 2 ⎦	black Shirley, Simeon, Sasson	*(6 counts)*
6.	Tray 2	Shirley, Sarah, John	*(hold 6 counts, then quickly):*
7.	*	Sloppy Joe's	*(4 counts each)*
	*	Grandmother	
	*	2 women in field	
	*	mother and son (old)	
	*	wistful girl	
	*	mother and son	
	*	women in knickers	
	*	Babette's mother	*(8 counts)*
	*	fashionable woman	*(hold during tape):* 93

Tape on (John's voice)

First an emptiness like a great white bird soared through her. Then she began to think about particulars — the quality of his intelligence at the moment . . . ., his insight into the nature of her struggle, his refusal to go along with her desperate . . . .

He had dragged it all out of her. Now she had to pay. Yet it was a relief that he was now carrying the ball. It was *his* turn to . . . . and not dance the fandango in . . . . And there was still so much she didn't know, which, if known, might have made her act differently. How much of the problem of their differences was real and how much was a smokescreen to conceal . . . . ? Her mind clouded when she tried to answer.

She had set him an impossible task. " . . . . to allow me to . . . . when I need to," she had told him. He had reminded her that *she* was not so . . . . . of *his* . . . . She pleaded special circumstances. They argued. His voice was hard and curt.

The die seemed cast. Yet in some way she trusted him. He would . . . . They would meet again. If only he could say, "But we really . . . ." Which was all very well for *her* to say, having jumped the gun in . . . .

Then that terrible accusation of his. She couldn't even repeat it, it . . . . Yet it posed another question: "Is it possible that I have really . . . . that I will never make . . . . Only in this way . . . . survive." So be it. There are worse ways to live. Being so . . . . may very well . . . . She felt, however, little conviction.

255

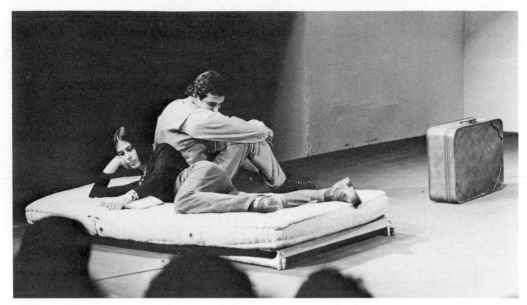

94

95

And finally, she grew calmer, almost resigned. They had both been . . . . . — her terror and the . . . . — slowly eroding . . . . and regard him . . . . and pleasure.

Tape off

8. Lights up
   Tray 2   **black**
             (*Yvonne enters, wearing green corduroy pants and long-sleeved purple blouse. This section has John and Yvonne doing stop-motion poses in relation to each other and the objects.*)   94

   Narrator: (*40 second intervals; begins 40 seconds after Y's first pose*)
   (Shirley)   When he came in that night she knew something was amiss.
               She wasn't hungry yet and was not through working.
               He had waited for her.
               She tells him about the article. If he is surprised he doesn't show it.
               As they pass each other in the hall — she on the way to the bathroom, he to the kitchen . . . .
               The light bothers him. He moves his chair.
               He talks for a long time. In spite of his urgency she finds her mind wandering.
               She has already asked him what he intended to do. She would have to ask him again.
               She stands lost in thought. He interrupts her reverie.
               She is suddenly struck by the absurdity of the situation. Her laughter is infectious.
               Should she keep her peace?
               He touched her on the arm gently and said "I'm sorry I upset you."
               She is tempted to turn her head away to hide her feeling.
               He starts to leave. She asks him not to.
               As she slowly turns her gaze toward him . . .
               Her mind reels from the enormity of her act.
               She searches for the right words.

9. Lights fade
   Tray 1 ⌉   Somehow she suspects that she has failed miserably again. She
          | has refused to tell herself what she wanted. "Let him figure it
          | out for both of us!"
   Tray 2 ⌋   family (hold long enough for above to be read, then change to):
         *   two women (remains during

10. Tray 1   She knows the crucial moment was when she said 'Hold me.'   95

When thinking this over she
became confused and agitated,
then gave it up in disgust and
went out to the museum.

96

Tray 1		When thinking this over she became confused and agitated, then gave it up in disgust and went out to the museum.
11.	Tray 1 ⌉	**black**
	Tray 2 ⌋	*Two successive slides of* **Pantheon** *are shown during paragraph 1:*
	Narrator:	*paragraph 1*

She visited the Pantheon at different times of day. She didn't respond when he beckoned to her to come over to listen to the recorded lecture on the earphones. She knew that to know who was buried there would not make the visit any more meaningful to her. She stood in the great expanse of floor and enclosed light and felt her mind soar.

12.
Ten slides are shown in quick succession during paragraph 2:

* **Cluny Tapestry**
* **Etruscan fresco** 96
* **Pillars**
* **painting of Coliseum**
* **painting of Roman scene**
* **Versailles**
* **Versailles**
* **Grand Canyon**
* **Las Vegas**
* **Borghese Gardens** *(remains during paragraph 3)*

Narrator: *paragraph 2*

By the end of the day she was sick of madonnas holding up their male infants, saints holding their bloody foreheads, martyrs holding their heads, angels holding their fingers up, duchesses holding up their robes, dukes holding their falcons, soldiers holding their spears, lions holding up banners, and virgins holding up mirrors. "Everything is about seduction or death. . ." But then she thinks of her own recent situation and the word 'resignation' springs to her mind. But she knows she can't resign herself to it and must sooner or later have a confrontation or simply end it. She would not add her name to his collection of questionable friendships.

13. Narrator. *paragraph 3*

The phantom jets roared overhead in formations of six. The cab driver seemed very impressed with the display and called her attention to each new entry in the sky above them. They had to stop at an intersection to allow a convoy of tanks to pass. She thought of the tumbrils on the way to the guillotine. She was glad to go, though the crude reminder of military realities had no bearing on her feeling. "America doesn't have to persuade anyone of her aggrandizement. Everyone knows. The great democracy is careful not to parade her death-power too flambuoyantly in the streets of America. Even the cab drivers would be embarrassed."

She lived there for a month
without seeing anybody she
knew. She talked only when
buying food or dealing with
tradespeople. She never heard
or spoke her own language.

In short, suddenly she found
herself in a bad way.

97

14. Tray 1   **Las Vegas**
    Tray 2   **women and cat** *(remains during 15 and 16)*
    Narrator: *paragraph 4*

After three days in that city she began to panic. How was she to face him when he arrived? What she had not allowed to intrude on her consciousness at home was now a reality; she couldn't go on with it. Even this brief interlude was enough to make her aware of a tremendous relief and renewed purpose. She had to tell him. She felt at once anxious and happy. By the time he arrived she was quite hardened in her resolve. She managed to be there for several days; then at their first meeting they had it out. She was amazed at her change of heart. How had she stood it for so long? They agreed that of course they would go on working on the project, but she had a sneaking presentiment that she would not even be able to manage that. "Is love really so blind?" she asks herself.

15. Tray 1   She lived there for a month without seeing anybody she knew. She talked only when buying food or dealing with tradespeople. She never heard or spoke her own language.

16. Film on   **Ocean and beach** *(superimposed on left-hand slide projection)*
       *   In short, suddenly she found herself in a bad way.   97

17. Tray 1   **black**
    Tray 2   **black**

18. Tray 1   The light from the open doorway shows a man and woman coming from the other direction.
       *   A nameless grief swept through her again and again.
       *   She pretends to sleep.
       *   "What movie?" she replies thickly.

"2001."

"Oh yes, of course."

    Tray 1   Now when she looks at the work all she can see are the flaws. That part is too long, that too short, that too quick, that too slow.

    Tray 2   "Carriage Discreteness".
    Tray 1   In the middle of the night she wakes and begins to fondle his cock.

    Tray 2   **black**
    Tray 1   In the morning he was hugely depressed.
       *   "I'd like to kick your ass in!"

    Film off
    Lights up

19.   *   **black**

Shirley delivers monologue (while J and Y sit in chairs facing audience)

"Alright, so I made a mistake. I thought I could just knock it off. I mean I thought it would be a cinch — I could do it all by myself. I would just go up there, set it all up myself, do every-thing — dance, talk, slides, everything — and come out like a breeze. I mean I thought it was going to be a breeze, that's the word, breeze. And I would be none the worse off after I did it. Only it just wasn't the case. I went up there and to begin with there was a blizzard and the bus was slipping and sliding all over the road and the bus driver was cursing about the lousy bus and the defrosters on the windshield weren't working and he had to keep getting out of the bus to chop the ice off the window.

The first one was alright. I got to like him after awhile. He said *he* vacuumed his house all the time. And he was married. The second one was too cheerful. I didn't believe a minute of it. The third one came at me as if he wanted something and he sat too close. The fourth one was enormous and didn't say much. Then the meditation group threw me out of the room where I was trying to collect myself and I began to pace around like a lion-ess tired of waiting for the kill. Then afterwards the fifth one asked twenty questions. My patience was diabolical. When it was all over I found myself downstairs raging around in the icebox. I had begun to bleed and felt a little relieved on that score but otherwise totally hyped up. My mind was racing. I couldn't get rid of the dream that had been bugging me all day and couldn't make any sense out of it. I had arrived in London from Paris. I went very briefly to the house of friends. They urged me to visit a certain museum in the few hours I was going to be in London before having to catch my plane home. An unknown man took me with my suitcase in a car and dropped me off at the museum. He then drove off with my suitcase. The museum turned out to be a nearly deserted old mansion. I walked up one staircase after another vainly looking for exhib-its. Pausing on a landing I peeked through a crack in a locked door and saw a number of people in a large room one side of which was completely enclosed by glass. They were all peering down through the glass as though they were in the observation deck overlooking customs at Kennedy Airport. I continued up more flights of stairs, now accompanied by another unknown man. I decided I had stayed there long enough and also wanted to ditch this man, whose attentions were becoming unpleasant. I started back down the stairs, came to a dimly lit place and warned the man that a step was missing there. Then I was out-side looking for a taxi, really worried now because I had so little time and afraid that I would not be able to locate my suitcase. I found what looked like a cab. The cabby was a man with a bulky briefcase that was fastened with a complicated arrangement of straps. He drove me to a house not far away. We went inside and observed a man and a woman sitting in the living room. The man I was with proceeded to arrange his briefcase so that the straps became hoses out of which flowed carbon monoxide gas. He was about to murder the innocent couple. I was horrified, but couldn't decide whether I was in collusion with him or was observing the event. I woke up.

The next day the first one drove me thirty miles to the other place. The drive was a pleasant interlude. He told me about his eidetic images . . . uh, no, forgive me. He told me about a recurrent event in his life. It was an event that always left him with a remarkable feeling of peace. Totally unaccountable and unexpected. At such times a tremendous relief flowed through his whole body. I didn't know why he was telling me all this, but I believed him.

Then he abandoned me at the boy's school. I had to start all over again. I set the show up in record time, then did it for 200 pubescent boys. I felt like a stripper. My breasts had never seemed so big. I knew I *had* them. They had never seen the likes of me. They probably would never forget me. I would come back to haunt their mother-fucking testosterone dreams. "What the fuck am I doing here?" I wanted it to be over I wanted it to be over I wanted it to be over I wanted it to be over . . . . . To cap it all off the ninth one accompanied me on the bus back home. I slept most of the way. When I woke up he expounded his ideas about education. Victimized once more victimized once more victimized once more . . .
No, it wasn't a breeze."

Slow-motion fight between Yvonne and John while Shirley shuffles papers on floor.
Shirley stands downstage center with microphone and says "That's her fantasy. If it were mine I'd do it differently." She has a screaming fit, then says "No, that isn't it either." She opens her mouth and 'tries' to scream, then says, "I just can't do it tonight." John starts to rearrange chairs. Shirley goes to him and says "Her unrelenting inten . . ." Yvonne looks up from where she has been shuffling papers, stands up, coughs, watches Shirley lie down on mattress. John looks at Yvonne. He says "So?" Yvonne says "Oh," They then both help Shirley up. All 3 walk to chair. John and Yvonne help Shirley jump over the back and onto the seat. Shirley turns face to audience and giggles. All 3 take positions in a triangle for 'Conversation', John sitting on floor with back to audience. 'Conversation' consists of gestures and facial expressions encountered during normal conversation. Only one person is active at a time.

5 minutes after Conversation begins

20. Tape on   *begins with phone ringing. Yvonne's voice answers phone:* "Hello. Oh hi, hi . . . Yeh, I just got it in the mail. You want me to read it? Well I'll try, but your handwriting is sort of hard to read . . . OK, here goes:

263

98

'This is the poetically licensed story of a woman who finds it
difficult to reconcile certain external facts with her image of
her own perfection. It is also the same woman's story if we say
she can't reconcile these facts with her image of her own deformity. *(a.)* She would like to engage in politics, but she can't

Tray 3   *(a.)* They thought her shit was more important than she was.
          Her shit got more attention than she did.

decide whether to join the big woman or the hunch-twats. The
big women have a lot to offer, but she has discovered essential
weaknesses in their proposal to use wads of counterfeit money
for doorstops? What is this . . . boxtops? Oh . . . box-stops.
(b.) Neither is she attracted to the naive notion of hunch-twats

*   *(b.)* box-stops

that every connection brings bed-chains. Not that it's a matter
of victims and oppressors. She simply can't find alternatives to
being inside with her fear or standing in the rain with her self-
contempt. *(c.)* How long can you go on this way, mmm? You

*   *(c.)* Sit tight.

still think it's all going to come out right, don't you? For instance, if you get up in the morning and feel your feelings well
enough you will receive the right gifts from heaven without
ever having to ask for them or even define them. It should be
smooth sailing now, right? *(d.)* Just deciding which side you're

*   *(d.)* Is she for or against herself?

264

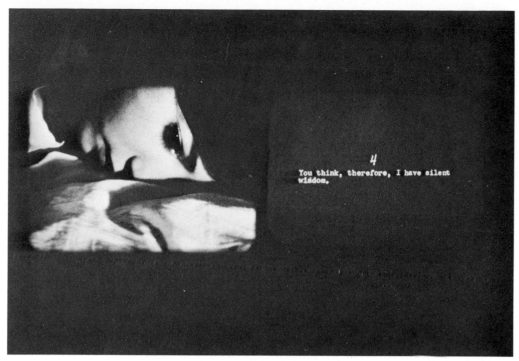

99 Film and slide being projected simultaneously – Sarah Soffer

on should insure that all the best things in life will beat a path to your door. Right? After all, you've paid your dues, haven't you? What do you want?
Her pretense of innocence must end. *(e.)* Nothing is new any-

*   *(e.)* She feels like a fool.

more, thank god. Now at last she can use her head and her eyes. If the mind is a muscle then the head is a huntress and the eye is an arrow. *(f.)* Thanking you for your immediate attention to

*   *(f.)* **black**

this matter, I look forward to hearing from you at your earliest possible convenience. Respectfully . . . . . blah, blah, blah.'
Yes, I think it's pretty good. I think they'll get the message."

followed immediately by ear-splitting thunder and flashes of lightning.

21. Lights off
      Film on   **Sarah in bed.** *Thunder and lightning continue until no.12 ("I despise you") when thunder fades out.*

22. Tray 2   How bad can it get? Listen:
      *   1 I appear to be self-sufficient.
      *   2 I can behave as though you don't exist.
      *   3 My face conveys a congealed intelligence.
      *   4 You think, therefore, I have silent wisdom.   99
      *   5 If I were wiser life might be unbearable.
      *   6 I am a stern and unrelenting judge and critic. I do not forgive.

Tray 2		7 I use my energies for the solemn enforcement of absolute sameness. I do not tolerate frustration of any kind.
	*	8 I refuse to compromise with a world to which I have been a total stranger from the beginning.
Lightning stops —	*	9 And if I make occasional concessions, I will not grant this privilege to others.
tape begins	*	10 It is time for me to be silent, methodical, resentful, gloomy.
to	*	11 You are a sap to feel close to such as me.
fade	*	12 I despise you.
Film off	*	13 I shall remove myself from your offerings.
	*	14 I shall appear self-sufficient.
	*	15 I shall appear to need nothing.
		YOU LEAST OF ALL, SAP.
	*	16 I shall become still, feign death.
	*	17 One false move and the jig's up.

23. Tray 1 ⎤ My life is such a mess.
    Tray 2 ⎦ Dummy.

24. Tray 1 ⎤ She longs for release from her compulsion to not enjoy all this.
    (remains during 25)
    Tray 2 ⎦ **2 children**

25.   * **Luxembourg Gardens** *(remains through 26 and 27)*

26. Tray 1   **black**
    Narrator: *paragraph 5*
    The places for sitting in the Luxembourg Gardens are individual chairs rather than benches. So one can make small adjustments in placing oneself in relation to a companion or the total view.

27. Tray 1   He sees her and tries to run away, but it is too late. She has already caught sight of him.
    *   It was impossible to face him. Everytime she turned to face him he changed his position so that they were always side by side in a 45°angle.
    *   He dismisses the lascivious thought. "So what if she has younger looking breasts than Beatrice?"
    Tray 1 *   He tells her about his eidetic images.
    Follow
    spot on   *Yvonne and John sitting in chairs.*   92
    Narrator: paragraph 6
    He tells her about his eidetic images. She listens intently, watching his graceful quick gestures, his darting eyes, the mouth moving, pursing, curving, opening, the slender fingers curving around the cigarette. Her eyes devour him. Her mouth becomes hollow with expectation. She moves her knees cautiously so that they are further apart. He doesn't notice, or pretends not to. She holds back, continues to listen, and the sensations pass.

    Light off

266

100

	*	**Young man**
	*	**John's father fishing**
	*	**Sasson in cap** (remains during
28.	Tray 2	**Shirley, Simeon, Sasson** (remains during
29.	Tray 1	**John, Shirley, Sarah** (remains during
30.	Tray 2	She shows him her dance.
31.	Lights up	
	Tray 1⟧	**black**
	Tray 2⟧	**black**
32.	Tape on	*Yvonne performs* Three Satie Spoons. *At end of music, lights* 100 *fade.*
33.	Tray 1	**Why doesn't he say something?**
	"	**black**
34.	Narrator:	*(5 second intervals)*
		He stares over her shoulder.
		She turns away.
		Laughing, she struggles to keep the door closed.
		He can't bring himself to ask her to go away with him.
35.	*	In her fantasy she speaks to his penis. Contingent on what she says, it enlarges and decreases in size. The man does not otherwise move in his reclining position. Neither does he speak.
	*	**black**

267

36. Narrator: Overcome by confusion she breaks off abruptly and runs from the room.

37. Tray 3   *succession of* **40 stills from Psycho** *ending in* **black** *during*
    Narrator: *paragraph 7*

She stumbles out of the theater. Her disgust with the film and actual nausea drive her body into the street. She recalls roughly the location of the hotel and starts walking in that direction. Her gut burns and she has to keep spitting out the bitter saliva that collects in her mouth. The streets are dimly lit and deserted, the houses shuttered and silent. She wonders if she will find the hotel in time. At a certain point, not having seen any familiar landmarks for awhile, she realizes that she is lost and experiences a powerful exultation. The discomfort of her body, the presence of the night, her solitude — all give her an acute sense of the moment. She finds a vacant grassy lot, gropes her way past the open door of a parked truck, and vomits. Relieved, she straightens up and sees the looming outline of a huge gas storage tank and remembers standing in the street across from the hotel early that morning watching two men on a scaffold painting the tank orange. She then knows that she is now only a block away. Almost regretfully she goes directly to the hotel, willing to take care of her body, reluctant to terminate being lost in the sleeping town.

Tray 3

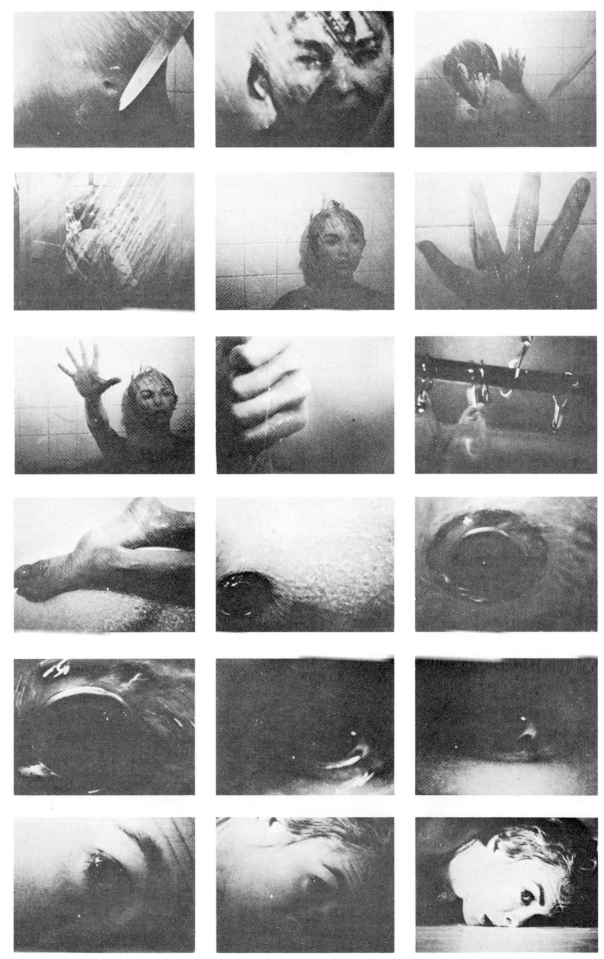

38. Tray 1 ⎤ On the way back to the city she was careful not to touch him as
                they sat in the back seat of the car.
     Tray 2 ⎦ **Mont St. Michel**
     Narrator *paragraph 8*
                On the way back to the city she was careful not to touch him as
                they sat in the back seat of the car. When he unconcernedly —
                or calculatingly (she couldn't tell which) — shifted his position
                so that his knee grazed her thigh, she carefully disengaged her-
                self from contact. By the time they arrived in town he occupied
                most of the seat, and she had squished herself into a cramped
                tight ball. She was enraged.

39. Tray 1 ⎤ As the truth becomes more clear to her she decides to confront
                him.
     Tray 2 ⎦ **black**

40. Lights ½ up
     Tray 1 ⎤ She stands in the doorway, a brooding intensity disfiguring her
                features. *Yvonne enters and mimics position of*
     Tray 2 ⎦ **woman leaning** *(remains during 41)*

41. Tray 1   She had caught his cold. Injury to insult.

42. Tray 2   **group of men** *(remains during 43)*
                John enters, sits, reads.

43. Tray 1   Unshaken by her pronouncement he continues to read. *(remains
                during 44)*

44. Tray 2   **man at desk** *(remains during 45)*

45. Tray 1   She regrets that he can't take pleasure in a friend's success.
       *   As he comes toward her, her mind reels with a deluge of ques-
                tions. Should she keep her peace? *John approaches Yvonne.*

46. Tray 1 ⎤ Motionless, she lets his caresses play over her while her eyes
                close with pleasure.
     Tray 2 ⎦ **black**

47. Tray 1 ⎤ But she feels her jealousy acutely. The knowledge of their past
                urbanity and mutual congratulations releases slivers of jealousy
                through her mind in a slow drip.
     Tray 2 ⎦ **John and Yvonne** *(remains during 48)*

48. Tray 1   She starts to leave, then changes her mind and rejoins him.
       *   *Yvonne starts to leave, then returns.*
                The demonstration stretches for miles below them.

49. Tray 1 ⎤ **black**
     Tray 2 ⎦ **Yvonne and John** *(remains during 50)*
     Narrator: She tries to make him see it as she does.
                He turns away from her, his face suddenly expressionless. He
                reaches for the revolver. *John reaches for gun.*

She draws away from him in disbelief and horror. *Yvonne does this.*

He lets the gun fall to his side. *John picks up gun.*

50. Tray 1   Who is the victim here?

51. Tray 1 ⎤   He presses his face and chest against the wall. He gives way
                without shame to a fit of uncontrollable sobbing. *(remains*
                during 52) John leans head into upraised bent arm against back
    Tray 2 ⎦   *wall.*
                black

52. Tray 2   *succession of four slides:* **John's mother as**
    *   **child**
    *   **adolescent**
    *   **young woman fishing**
    *   **mother with husband and infant** *(remains during 53)*

53. Tray 1   *She is sorry she upset him.*
    *   "Oh Christ," she thinks. "Now he'll never screw me again." She
              is determined, however, not to back off. She will take the bull
              by the horns, so to speak, and try again . . . His performance
              was magnificent. Afterwards she wept. Then she slept. As a pool
              of warm water spreading in the sunlight.

54. Tray 1 ⎤   **black**
    Tray 2 ⎦   **Brittany coast** *(remains until the end of paragraph 9)*
    Narrator: He buries his head in her lap.*(He does this.)* She strokes his hair.   102
                So they sit there, motionless, for a long time, clasping one
                another closely.
                paragraph 9
                Then she remembers what the scene had reminded her of. The
                sky with its leaden clouds, the wet spray of the sea, the hollow
                thud of the surf against the wet rocks. The two weeks had fled
                past them. She didn't remember a single argument, not even
                the kind of manoeuvering for brief privateness that people do
                when they are together constantly. At this remove it seemed
                impossibly idyllic. Looking at those two weeks against the back-
                drop of later events, she was at a loss to understand the nature
                of his feelings. She herself felt like a fool thinking about it —
                deceived and humiliated. But she also felt a terrible loss. There
                was no denying her own happiness and sense of completion at
                the time. Had he ever felt such things in her presence — for even
                a single moment? She wondered.

55. Tray 1 ⎤   What do you want?
    Tray 2 ⎦   **black**

56. Tray 1   They decide to continue working together.
    Lights up
    *   **black**

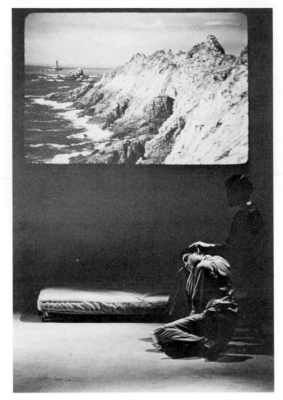

102

57.   *John and Yvonne perform* Walk, She Said. *Both then "mark"*   103
        Trio A. *Then John performs it "full-out." After John gets up*   104
        from upstage roll, tape on. It consists of 3 piano sonatas by
        Edvard Grieg, played by Philip Corner. The first one is "Native
        Land." John finishes his Trio A *just before the final bars.*
        Yvonne enters and performs Trio A *on the music. The other*
        two sonatas are "Arietta" and "Thanks."

103 *Walk, She Said*

104 *Trio A*

58. Lights off   *as Yvonne finishes on 5th "dee, da-da dum" of "Thanks"*
    Film on   **Ocean and beach** *as before.*

59.   *on 6th "dee, da-da dum":*
    Tray 1   Several years later she would ask him "Where were you when I was giving birth to your child? After all I did it for you." He hit her across the face.
           11th "dee, da-da dum":
      *   ENOUGH!
           Then on successive beats:
      *   He laughs out loud.
      *   Now she is thinking of his penis again.
      *   **black** *(hold)*
      *   She sighs with relief. Now that she knew the truth about her feelings she was free to love him again.
      *   **black** *(hold)*
      *   I've always liked ocean endings. *(next-to-last musical phrase)*

60. Lights come
    slowly up at
    end of music
         *   **black**
    Film off   E N D

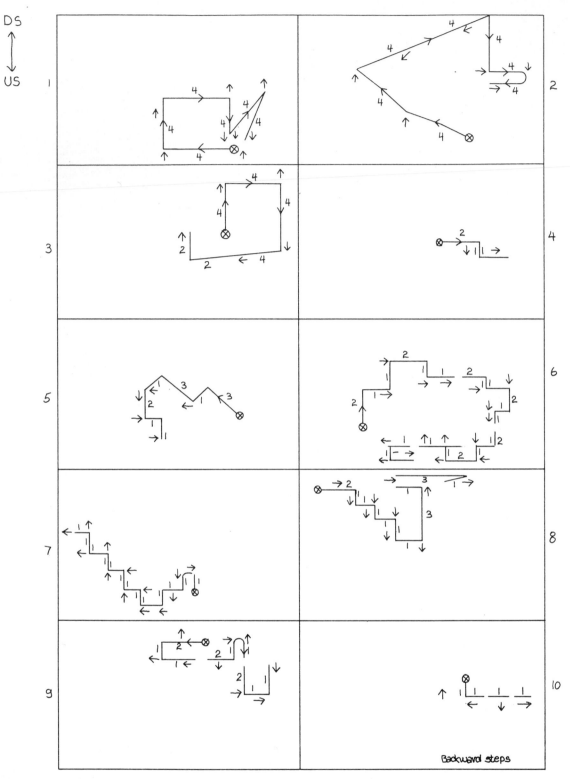

Diagram of *Walk, She Said*, first performed in toto during *Performance* at the Whitney Museum (*page 242*), later in *Lives of Performers* (*page 213*). The unattached arrows indicate the directions in which the torso and head face (at the end of each 4-count measure). The numbers denote number of steps in a given direction.

Late random notes and quotes on four points of focus: Performance, Autobiography, Fiction, Media

"For me the body alone is no longer the main focus. I'm interested in private experience and the problems of projecting and transforming it. But I think I still put things together in the same way. My content is different, but I have the same ideas of duration and continuity. I call myself a choreographer because as such I first discovered my artistry and formal methods for framing it. I also like the concrete kind of problem-solving that the word choreography encompasses. Besides there's still dancing in my work."

Performance, A Conversation edited by Stephen Koch, Artforum, December 1972.

After *Rose Fractions* of 1969 I began to have a new concern with performance, with different levels of performance, and later with the idea of "performance-work" as a background or justification for fiction. Right now I'm trying to develop a certain kind of narrative, and since my work in a broad sense has always been autobiographical, one point of departure is my own persona of performer, as previously my own body was a point of departure.

The easiest way for me to think about character is from my own point of view. One result of this is that all the performers become extensions of this point of view, sometimes interchangeably. There are no clearly delineated lines of character, except where the performers are allowed to be themselves. Sometimes both of these things happen at the same time, as in *Lives of Performers* when they sit around talking and using their own casual social mannerisms while the voice on the soundtrack invents what they are talking about, pieces of jumbled autobiography.

Autobiography, as I use it, is a rich source of material, and like all material, can be manipulated: fragmented, redistributed, magnified, analyzed, juxtaposed. I am a performer, a dancer, a director, a person who has been through shit and come up smiling, etc. The actuality of these roles lends a credibility to what otherwise I would have to invent totally from my imagination, which I'm not prepared to do. Autobiography saves me needless work. When it is distributed among a number of people, as in *Lives of Performers*, or depersonalized by the use of the third person pronoun, as in *This is the story of a woman who . . .* , it has the possibility of becoming more objectively biographical, and finally, fictional.

I like to think that I have a careful screening process operating to exclude personal material that applies uniquely to my experience. What passes my screening must somehow be identifiable with probabilities of experience of you, the audience. Surgery, no; illness and thoughts of suicide perhaps; love, pleasure, rage, self-doubt yes. (When and if I become aware of a prevalence of intestinal difficulty in the population of my audience, then maybe I will consider dealing with that as material!)

I kind of have my feet in two different places. I go back and forth between documentation and fiction.

I shall quote something Jonas Mekas wrote which pleases and flatters me, but also raises some questions:

> "The evening, for me, became a meditation on the cliché, on melodrama, on memory, on feelings, on language. It also had something very personal. It all pointed to some very personal experience of Yvonne herself, with man-woman relationships, doubts, re-evaluations, reconsiderations, questionings. It was a very personal looking into the meanings of one's actions, expressions, movements. Yes, it was a very personal piece about certain areas of experience that are not touched too often by artists because they are very difficult to tackle, formally. This content can be caught only by a certain kind of form, a form that is very very dangerous, a form that can collapse on you any moment, leaving you with a pile of nothing. A form that needs a certain kind of fusion of the utmost rigidity and the utmost openness, and this kind of openness has always been one of the peculiar gifts of Yvonne's genius."
> (*Movie Journal*, Village Voice, May 4, 1972)

My work is personal, but not strictly autobiographical, if for no other reason than that I don't intend it as such. It contains many autobiographical elements, sometimes identifiable, sometimes not. One way it is saved from being autobiographical, or *merely* personal, however, is by being so frequently pushed into the realm of fiction. Which is where cliché comes in. The degree to which I can interject the familiar — in language, artifact, and reference — is the degree to which the purely personal factor in the work can be offset and distanced. Sometimes this familiarity verges on cliché (the gun, the letter, "Is love really so blind?"); sometimes it goes beyond cliché (the letter, the suitcase, "But she feels her jealousy acutely."). References to others' work function in the same way: the use of movie stills from Pabst's *Lulu* and Hitchcock's *Psycho* relieves *my* work of the danger of insularity and solipsism; documents of fiction put to new fictional use.

But fiction is created not only by this resorting to the familiar. *Incongruity* can transform the banal into the fantastic: 1. Two images — familiar in ambience but incongruent in time — when juxtaposed, create a third reality. 2. The use of two plausible, but conflicting readings of the same image moves meaning from one reality to another, from a semblance of truth to a confirmation of fiction. 3. Discrepancy between emotional neutrality of image and emotional stress of simultaneous text subverts the "authenticity" of both.

276

And then, of course, the fictional thrust sometimes reverses itself: A "real" family photo is juxtaposed with a "fake" family photo. Two members of the latter also appear in the "real" photo. Or one person in the real photo and two in the fake are actual performers in the work. A cross-sectioned slice of truth made as strange as fiction.

I used continuous verbal material as early as 1962 (*Ordinary Dance, page 288*), film and slides in 1966. How is my use of these things different now? As for texts: The text now functions to construct a fictional continuity and cohesiveness. In the past it was an independent element that was meant to enrich a sequence of events and very often replaced music. It provided an emotional or dramatic fabric that I had not necessarily been concerned with in the making of the dance, a filling in of crevices with a content that the dance itself did not supply. Sometimes the text contained a thorough exploration of a given content, a cataloging of a body of information in as complete a way as I could (the William Bentley diary used in *Parts of Some Sextets* – *page 55*). This was not the way I went at dancing at all, at making movement. The physical aspect of my work had always been more erratic and eclectic; I didn't always feel the same obligation to make the dances hang together in a contextual way. But the texts fulfilled what obviously was some kind of need.

Film and slides now too project the imagery and content of an elusive story. Slide projections of text are a recent development. My process requires that I make certain distinctions for myself: What do I want the audience to do: *read* or *hear* textual material? When should such material be heard as a *recording* and when should it be heard *live*, i.e., from the lips of the performers themselves? In film should the spoken words be *in synch* or *out of synch*, or should there be *voice-over narration*? (This last decision is often based on economics.) Should the performer *read* the words, *recite* them, or *paraphrase* them? These decisions are usually contingent on the nature of the material itself (such as length) and/or the context within which it is to be presented. The particular construction of a given sentence may be more important to me than a quality of "ad libbing", or vice versa.

In my live shows I look for a certain amount of diversity. I wouldn't like the audience to have to read all night; better they stay home with a good book. We do have the metaphor, however, "in one ear and out the other", which doesn't exist in relation to the eyes. When I want to be certain of strongest impact from a given text, when I want to avoid the possibility that the words merely "wash over" the audience, I present the material in printed form. Four-letter words, erotic, and more emotionally "loaded" materials are dealt with in this manner. The complicity of the audience in being "face-to-face" with such material is an important factor in the quality of impact.

One outcome of these considerations in making a film is that any one choice automatically puts that part of the film into some kind of convention, such as the *acting* of the narrative film, the *inter-titles* of the silent movie, the *sub-titles* and *dubbing* of the foreign language film, the *voice-over* of the documentary and the flash-back, and the *face-front-to-camera delivery* of Godard.

Some people are overly affected by the solemnity of some of my subject matter. It seems to me that this can happen when one separates content from context, or the means by which the content is projected. For instance, the line "Her shit got more attention that she did" is one of the most awesomely horrible pieces of text in all of my oeuvre. But when it gets isolated as a slide projection in the middle of an eccentric taped reading — well, something else happens: it becomes pitiful and absurd *as well as* horrible.

Supposing I had placed that line next to the film of the little girl lying in bed? Would I have gotten bathos? Sometimes I feel like a cliff-hanger about to plummet into a sea of my own grease.

99

Some words about *Inner Appearances* (*page 251*): Originally made for a female, it was performed as an independent work and also incorporated into *Performance* and *This is the story of a woman who* . . . After I began to receive feedback about the political overtones of the piece — that the vacuum cleaner stood for women's oppression, that it was a statement about "women's lib" — I had to re-think the whole thing. I felt very ingenuous in not forseeing this response. I usually live alone and I occasionally use a vacuum cleaner to clean my house. I have never felt oppressed by having to accomodate certain hygenic needs in this manner. Well, I thought, if it's going to be received as a political statement then it must be made more radical. My solution was to re-write it for a male performer. The problems involved were fascinating and staggering.

I made four different versions of it and continued to have problems. I consulted male and female friends, and they confused me further. It was impossible as a rule-of-thumb to simply change the gender of the pronouns. This would have resulted in some cases in readings that were physically untenable, but these were simple to take care of compared to dilemmas over cultural transpositions. For instance, the second paragraph originally read ". . . Now she is reviewing the conversation in her mind. 'He doesn't take me seriously. God-damn him!' Her mind works in spirals behind the eyeshade." In my first attempt I simply transposed the pronouns so that the inside quote read "She doesn't take me seriously. Goddamn her!" I made similar changes in other paragraphs, then showed the whole thing to a male friend. His response in effect was that the same readings when applied to both male and female made for a 'strong woman' and a 'weak man.' I naturally objected. If a woman is 'strong' for revealing her humiliations and vulnerabilities and a man 'weak' for doing the same thing, then that just points up our need for new values.

I felt suddenly like a missionary: *Inner Appearances* would give men permission to be as human as us women and give women a vision of such a man. Then I started to show the stuff to others and the response kept coming back: For a man to have such feelings is one thing; for him to reveal them puts him in a 'bad light.' It was hard to ignore the prejudice attached to the expression of inadequacy on the part of a man.

For a while I stuck to my guns: A woman's complaint about "not being taken seriously" by a man is so ordinary as to be commonplace, and women's anger over this has become similarly familiar, thanks to the women's movement. However, "She doesn't take me seriously. Goddamn her!" as spoken by a man is by no means culturally commonplace at this time. The line jumps from the page with an urgency that the female version just doesn't have. On reading this one asks either "What is wrong with him?" or "Why is he so vulnerable?" Thus the male version is highly political in the question it raises, while the female version is not. Now I really had to ask myself "Just how radical do you want this to be?"

If *Inner Appearances* were to stand as a singular work, I would make its stance as extreme as I could imagine. But I had to take into consideration that, since it formed the beginning of a larger work and introduced the sole male performer in that work, I had to make some concession toward making him a less culturally controversial person. (A small psycho-analytically minded voice in me says I had to make him heterosexual rather than homosexual. I am not prepared to elaborate on this notion. I am afraid that my own prejudices are at stake. And I still don't know if the small changes I made really effected that psychological change.)

So I made several concessions: 1. "She doesn't take me seriously. Goddamn her!" of the second paragraph became "She hasn't changed a bit," he muses. 2. In the paragraph beginning with "Again he thinks about making love . . ." *she* remained the performer in *his* gaze as in the female version, rather than *he* becoming the performer for *her*. I couldn't make him that narcissistic. (*page 252*)

One last comment on *Inner Appearances*: THE VACUUM CLEANER! In the spring of 1973 John Erdman and I did live work about performances of an abridged version of . . . *woman who* . . . called *This is the story of a woman and man who* . . . The vacuum cleaner, which was a different kind of machine in each place, elicited many gender-oriented remarks. The industrial vacuum cleaner was called "man-size", the little electric broom was thought appropriate because it was so "phallic", etc. The image of a man vacuuming was obviously too extraordinary to pass notice. I had never encountered such remarks when I had performed the work myself.

IX Flashback

Some of the photos in this chapter are not of first performances of the works listed. In such instances place and date of photo are given. For date of first performance, see Chronology, page 331.

1961-62

Three Satie Spoons: My first dance, a solo, its repetitive structure based on a version of the aleatory score of John Cage's *Fontana Mix* as presented by Robert Dunn in his workshop of 1960-61. The music was Satie's *Trois Gymnopedies*. It is still in my repertoire.

KQED-TV, San Francisco, Aug. 1962.

Gymnopédie I

1		red	4	10		violet red	4
2	2		4	11	6		4
3		blue	4	12	7	red violet	4
4	3		6	13	8		6
5		green	3	14	9	blue	3
6	4		5	15	10	blue green	5
7		blue green	5	16	11	blue	5
8	5		5	17	12	violet	5
9		violet	3	18	13		3

red   Index fingers touch cheeks, then stretch mouth, right finger releases mouth, draws line down front of torso to side. ~~Torso tilts left~~; left finger draws same line on down left side - back of left leg to plié. Torso rounds forward & around to right side, straightens as right index finger draws line up back of right leg.

blue   Left index finger draws line down back of left leg to plié; large jump with left leg thrust to side at last minute before landing in squat - hands on floor to right of feet.

green   Begins in position last described above. Left leg extends to back (along floor) come back. Right leg slides forward until straight, then returns. Right leg slides between hands until it is wrapped around left hand, draws left hand over to left foot. Weight is then placed upon right foot, hands grasp left foot and pull it high up on right thigh as right leg straightens to standing position while making full turn to left - ending up facing front again. →

violet   Hands on hips. Left leg turns in & moves to side. Left leg bends, foot relaxed then standing leg pliés →
Standing leg slowly straightens as entire body moves enmasse to horizontal position.
Repeat index finger operation as in (—).
As left finger travels down left side, left leg straightens & then torso moves up.

282

Gymnopédie II

1	blue	4 ⎤8	9			4
2	blue	4 ⎤8	10	blue red purple		4
3		4 ⎤	11	green		2
4		2 ⎤	12	green		6
5	green purple	9	13			5
6		4	14	red purple		4
7	blue	9	15			1
8	red purple	3				

green   arm movements

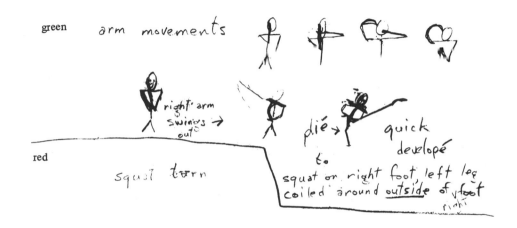

right arm swings out →

red   squat turn

plié → quick dévelopé to squat on right foot, left leg coiled around **outside** of right foot

purple   weight on left foot in squat with left foot in crook of right leg. Arms slowly meet overhead. Lie down on side, arms supporting slightly raised torso; lie completely on side, right arm underneath, forearm extending out, palm up, for balance. Fall over on back, legs come up, right arm remains constant.

blue   Stand. Alternate extending trembling bent leg — ending in pointed-foot thrust while arms take various positions — folded; hands on hips, behind head; one hand on hip, one hanging

Gymnopedie III

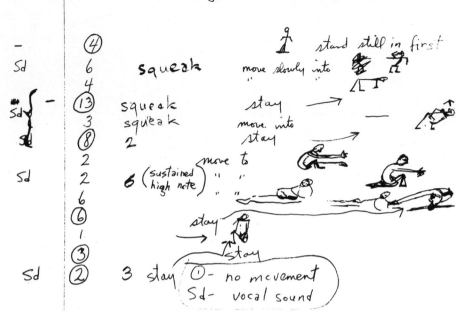

−	④	stand still in first
Sd	6	squeak move slowly into "
	4	
#Sd	⑬	squeak stay
	3	squeak move into
	⑧	2 stay
	2	
Sd	2	6 (sustained high note) { move to " " "
	6	
	⑥	
	1	stay
	③	stay
Sd	②	3 stay ① − no movement
		Sd − vocal sound

Gymnopedie III

Sd	④	
	6	Squeak
	4	
Sd	⑬	Squeak
	3	Squeak
	⑧	"The grass is greener when the sun is yellow"
	2	
Sd	2	Sustained high note
	6	
	⑥	
	1	
	③	
Sd	②	"ah-ooow ah-ooo"

The Bells: A solo. I remember two movements: one where my right hand 'collided' with my nose, the other during which I uttered the line "I told you everything would be all right, Harry" while twiddling my fingers in front of my face. The dance was repetitive with many changes in frontal orientation.

Satie for Two: A duet with Trisha Brown, same structure as *Three Satie Spoons*. The music was Satie's *Trois Gnossiennes*.

Three Seascapes: Solo in three parts: 1) Running around the periphery of the space in a black overcoat during the last movement of Rachmaninoff's *Second Piano Concerto*. 2) Traveling with slow-motion undulations on an upstage-to-downstage diagonal during La Monte Young's *Poem for Tables, Chairs, Benches*. 3) Screaming fit downstage right in a pile of white gauze and black overcoat.

Judson Church, N.Y.C., Jan. 29, 1963.

286

Grass: Duet with ballet-trained Dariusz Hochman. I remember nothing about it other than that it was dedicated to the Great Wallendas.

Dance for 3 People and 6 Arms: A trio consisting of an improvised sequence of pre-determined activities, performed by Trisha Brown, William Davis, and Y.R. (Judith Dunn replaced Trisha in a later concert at Judson Church, July 6, 1962). My notebook contains the following:

Movements:

1. Walk in plié while hands are placed on body, accompanied by sound — high-pitched, slightly varying in pitch, ah-ah.

2. Bent-over run with swimming arms ending in parallel relevé with arms overhead, limp wrists, into forced arch plié with other leg passing front and back with arm crawl, into ponché arabesque.

3. Turned-in attitude traveling from upstage to d.s. with spread-eagle arms finally drawing body around in turn. (Must be completed each time.)

4. Turn with hands globed on body, looking back at flexed foot which draws focus around so that it ends with rounded back, head down.

5. Slow vague plié-relevé. Limp arms.

6. Sharp piqué on right leg — 2nd position, arms spread-eagle, relax, scratch arm, face right, relevé with right palm gliding up nose, begin to descend, suddenly drop — scratch arm walking in circle to right. When facing original direction suddenly take stance in parallel plié with head thrown back.

7. Travel sideways with one foot limp, barely touching the floor while the other foot steps across in plié and receives weight of body. After 2 or 3 of these steps limp leg bounds up in turned-in jump. Resume previous mode of travel.

8. Foot-play with one hand "consciously" moving the other hand about the body. Hands alternate being "animate" and "inanimate."

9. "Flapper" — very relaxed traveling forward alternating 4th position with arms limply doing porte-de-bras over the head.

10. Running entrance sequence — from upstage left run to d.s. right; squat, come up straight to relevé with hands clasped across midsection, torso bent to left with head still upright; idiot collapse; no.4 turn to right; bend over — clasp ankles — bourée in circle to right; come up on left leg clasping right ankle in right hand with left shoulder raised, left arm bent in with limp wrist and hand; release right leg in sharp battement to side while left arm shoots straight up; collapse downward vibrating head and left hand into

287

4th position squat right foot front; travel to right in squat "glissade-change" twice with left arm circling undulating head.

Actions:

11. Walk rocking from side to side while without the cognizance of head one hand tries to clasp the other. When head perceives the action, hands quickly separate. Vary dynamics and levels.

12. Move arms as fast as possible while descending as slowly as possible until prone on floor.

13. "Blam-blam. Blam. Blam-blam." accompanied by flat-footed jumping about. When one person starts it, the other two must join in — all 3 gravitating toward each other. As soon as one stops, the others must stop and resume previous activity.

Positions:

14. "Ghoul" — only upstage.

15. Twist with eyeballs up — perched on one leg. Placed either d.s. right or d.s. left.

The dance began with the three performers standing quietly upstage equally spaced facing out at the audience. After a moment they did no. 3. After doing the turn downstage each one was on his/her own, making spontaneous choices of material and duration for the next 15 minutes. The total duration was timed by the lighting person, who brought the lights down at the end.

Ordinary Dance: A solo accompanied by an autobiographical monologue spoken by the performer:

It began in 1934. I think it was November 1934. Or it was November 24, 1934? College Avenue was before my time. Geary Street. That's the impression I got. Yes. Geary Street with too much sun and windows open to the sea. No birth certificate. Then came the dark alley of 1914 and the empty elevated lot of Golden Gate Avenue. A fire started in a drawer. No more fires, no no. Los Gatos and Daly City belong in here somewhere: singing among the deaf-mutes. And of course, Sunnyside, but I won't go into that — no point. Seventh Avenue with Parnassus looming above Hugo Street: It always glittered over there. Oh yes, I forgot to mention Gilroy: the two-wheeled cart which moved the earth.

1941 - 1942. The story gets denser around here. 1-2-3-4-5. MacDonald, Barrett, Myers, King, Myers, McCarthy, Kermoian, Pepina. 5-6-7-8-9. I'm not going to be able to talk for awhile.

Uh. Let's see. Panhandle, early morning. Uh, let's see. Panhandle, early morning. White, white, white. Uh, let's see. Panhandle, early morning. White, white, white. White, whaat, whaat, whaat. Whack whack whack, whack whack whack, whack whack WHACK! Oh yes, I forgot to mention Detner.

It's going to get cosmic any minute now. Yes. Here it comes: Roosevelt. Gravel and industry. But not for long. September, 1952. Pierce St. Then came the long haul to the riverside bloodstream looped through with portwinesap.

Oak St. Scott St. Over the bathroomed tunnel. But I'm really not telling you much lately, am I. Nevertheless, it does go forward. 1956: After the moon-milked water shock: Bank treatment. 21-25-63-57-14. So, that's the story. Oh yes, I forgot to mention North Pinegrove. Also 88th Street. But I'll have to demonstrate that.

KQED-TV, San Francisco, Aug. 1962. End of *Ordinary Dance*.

1963

We Shall Run: A seven-minute running dance first performed by Trisha Brown, Lucinda Childs, Philip Corner, June Ekman, Malcolm Goldstein, Ruth Emerson, Alex Hay, Deborah Hay, Tony Holder, Carol Scothorn, John Worden, Arlene Rothlein, to the *Tuba Miram* of the *Requiem* by Berlioz.

Wadsworth Atheneum, Hartford, Conn., March 7, 1965 — Y.R., Deborah Hay, Robert Rauschenberg, Robert Morris, Sally Gross, Joseph Schlichter, Tony Holder, Alex Hay.

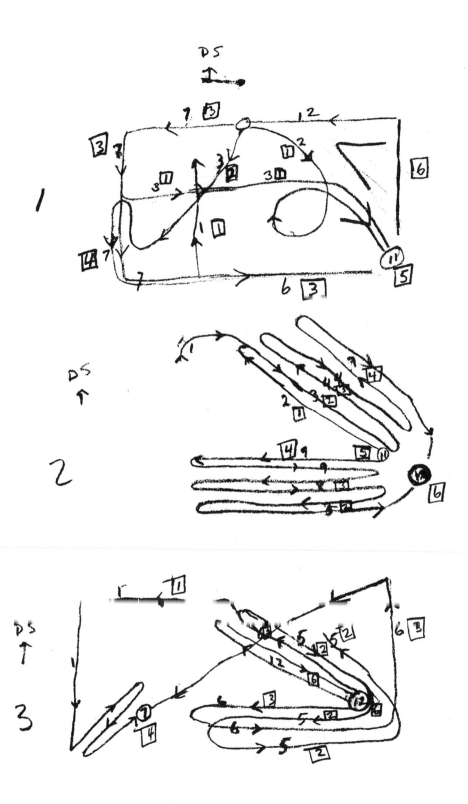

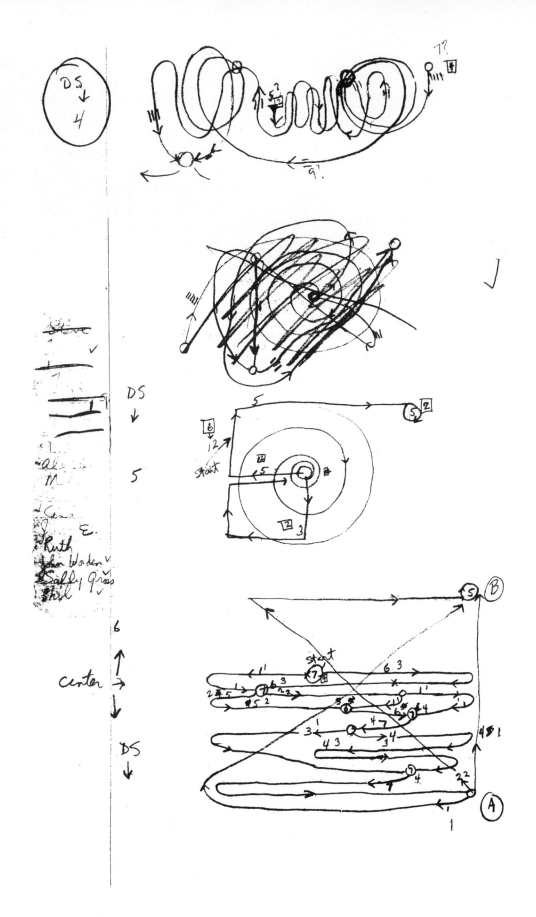

Word Words: A collaboration with Steve Paxton, a 10-minute sequence of movement performed first by Y.R., then by Steve, then by the two of us simultaneously. It was performed only once, Judson Church, Jan. 29, 1963.

Terrain: page 12

Person Dance (from Dance for Fat Man, Dancer, and Person) was listed on a program for a group concert that took place at the Pocket Theater, N.Y.C., June 10, 1963. Not only do I have absolutely no memory of performing this, but *Dance for Fat Man, Dancer and Person* was never made! It must have been a solo. And the title seems to have anticipated my concerns of 1970.

Room Service: A collaboration with sculptor Charles Ross involving three three-member teams playing follow-the-leader in an elaborate environment created by Ross and manipulated by him and two assistants. The performers were Ross, Marty Greenbaum, Lulu, Lucinda Childs, Carla Blank, Sally Gross, Felix Appeli, Ruth Emerson, Alex Hay, Tony Holder, Alfred Kurchin, and Y.R.

Shorter End of a Small Piece: A group work using a part of Charles Ross's environment. Contained elements that later went into *Dialogues*, such as the persona in black dress and the running men. (page 296)

1964

At My Body's House: A solo utilizing wireless sound transmission engineered by Billy Kluver to amplify my breathing via a contact microphone taped to my throat. The dance began with me standing still for three minutes during very loud Buxtehude organ music. This was followed by small, rapid footwork. At one point I told a story about an elephant from *The Diary of William Bentley* used in *Parts of Some Sextets* (*page 55*) (When I performed this solo in Stockholm I told the story in archaic Swedish.)

Stage 73 N.Y.C., March 2, 1964 (Marks on floor had nothing to do with the dance.)

Dialogues: A piece for four women and three men (Alex Hay, Tony Holder, and Steve Paxton). The men do nothing but run on and off the stage for the duration of the piece. The first section consists of two identical simultaneous solos by Judith Dunn and Y.R. during which we engage in the following dialogue:

Yvonne: We are desperate.
Judith: Speak for yourself.
Y: I need help.
J: I am going to call for help.
Y: Help help.
J: Go get help.
Y: Help help.
J: I am angry.
Y: No, I am ecstatic.
J: I am always anxious.
Y: No, I have needed something for years.
J: Help help.
Y: Help us someone, won't you.
J: I am distraught.
Y: No, I am thirsty.
J: I am up against a wall.
Y: No, I am abandoned.
J: I am really happy now.
Y: Look look.
J: Look at us.
Y: Help help.
J: Go get help.
Y: Go look for help.

J: I need help.
Y: Who's happy here.
J: I am so hungry I could eat a whole pig.
Y: Help help help.
J: I am afraid.
Y: No, I am satisfied.
J: I am exhausted.
Y: No, I am gadget-happy.
J: I am terribly concerned about that orphan I
   left in the oven.
Y: No, I am sexy.
J: I am so sexy I could eat a whole pig.
Y: I am so hungry I could eat a whole.
J: I am so cold I could eat a whole pig.
Y: No, I am terrified.
J: I am impossible.
Y: No, I need help.
H: Help help help.
Y: Won't someone help.
J: I am torn between lust and loyalty.
Y: I am torn between duty and ennui.
J: I am torn between decency and fear.
Y: I am torn between aversion and immobility.

296

J: I am torn between paralysis and desire.
Y: I am torn between indolence and action.
J: I am torn between expectation and possibility.
Y: I am torn between fantasy and foreign currency.
J: I am torn between vengence and cupidity.
Y: I am torn between memory and management.
J: I am torn between idealism and higher calculus.
Y: I am torn between love and aversion.
J: I am torn between urgency and responsibility.
Y: I am torn between obligation and experience.

J: I am torn between corruption and purity.
Y: I am torn between sainthood and hedonism.
J: I am torn between divorce and adultery.
Y: I am torn between adultery and sodomy.
J: I am torn between sodomy and sedation.
Y: I am torn between sedation and dialectics.
J: I am torn between dialectics and diuretics.
Y: I am torn between diuretics and love.
J: I am torn between love and listening.

The second section has Lucinda Childs and Y.R. improvising a conversation consisting of questions ("How wide was it?") and answers ("Two hours, 20 minutes"). The third and final section was performed by Deborah Hay and Y.R. Over and over again we went from a standing position – side by side – to a squat, then stretched out on our sides in a "stack", flopped over our bellies, and then stood up. Throughout this we carried on the following dialogue in falsetto voices:

Yvonne: That was so lovely.
Debbie: Yes yes that was so lovely.
Y: It was so lovely it will make me think about it a lot.
D: In fact we will write about all that thinking.
Y: Yes it is so lovely to have thinking.
D: Yes yes yes it was unbelievable it was so lovely.
Y: We have changed.
D: Yes yes we have really changed.
Y: Yes yes yes yes we have changed together.
D: It is so lovely to have changing.
Y: Life life yes life is all about lovely changing.
D: Yes yes we weren't always like this.
Y: We must remember to write about our lovely changing.
D: We must tell people that changing is not for everybody.
Y: Will we always be so lovely.
D: Will we always be so lovely.
Y: I understand much more about it now.
D: Will we always be changing.
Y: We have always been changing and lovely.
D: Everyday we become more lovely.
Y: Growing yes growing is lovely changing.
D: We are always growing while we are changing.
Y: Thinking about that lovely growing brings on more changing.
D: Oh yes I feel it coming.
Y: We were changing even while it was growing.
D: Oh yes I feel it coming and growing.
Y: It was growing all the while we were changing. and we didn't even see it.
D: Oh yes my thinking is changing even while it is growing.
Y: It was changing and growing even while we were thinking and our thinking continued.
D: Oh yes I am changing and changing while it is growing and growing.

Y: As our thinking was changing our changing in thinking was thinking about its growing and changing in growing.
D: Oh yes I am about to be thinking about its growing and how it is growing so loving.
Y: While we were so busy changing it was growing so loving.
D: Oh yes it is so loving now that I am thinking about its growing so loving.
Y: It was growing so loving even as we were thinking about stopping its growing.
D: Oh yes it is becoming more loving even as I am more becoming.
Y: It was growing so loving and was still so growing that we were considering stopping our thinking.
D: Oh yes I am continuing to be becoming because it is so loving.
Y: Its becoming was so growing that our loving was stopping.
D: Oh yes its becoming is so growing that there is no stopping my changing.
Y: What was happening when the changing was stopping?
D: Oh yes its growing is about to be filling my becoming.
Y: Its growing was overflowing our thinking.
D: Oh yes its flowing is filling up my loving.
Y: Was it really so lovely?
D: It was unbelievable it was so lovely.

Some Thoughts on Ímprovisation: An improvised solo with a spool of white
thread, it had a taped reading of an essay I had written after dancing at the Green
Gallery during an event by the artist James Lee Byars. The essay reads:

> Well see, it's like this see. I get into this place and I size up the situation.
> That doesn't take much doing. You just size up the situation, and you
> let your blood flow and then there is an obvious opening: There is an
> aisle completely surrounding the platform of boxes, an aisle between
> the platform and the people standing against the wall. So I walk. And
> while I'm walking I'm sizing up the situation. There's all this slow
> stuff: two people unrolling scrolls over the platform. One has a bird's-
> egg head and the other has an original Balenciaga. The ideas come, and
> the impulses, and the anti-impulses. I think first come the impulses.
> These are purely physical. They are the pulse and tongue of the body
> in the place, in the space of the place. They are the invisible strings
> that extend from outstretched fingers to the limits of the place. They
> are the heat that flows from the armpits to an object in the place. They
> are the swellings and contractions of the damp gaze that can be turned
> on and off.
>
> So I keep on sizing up the situation, see. And I keep walking. And I
> make decisions: He has left the room, I will run; she is standing stock-

still, I will bring my head close to hers; that man is moving his arms around, I will do as he does; the wall looms close, I will walk until I bump into it; my black dress is white from the wall, I will brush it off; they are finished, I will rest in this position for a long time; the man is using the magnifying glass, I will look at him from the other side; he and she are standing together, I will stand with them; the woman removes her cellophane bag from the reach of my steam-rolling foot, I WILL NOT MAKE AN ISSUE OF IT.

I can choose not to carry thru an impulse. On what basis is such a choice made? Sometimes I know:

The scrolls are made of white paper mostly. The boxes are a snowy field. The walls rise white and flat. His bird's-egg head gleams whitely. Her cameo face is placid. I share a common impulse with many people in the room: We want to defile, to desecrate, to shit on this whiteness, to crush this fragility, to smash this silence, to silence this shrieking purity. Enough poetry. Anyway, the thing is that I DON'T HAVE TO DO IT. Any of it: all that smash and smudge, I choose not to do it. I choose to play the game his way and in so choosing I am freed from wanting to destroy his image. I become powerful and happy. I become knowledgeable: I know what is appropriate to do. I find his image beautiful.

Improvisation, in my way of handling it, demands a constant connection with some thing — object, action, and/or mood — in a situation. The more connections are established the easier it is to proceed. The idea of "more" or "fewer" connections is related to one's degree of awareness of the total situation, including audience. One definition of a connection is a lifeline from "it" to me that conducts a flow of stimuli and ideas. When the lifeline breaks, I flounder about, looking for another one. Not finding it, I lose all reason for being there at that moment, become frantic, grasp at unkinesthetic memories of previous moments, lose my freedom, work mechanically and am miserable, and in misery drift deeper into a murky ambience of non-distinctions.

Of course it is not always clear, even to oneself, whether one is "connecting" or not. The line is variously slack or taut, and one can never be sure just how connected one is in any objective sense.

That's another thing: One must take a chance on the fitness of one's own instincts. It seems to me I've said that before, but it's not enough to know something once; you have to know it all over again in a different context. In the improvisation, at the moment of moving into an action; one must behave and feel as though no other choice exists even while running the risk of acting out a thoroughly private illusion — incomprehensible to anyone looking on. Regret reveals itself instantly and undermines whatever is happening on top of it. Regret garrotes the imagination. I like that. I'll say it again. Regret garrotes the imagination. The Spaniards used the garrote to choke people to death.

For instance, right now (and maybe generally) I use a mock-innocent, self-conscious style. If this were to take shape in an analogous way in an improvisation, I must carry it thru with utter conviction until an exit or turn-off point reveals itself. Lack of conviction can work only when it is consciously exploited and elevated to respectable membership in the improvisation. Like saying "Look at my dirty underwear. I forgot to change it today, but you see, it too exists." An improvisational equivalent of dirty underwear might be the letting go of one's concentration and just *being* there looking at the people who are looking at you. So what's wrong with dirty underwear? But remember, a little bit of dirty underwear goes a long way. Haw Haw.

Sometimes, especially when working with another person, the improvisational situation can produce a helluva lot of anxiety. What is he going to do next, will he pick up on what I do next, should I ignore him, should I interfere with her, even when she's got something great going, have we gone too far with a particular line of action, why isn't this working for me now and what can I do about it?

The anxiety also comes when I don't want to be there — here — right now. If I don't want to be here right now, God help me. Or something like that. The funny thing is that if I knew — right now — that I don't want to be here — right now — then I could play with *that* and possibly turn it into being here right now. But unfortunately, knowing that you don't want to be here right now usually comes too late to do anyone any good, until maybe next time. Then maybe you can do something to insure that you will want to be here right now, like think of Charlie Chaplin or just plain be here right now. Next time I am going to try something new: I am going to say "It has never been this way before; ain't it grand."

But to get back to improvisation with another person: One's sense of fitness here becomes very precarious indeed. Conditional to whatever problems and limitations have been prescribed, one's concentration is generally divided, more acutely so than in an improvisation with many people. In a many-peopled situation you feel responsible mainly to yourself; you assume that the total picture will pretty much take care of itself by virtue of the multiple individual involvements. Whether the picture can or does take care of itself in actuality is a moot point, the real point being that it is well nigh impossible to keep tabs on everyone else's carryings-on so you may as well concentrate on your own, leaving the door open for other people to come in or for yourself to rush out if need be.

But with a single other person, every move counts, and counts in a way that one can see or sense immediately. One has here the possibility of almost as much awareness as if alone, but not the degree of control, for one's range of choice is partially contingent on the unknown factor of the other's moment-to-moment decisions.

Yet at the same time my own every action and decision brings to bear an element of control and certainly influence, thus returning to my hand a limited power to push the thing where I want it to go at that moment. If I seem to be concerned with the idea of a power conflict, I am not (though the possibility exists). As frequently happens, two people in an improvisation are as much pushed by *it* as by each other. When it goes forward it moves with an inexorable thrust and exerts a very particular kind of tension: spare, unadorned, highly dramatic, loaded with expectancy — a field for action. What more could one ask for?

Part of a Sextet: page 45

Incidents: A collaboration with Larry Loonin at the Cafe Cino. I remember balancing on two piles of books while Larry read an FBI report. We also repeat- *46, 48* edly requested that the audience move their chairs from one side of the room to the other.

Part of a Sextet no.2 (Rope Duet): pages 48, 49

1965

Parts of Some Sextets: page 44

New untitled Partially Improvised Solo with Pink T-Shirt, Blue Bloomers, Red Ball, and Bach's Toccata and Fugue in D Minor: Just so! (At its premiere at the Wadsworth Atheneum I had forgotten to bring a red ball and had to substitute a tin can.)

1966

The Mind is a Muscle, Part I (Trio A): pages 63, 75

The Mind is a Muscle (1st version): page 62

Carriage Discreteness: A large group work that appeared in the series called *Nine Evenings — Theater and Engineering* at the 69th Regiment Armory in New York City (the same armory that housed the Armory Show of 1913)

Yvonne Rainer   Objects
~~Items~~ to be manipulated in CARRIAGE ~~Discreteness~~ Discreteness

No. of items	Object	Dimensions
1. 100	wood slat	48" x 1½" x ¼"
2. 100	foam rubber slat	
3. 5	wood sewing machine top	28" x 16½" x 1¾"
4. 5	foam rubber slab	
5. 6	mattress	72" x 36" x 4¾"
6. 3	wood box	
7. 2	elevator weight	
8. 2	foam rubber cube	4½ x 8¼" x 5"
9. 2	polyeurythane cube	
10. 3	plywood slab	48" x 48" x 1/8"
11. 32	masonite slab	" "
12. 3	foam rubber slab	" "
13. 2	wood plank	10' x 10" x 1½"
14. 2	foam rubber plank	
15. 2	masonite plank	8-10' x 10" x ¼"
16. 2	flush doors	80" x 30" x 1½"
17. 2	~~plywood~~ masonite sheet	8' x 4' x 3/4"
18. 2	foam rubber	
19. 5	Carl Andre's styrofoam beam	
20. 5	sheet metal	8½" x 11" x 1/16"
21. 5	typewriter paper	
22. 2	bull horns	
~~23. 36~~	~~red rubber balls~~	
~~24. 30~~	~~gray or white rubber balls~~	
~~25. 34~~	~~super balls~~	
	1 super ball	
26. 1	swing, suspended from the ceiling	
27. 2	"Hollywood Premiere" floodlights	
28. 5	wood beam	15 X 13 X 60
29. 5	foam rubber beam	
30. 1	brick	
31. 1	foam rubber brick	
32 1	sheet of cardboard	4 x 8
33. 1	sheet metal	4 x 8

303

CARRIAGE DISCRETENESS

A DANCE CONSISTING OF TWO SEPARATE BUT PARALLEL (SIMULTANEOUS) CONTINUITIES AND TWO SEPARATE (BUT EQUAL) CONTROL SYSTEMS.

I. PERFORMER CONTINUITY CONTROLLED BY ME FROM A PLACE REMOTE FROM THE PERFORMING AREA WHERE AT THE MOMENT OF PERFORMANCE I DECIDE THE ACTIONS AND PLACEMENT OF PEOPLE AND OBJECTS AND COMMUNICATE THOSE DECISIONS TO THE 10-ODD PERFORMERS VIA WALKIE-TALKIE.

2. EVENT CONTINUITY CONTROLLED BY TEEM (THEATRE ELECTRONIC ENVIRONMENTAL MODULAR SYSTEM) IN ITS MEMORY CAPACITY. THIS PART CONSISTS OF SEQUENTIAL EVENTS THAT INCLUDE MOVIE FRAGMENTS, SLIDE PROJECTIONS, LIGHT CHANGES, A TAPE RECORDED CONVERSATION; AND AUTOMATED MOVEMENT OF A BALLOON, PLEXIGLASS GLOBE, LUCITE ROD (ILLUMINATED), BLACK-LIT MATERIAL, GARBAGE PAIL, TIN CAN, COLLAPSIBLE WOOD PARTITION; AND CUED MOVEMENT OF A MAN IN A SWING AND 4 PEOPLE IN THE AUDIENCE, 2 OF THEM MAKING SOUNDS THROUGH BULL HORNS.

in technical collaboration with Per Biorn, Herbert Schneider, Anthony Trozzolo, and   Winslow

performed by :

1 Carl Andre   2 Becky Arnold   3 Rosemary Castoro

4 William Davis   5 Lette Lou Eisenhauer   6 June Ekman

7 Dm Iverson,   8 Katherine Iverson,   9 Julia Judd

10 Michael Kirby   Alfred Kurchin   Benjamin Lloyd

Tom Lloyd   Meredith Monk   Steve Paxton   11 Carol Summers

Lewis

Statement from program:

     I have become interested in the idea or effort and in finding precise ways in which ~~it~~ *effort* can be made ~~observable or invisible~~. *evident or not*

Program of events for *Carriage Discreteness*

Preliminary setting: "House" lights off, stage lights up bright. (This arrangement must take place at least 20 minutes before curtain time, as the house lights cannot operate without a 20-minute 'rest'.)

1. Black-out
2. Stage lights up dim
3. Slide no.1 (screen no.1) Rainer flier
4. Slide off
5. House lights on (cue: bull horn)
6. Tape on (13½ minutes)
7. Tape off
8. House lights off (cue: bull horn)
9. Projector on (screen no.2) (25 seconds)
10. off
11. Super Trouper no.1 on
12. off
13. Slide no.2 on (screen no.1) Chou en Lai
14. Slide off
15. Lucite rod crosses (upstage to downstage)
16. Lucite rod finishes
17. Lights up extremely bright
18. Slide no.3 (screen no.1) Stockholm flier
19. Slide off
20. Light change (slightly dimmer)
21. Film no.1 on (W.C.Fields) (screen no.1) (4 min., 40 sec.)
22. off
23. Slide no.4 on (screen no.1) Grandstand riot
24. off
25. TV system on (camera no.1, screen no.2) (20 sec.)
26. off
27. Super Trouper no.2 on (8 seconds)
28. off
29. Balloon goes up
30. Balloon comes down
31. Lights down extremely dim
32. Ultraviolet crosses
33. Ultraviolet finishes
34. Lights up bright
35. Foam rubber slats come down from ceiling
36. Slide no.5 on (screen no.1) Morris-Rainer flier
37. off
38. Lights down to dim
39. off
40. Slide no.6 on (screen no.1) Ice skating clown
41. off
42. Super Trouper no.2 on
43. off
44. Luminol interaction   1min.
45. Super Trouper no.1 on
46. Slide no.7 on (screen no.1) Rainer, London flier
47. off
48. Screen no.1 falls down
49. Globe cross (same direction as lucite rod)
50. Finish
51. Super Trouper no.1 off
52. Film no.2 on (Cagney – screen no.2) (3 min. 15 sec.)
53. Film image off, sound continues
54. Sound off, film off
55. Slide no.8 on (screen no.2) Gordon. Rainer, Paxton flier
56. off
57. Slide no.9 on (screen no.2) Gazelles
58. off
59. Super ball drops
60. Slide no.10 on (screen no.2) World's Fair Ruins
61. off
62. Swing
63. Lew and Benjamin
64. Super Trouper no.1 on
65. Swing begins
66. Swing stops
67. Super Trouper off

1967

Convalescent Dance: *Trio A* performed by me in a convalescent condition.

1968

Untitled Work for 10 People: A collection of activities – group and individual – having an indeterminate structure and taking place in two large adjacent rooms. Some of the activities were from the soon-to-be-performed *The Mind is a Muscle*. The place and duration of many of the events were determined by various pre-arranged rules. The piece was made for the students of the New York University Dance Department.

The Mind is a Muscle (final version): page 63

Performance Demonstration no.1: page 109

North East Passing: page 117

1969

Rose Fractions: page 116

Performance Fractions for the West Coast: three performances arranged by Ace Gallery, each one the culmination of five days of work with thirty people in three different locales: Vancouver Art Gallery; Mills College, Oakland; and the Music Conservatory Building in Los Angeles. Contained material similar to that used in *Rose Fractions*: "People Walls," a large figured carpet, a six-foot wooden frame on four short legs. Each performance ended with my performance of *Trio A* to the Chambers Brothers. This now seems an unfortunate juxtaposition of "professional" and "amateur" activities.

Connecticut Composite: page 126

1970

Continuous Project — Altered Daily: page 129

WAR: page 161

Judson Flag Show: page 170

1971

Grand Union Dreams: page 189

Numerous Frames: A piece made for 50 people and a small stage. Consecutive entrances and exits, usually by two people at a time; one person reads or says something to the other ("I dreamed of my mother last night, and of my wife. My wife was crying for me."); either both leave, or only one, in which case that one then has an encounter with a new person who enters. Some of the exits were up the aisles through the audience. Once having left, each person did not reappear, so there was a continual emergence of new people. Some of the verbal material was from *Grand Union Dreams*. I shall never forget one 12-year old girl saying to another "I am not afraid to die, but I don't want to."

1972

1973

X Scrapbook

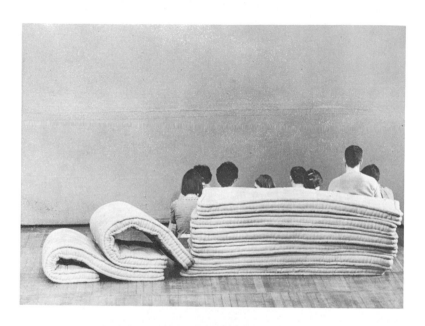

312

Ann Halprin's
Summer Workshop
1960, Kentfield, Calif.
1. Shirley Ririe
2. June Ekman
3. Sunny Bloland
4. Ann Halprin
5. Lisa Strauss
6. Paul Pera
7. Trisha Brown
8. Jerrie Glover
9. Ruth Emerson
10. Simone Forti
11. Y.R.
12. A.A. Leath
13. unknown
14. Willis Ward
15. unknown
16. John Graham

Dressing room
shenanigans after
rehearsal of
Rose Fractions
(Barbara Lloyd
is absent)
1. David Gordon
2. Jennifer Tipton
3. Y.R.
4. Heywood Becker
5. Susan Marshall
6. Frances Brooks
7. Steve Paxton
8. Judy Padow
9. Becky Arnold
10. Douglas Dunn
11. Fredric Lehrman
12. Frances Barth
13. Barbara Jarvis
14. Rosemarie Castoro

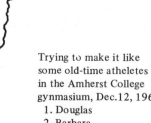

Finale of
Parts of Some Sextets
at the Wadsworth
1. Robert Morris
2. Lucinda Childs
3. Steve Paxton
4. Y.R.
5. Deborah Hay
6. Tony Holder
7. Sally Gross
8. Robert Rauschenberg
9. Judith Dunn
10. Joseph Schlichter

Trying to make it like
some old-time atheletes
in the Amherst College
gynmasium, Dec.12, 1969
1. Douglas
2. Barbara
3. Becky
4. Steve
5. David
6. Y.R.

314

Page 311 above: Fredric, Doug, Marilyn in *North East Passing*
Below: *Parts of Some Sextets* at the Wadsworth

Page 314: The two newspaper photos on the opposite page were projected from slides during *Rose Fractions*
Above: Chou en Lai in a happy mood
Below: Publicity shot (in the N.Y. Times) prior to N.Y. Dance Marathon, Feb., 1969. From L. to R.: Merce Cunningham, Erick Hawkins, Paul Taylor, me, Don Redlich, Twyla Tharp, Martha Graham, Jose Limon

Page 315: Dancing with Jimmy Waring in his *Dromenon*, 1961

Page 316: Jill Johnston and I improvise at the Washington Square Gallery, July 31, 1964

Page 317: Facsimile from issue of Les Levine's *Culture Hero* devoted to Jill

Page 320: Mama and Daddy start living together in 1925
Below right: With my niece, Ruth, in 1956

Page 321 above left: One of my favorite pictures. Trisha Brown and Steve Paxton in Trisha's *Lightfall* at Judson, Jan. 1963
Above right: Backstage during Dick Higgins' *Opera*, Dec. 1964. Lead brassiere by Robert Morris
Below: Me and Trisha, Barbara and David in a Grand Union Show, 1971

Page 322: Dachau

Page 323: Bonfire mound, Stanford University. This and the preceding photo were used as slides during *Rose Fractions*

TWO EVENINGS OF DANCES
BY
YVONNE RAINER
WITH

LUCINDA CHILDS * JUDITH DUNN * SALLY GROSS * ALEX HAY
DEBORAH HAY * TONY HOLDER * ROBERT MORRIS * STEVE PAXTON
YVONNE RAINER * ROBERT RAUSCHENBERG * JOSEPH SCHLICHTER

PROGRAM

WE SHALL RUN (3/4)
   MUSIC: BERLIOZ (FRAGMENT OF "REQUIEM")
   RUN BY LUCINDA CHILDS, SALLY GROSS, ALEX HAY, DEBORAH
   HAY, TONY HOLDER, ROBERT MORRIS, YVONNE RAINER,
   ROBERT RAUSCHENBERG, JOSEPH SCHLICHTER

NEW UNTITLED PARTIALLY IMPROVISED SOLO WITH PINK T-SHIRT,
BLUE BLOOMERS, RED BALL, AND BACH'S TOCCATA & FUGUE IN
D MINOR

PART OF A SEXTET
   DUET DANCED WITH ROBERT MORRIS

INTERMISSION

PARTS OF SOME SEXTETS - NEW WORK BY YVONNE RAINER
   COMMISSIONED BY THE WADSWORTH ATHENEUM
   TEXT: THE REV. WILLIAM BENTLEY
   DANCED BY LUCINDA CHILDS, JUDITH DUNN, SALLY GROSS,
   DEBORAH HAY, TONY HOLDER, ROBERT MORRIS, STEVE
   PAXTON, YVONNE RAINER, ROBERT RAUSCHENBERG, JOSEPH
   SCHLICHTER

AVERY THEATRE, WADSWORTH ATHENEUM, HARTFORD, CONNECTICUT
SATURDAY, MARCH 6TH, 8:30 P.M., SUNDAY, MARCH 7TH, 5 P.M.
THESE TWO EVENINGS SPONSORED BY SUSAN MORSE HILLES

RAINER

BY JILL JOHNSTON, DANCE CRITIC, VILLAGE VOICE

I CAN'T REMEMBER THE FIRST TIME I SAW YVONNE RAINER.
I KNOW THAT SHE CAME TO NEW YORK, FROM CALIFORNIA,
IN 1956, AND THAT SHE DIDN'T DECIDE TO BECOME A
DANCER UNTIL 1959 AND BY THAT TIME SHE WAS 24 YEARS
OLD. POSSIBLY I FIRST SAW HER ON THE STAGE OF THE
LIVING THEATRE DOING A SOLO CALLED "THE BELLS". THAT
WAS IN 1961. IT WAS A SIMPLE DANCE. SHE DIDN'T MOVE
AROUND MUCH. THERE WERE A FEW PHRASES THAT WERE RE-
PEATED SEVERAL TIMES. SEVERAL TIMES, WHILE MOVING,
SHE SAID "EVERYTHING IS GOING TO BE ALRIGHT --
HARRY." ON THE SAME PROGRAM SHE DID "THREE SATIE
SPOONS" WHICH WAS IN THREE PARTS AND SHE STOOD IN
ONE SPOT FOR EACH PART AND EACH PART CONTAINED
MOVEMENT ELEMENTS THAT REPEATED THEMSELVES. THESE
WERE HER FIRST TWO DANCE IN NEW YORK. SHE MADE
THEM BOTH AT A COURSE IN COMPOSITION TAUGHT BY
ROBERT DUNN AT MERCE CUNNINGHAM'S STUDIO. EVERY-
BODY AGREES THAT WAS AN EXCITING COURSE AND IT
OPENED UP NEW POSSIBILITIES IN DANCE AND ALL THE
NEW IDEAS REACHED THE PUBLIC IN 1962 WHEN THE
DANCERS AND PAINTERS AND COMPOSERS LAUNCHED A
SERIES OF CONCERTS AT JUDSON MEMORIAL CHURCH.

WHEN I SAW YVONNE'S TWO DANCES AT THE LIVING
THEATRE I WONDERED WHY THERE WAS SO MUCH REPETI-
TION. I WASN'T ACCUSTOMED TO EXACT REPETITION.
WHY SHOULD I WANT TO SEE SO MUCH OF ONE THING? BUT
YVONNE SAYS THAT REPETITION WAS HER FIRST IDEA OF
FORM. "SEEING IT AGAIN YOU CAN SEE MORE WHAT IT
IS." AND THEN I LEARNED ABOUT LA MONTE YOUNG,
THE COMPOSER, WHO WAS OBSESSED EVEN BEFORE HE CAME
TO NEW YORK, AS A STUDENT IN CALIFORNIA, WITH MUSIC
AS A CONTINUUM OF A SINGLE SOUND.

AND I HAD FORGOTTEN ABOUT GERTRUDE STEIN. THE NEXT
TIME I SAW YVONNE PERFORM, AT THE MAIDMAN PLAYHOUSE,
I HAPPENED TO BE READING STEIN'S "LECTURES IN AMERICA"
AND I LIKED WHAT SHE SAID ABOUT FAMILIARITY. SHE SAID:
"FROM THIS TIME ON FAMILIARITY BEGAN AND I LIKE FAMILIAR-
ITY. IT DOES NOT IN ME BREED CONTEMPT IT JUST BREEDS
FAMILIARITY. AND THE MORE FAMILIAR A THING IS THE MORE
THERE IS TO BE FAMILIAR WITH. AND SO MY FAMILIARITY
BEGAN AND KEPT ON BEING." AND NOW PEOPLE ARE VERY
FAMILIAR WITH THE SINGLE IMAGES OF CERTAIN CONTEMPORARY
PAINTERS.

AT THE MAIDMAN, YVONNE DID "THREE SEASCAPES." IN ONE OF
THE THREE SECTIONS SHE WORE A WINTER COAT AND KEPT RUNNING
AROUND THE STAGE AND SOMETIMES SHE WOULD LIE DOWN, THEN
GET UP AND START RUNNING AGAIN. THE ACCOMPANIMENT WAS
THE MOST ROMANTIC MOVEMENT OF RACHMANINOFF'S 2ND PIANO
CONCERTO. I THOUGHT IT WAS A SPOOF ON ROMANCE, OR
RACHMANINOFF, OR THE WHOLE PAST IDEA OF ROMANTIC MUSIC
WEDDED TO ROMANTIC DANCING. BUT SHE SAYS NO, HER IDEA
WAS TO SHIFT THE FOCUS FROM THE INTRICACY AND INTENSITY
OF THE DANCE (WITH THE MUSIC AS BACKGROUND, IN TRADI-
TIONAL PRACTICE) TO THE DANCE AS THE SIMPLEST THING SHE
COULD THINK OF TO DO, SO THAT ALL THE EMOTION AND COM-
PLEXITY AND VIRTUOSITY WOULD BE IN THE MUSIC. LATER
SHE DID THE SAME KIND OF THING IN "WE SHALL RUN", USING
THE BERLIOZ "REQUIEM", WHICH SHE THOUGHT WAS REALLY
GRAND AND HEROIC IN A BELIEVABLE WAY, THE PERFORMERS
RUNNING AND RUNNING, THE SAME EVEN JOG, AROUND THE
SPACE. THERE WAS, IN YVONNE'S FIRST DANCES, THIS CON-
CENTRATION ON A SINGLE, SIMPLE THING TO DO. ONE THING
AT A TIME. AND THEN ON THE NEXT THING. THAT WAS VERY
CLEAR IN "THREE SEASCAPES." THE FIRST SECTION WAS
RUNNING. THE SECOND WAS A HORIZONTAL JOURNEY ACROSS THE

STAGE, FEET PLACED AWKWARDLY FROM ONE STEP TO THE
NEXT, ARMS AND HANDS MOVING CONSTANTLY IN SPASTIC ANGU-
LARITIES, THE FACE SET WITH MANIC BEWILDERMENT. THE
THIRD SECTION SHE BROUGHT OUT THAT WINTER COAT AND
PUT IT DOWN WITH A LONG PIECE OF WHITE GAUZE AND HAD
A SCREAMING FIT IN A FLYING MESS OF COAT AND THE
GAUZE. I FIRST SAW HER DO THE SCREAMING FIT AT ROBERT
DUNN'S COURSE (IT WAS THE RESULT OF AN ASSIGNMENT TO
DO A 50 SECOND DANCE) AND IT SEEMED TO ME THEN INEV-
ITABLE THAT SUCH AN AMAZING SCREAM WOULD BECOME PART
OF A NEW MOVEMENT IN A DANCE SO UNLICENSED THAT PEOPLE
COULD AGAIN BECOME DELIGHTED AND CONFUSED BY A MEDIUM
THAT WAS WORN OUT BY OLD FORMULAS AND PRESCRIBED WAYS
MOVING.

OF COURSE, YVONNE WAS THINKING ABOUT THIS TOO. SHE
SAYS SHE WAS CERTAIN INTERESTED IN TESTING THE LIMITS
OF DANCE AS SHE KNEW THEM. THE SCREAMING, FOR IN-
STANCE, BELONGED TO A WHOLE GAMUT OF WHAT A CRITIC CA
CALLED "IRRESPONSIBLE NOISES" THAT SHE BEGAN TO IN-
CORPORATE AS EXPRESSIVE ELEMENTS IN HER DANCES. BARK-
ING, GRUNTING, MUMBLING, STAMMERING, WAILING. AND
SOMETIMES THE SENSE-TALK OF POETRY AND DIALOGUES.
WITHIN TWO YEARS YVONNE TESTED A LOT OF LIMITS AND
THAT INCLUDED UTILIZING THINGS SHE KNEW ABOUT --OTHER
INFLUENCES, LIKE IMPROVISATIONAL APPROACHES SHE
LEARNED AS A STUDENT ON THE WEST COAST -- AND PUSHING
THEM INTO SOMETHING MORE, OR LESS, TO SUIT HER PER-
SONAL DESIGN AND PURPOSES. THEN, WITH THE GREATER
COMPLEXITY OF HER FIRST LONG WORK, "TERRAIN", (1963)
ONE COULD SEE ALL THE THINGS THAT PREOCCUPIED HER
BEFORE THAT (AND SINCE THEN). IMPROVISATION, IN-
DETERMINACY, REPETITION, POETRY, ROMANCE, GAMES,
OBJECTS, DANCE MOVEMENT, NON-DANCE MOVEMENT, MANIC
BEHAVIOR, EXPANSIVE BEHAVIOR, "IRRESPONSIBLE NOISES."

AND WHAT MORE CAN YOU SAY EXCEPT THAT WHAT I'VE SAID
ACCOUNTS LITTLE FOR THE PRESENCE OF A DYNAMIC

PERSONALITY. THE FIRST IMPRESSION REMAINS: A LARGE
FACE, BIG FEATURES, FRAMES BY STRAIGHT BLACK HAIR, A
DEEP VOICE, A NARROW TORSO, SOLID LEGS, A KIND OF
FLAT-FOOTED WEIGHT, AND WITHAL THE QUALITY OF AUTHORITY,
OF APPEARING TO KNOW EXACTLY WHAT SHE WAS DOING AND
THAT NOTHING ELSE MATTERED AT EACH PRECISE MOMENT OF
DOING IT BECAUSE THAT MOMENT IT WAS THE RIGHT THING TO
DO.

MARCH, 1965

. . . .

TECHNICAL ASSISTANCE: ALEX HAY, ROBERT MORRIS, ROBERT
RAUSCHENBERG, AND WALTER STOCKER.

316

YVONNE RAINER

1500 words about J.J.! Good god (I've done 8 already) it would be hard for me to write that many about me. I shall just have to try to run off at the mouth nonstop, no niggling, no erasing, no adjustments, no getting the record straight, no trial by jury in other words: a rough approximation of the style of J.J. herself. Indeed. Stopped dead, whew. I can't remember where I first met her—sometime between 1959 and 1961. It says alot about me, that at that time I was picking up on people who were picking up on me, so my first conscious memory of her was at a dance concert at the 92nd Street Y probably one of those deadly dull affairs that everyone went to because of the general dearth and just to keep up and because we dancers had only just begun to take the first faltering step in trying to connect up to western civilization (those of us in our twenties in the early 60's) or certain aspects of it we hadn't yet realized that the 92nd St. Y was a cemetery that venerable repository of cranky ladies in Mexican jewelry and sagging boots with wizened faces not getting old with good grace in the audience and crazy ladies on the stage eking out their private agonies, fantasies and deprivations in the name of all that is or was holy and aesthitic. Their raptures, ecstacies and agonies even then or maybe especially then turned me off or turned me on to my own holy mission. Unbeknownst to me I was well on my way to joining their ranks. So I met Jill at this concert with Sally Gross, I forget whose concert it was, Jill evidently had just written something about me in the VV because I remember thanking her and she acknowledged my thanks something about there being no need for it and it was all very normal. The remainder part of this contact remains the clearest part of the memory because it was something that reoccurs periodically in my irregular meetings with JJ and at times drives me up the wall: It was the way she looked at me, the gaze very intent the expression indicating detachment, calculation, and bemusement. People with pale eyes always make me uncomfortable. I guess that is why I have a habit of looking at people's mouths during conversation; too many people in the world have pale eyes (and the Word is easier to deal with than whatever it is in them there eyes. HMM . . . I'll have to think about that.) In a strange way I have come to value that detached gaze of J.J.'s. It has come to mean Now there's a creature as strange as I am. I know very well it could mean anything or nothing at all but what it sometimes does is stop me cold in my presumption that everyone in the world is as

frantically engaged in the pursuit of sanity and rationality as I. (Is this about her or about me? I am managing to churn it out if not in a manner that I thought I might. Jill's early role in relation to me—that of self-style PR lady—unfortunately incurred a debt that I feel unequipped to repay in mind. My hindisght for the details of her life is very much blurred by self involvement and intense ambition. I remember lots of loft parties which we undoubtedly attended together and in the peripheral vision of my mind's eye I see her gyrating madly somewhere in the vicinity of my gyrations. Our party craziness overlapped for awhile. Mine died or withered or something long before hers did, I guess hers never did: it was simply that those big loft bashes gave out. People got tired, splintered, smaller scenes proliferated. I remember Jill lying on peoples' laps in a Volkswagen bus singing at the top of a drunken voice those British-American-revolutionary songs Prince Charlie, King George and all that and we ended up at the old Dom now the Electric Circus and Jill leaning over me and not getting the response she wanted saying, "O Yvonne, you're impossible." She always claimed that Bob Morris ruined me. I could tell her only much later in fact quite recently about how much I helped him out in that area. Now that I think about it a lot of things coincided or overlapped in our lives—JJ's and mine. Her entry into dance writing and mine into dancing. And our natural disasters or disasters de la guerre. One potent memory is me lying low in the critical ward of St. Vincent Hospital my then shrink by the bed helping me to open an envelope containing a feisty salutation from Jill in the St. Vincent psycho ward. I got out before she did that time. As far as I know we each had three official "dissolutions"—mine within a much shorter time span. I have come to consider mine breakdowns; I suspect she has a more transcendental view of hers, that they were breakups. Maybe because her ass is higher than mine. I entertain for this moment the quaint notion that people with low-slung asses have their feet on the ground. Of course by the fact of my own brief sojourn at Bellevue and also through direct observation while there, this notion cannot be entirely confirmed. The diet in mental institutions is not conducive to the maintenance of a high ass. (Notwithstanding that Jill emerged unscathed on that score.) Since I lost a lot of weight while there, could it be that The Ass Also Rises? Foo. Keep it light keep it light. One last foray: Jo Baer says that high asses are challenging. She ought to know.

I get very mad at Jill when she repeats something I say in her column or when I find out she's mad at me through reading the VV. She avoids direct communication. That's her trouble that's my trouble that's everybody's trouble. End sermon. Sorry Jo. Now I am remembering a dance that Jill and I actually really and truly did together at a place called the Washington Square Gallery around 1964. That gallery was something else: Ruth Kligman ran it; there apparently had been a huge bundle invested in it, it was 4 or 5 floors (no elevator!), the investment most conspicuous in the plushiest office I'd ever seen sitting like a throne atop a short balustraded berugged flight of stairs off the ground floor. You could tell the place was doomed as soon as you came in the door. The dance was to be a collaborative improvisation full of spontaneous determination and indeterminacy and chancey randomness. (O world forgive my perpetuation of these semantic pods of unnatural thought.) It was agreed that we would each do our thing. I forget what we called it. Jill had some muciz she wanted to use: Bach, Purcell, Monteverdi. She fortified herself with frequent guzzles from a bottle of vodka during the hour before the performance, making the professionals who were sharing the program somewhat uptight. Now there again my memory blurs: I really can't say what she did in that performance; I hardly can say what I did. Well let's see, I did some cathartic-type rolling around on the floor (I had very strong thighs then) coming up on the knees, falling back, also some rushing toward the front row of audience and flinging myself into a lap (one lap belonged to Larry Kornfeld, another another one David Bourdon's); did this several times. Jill and I converged at several points. I saw her waving around on the balcony, maybe hanging over the railing and I rushed over and tried to chin myself on the railing. Another time she was standing with her legs spread and I may have dived thru or twined around them. It was a time (early 60's, definite Halprin-Forti influence on improvisation) when if you saw someone's legs spread you dived thru. What else was there to do with someone's spread legs? Jill later said that she was very surprised at my trying to "relate" to her; she had really never expected anything like that. I have another image of Jill, perhaps not solely from this dance, of her doing her slow-motion giant behemoth thing, arms akimbo, head tilted to the side, face screwed up in intense concentration, torso over-so-heavily revolving from side to side. She was always making a lot of people

indignant, but a lot more people (and I secretly) admired her for it—like when she and Bob Morris did a thing at the Pocket Theater the previous year and flooded the stage. I didn't see the piece because I was on the same program and had to get into a G-string for an appearance in a Jimmy Waring extravaganza that followed their thing. Suddenly everyone was screaming about the water—how we'd all break out necks "out there" ("out there" means stage), and she was dead drunk on top of it to boot. The Jilly Bean had struck again. O and then for awhile there were some sad scenes when JJ became to drink too much and sometimes embarrass us at out-of-town concerts for some of us. I remember a particularly dismal one, perhaps it was the last, at Fairleigh Dickinson U involving Jill, me, and David Gordon in what I think was his last performance of his own work. There were 5 people in the audience. Becky Arnold was there seeing me for the first time. (Becky now dances with me.) Jill had a terrible time, the' microphones didn't work, her lecture didn't carry. It was just, after a blizzard. The VW that had picked us up at the bus station had skidded into a brick gatepost shaking us up quite a bit, then as soon as we got going again it skidded—very slowly dreamlike—into an oncoming

car. Jill got shaken around the worst—front seat next to driver. Banged head, scraped knee, sprained finger. I guess all that was before the performance. Remembering this gives me the shakes; I know one shouldn't tour in the winter in a car and I just got thru doing it again. Suicide.

Suddenly my 1500 words have taken on a melancholia. I can't pretend that in the last ten years Jill and I have not been thru painful times. Though I laugh at some of those times, it is not so easy with others. But it is true that many of the unpleasant experiences we shared were definitely some funny. Even your last VV column, Jill. And how about last fall—me sitting around after my most recent operation and you dispossessed of a home—the two of us getting up every morning, mooning over coffee cups, and fiercely engaged in a contest of who has more reason to be miserable. As usual I was determined to win. I must admit that your strategies baffled me. Perhaps it was a draw.

My life has now emerged along a different facet. I haven't seen you since that peculiar dinner at the Cookery—martinis, gibsons, and chicken salad—when you kept me in stitches with the first 10 pages of your memoirs and later I watched you get into your mother's walrus-car with the left side all bashed in. I hope you too have turned a corner.

If this isn't 1500 words then I don't know what is.

COMMONWEALTH INSTITUTE THEATRE

Michael White
presents

YVONNE RAINER

THE AMERICAN DANSEUSE
in a

CONCERT OF MODERN DANCE

MONDAY, 13th SEPTEMBER

at 8 P.M. (Doors 7·30)

ALL SEATS BOOKABLE ··· 10/-

from Advance Box Office, Bookstall, Main Entrance
(WESTERN 1852)

"SENSATION"... TIME MAGAZINE

318

Sleeping

Yvonne Rainer came to London in September – in front of a small audience at the Commonwealth Institute she talked, walked, screamed, danced, recited, contorted and somehow conveyed something of that taut, passionate articulate mixture of sensuality and purpose that one looks for so often but rarely finds. One of her pieces was called SLEEPING .....

"I want to make a dance about sleeping – yes make a piece about sleeping. I want to write a dance about sleep:

How many hours in sinking down in sleeping, how many years of hours in sleeping. What houses have I slept in, how many houses have I slept at, how many beds have I slept in, how many mattresses have I slept on.

Yes, a dance about sleeping – where I have slept, who I have slept with, what I have slept on – floor ground bed sleeping – all kinds of sleeping – animals near by trees traffic rooms.

How many nights of sleeping next to a room where someone was sleeping, how many nights of wondering about someone sleeping in the next room, how many nights of waking – waking and wondering about who was sleeping, how many nights with big ripe bodies in the bed, how many nights waking and touching then sleeping, how many nights waking and touching and no one, how many days sleeping sleeping, how many nights waking and listening to sounds of sleeping.

Listening then sleeping, sleeping and listening – breathing – how much breathing – alone together one at a time – breathing – slowly, heavily, sinking while breathing evenly slowly – sinking how much sinking, how many sinkings and rising up through the night to speak. How much speaking in the night speaking out in the night.

Where have I started up in the night – what house what town – started up out of deep sleeping to speak to rise up sometimes so slowly so heavily this rising up in the night in a strange bed next to a strange body, my own body strange, so strange. Those familiar beds, those unfamiliar beds, those one-night beds, those beds on the way somewhere in the night. How many sleepings like that. Those sleepings off the street, those second floor sleepings, that sleeping with the sound of the ocean, those sleepings high above the city, those sleepings with all that sleeping going on across the street.

Yes a dance about sleeping – men and women, children and animals. Fierce sleeping – fierce deep desperate sleeping, light sleeping, uneasy sleeping. Sleeping and dreaming. How many nights of sleeping and waking. How many nights of refusing to wake, refusing to sleep, sleeping and fighting to wake, fighting to sleep.

How many nights of sleeping and loving, sleeping and touching, entering and leaving; sweet ripe moving and sleeping, all that moving – big ripe bodies in the bed. How many mattresses wet with that moving, how many nights of that strange moving, that final sinking down into sleep.

I want to make a dance about sleep. Someday I will make a dance about sleeping. Not right now."

YVONNE RAINER
1964

from I.C.A. Bulletin, London, 1965

wait for tonight!

e group of startled Pressmen,
g like a mad dog.

she picked up cameras and equip-
and started running through the
dumping camera cases in dustbins,
hide and seek behind walls,
g up the back of parked cars and
g off their roofs.

was my way of demonstrating my
tion with you all," she explained.
ght, anything could happen.

y's
d

f course

But the pictures **freeze a**
fast-moving bit of time (the
Julie Christie film " Darling "
is another segment of it),
much as Toulouse-Lautrec's
sketches caught the turn of
the century Paris cafe life.

There are the inevitable
names — **Jean Shrimpton,**
Andrew Oldham, John
Lennon, Mick Jagger, Brian
Epstein,

Loftier

There is pop artist **David**
Hockney, hat designing,
boutique owning **James**
Wedge, fashion designer
Gerald McCann, actor
Michael Caine, interior
decorator **David Hicks.**

There is **Chrissie Shrimp-**
ton, models **Sue Murray** and
Celia Hammond, Rudolf
Nureyev—plus a few remoter,
loftier figures of the period
like **Lord Snowdon** and **Cecil**

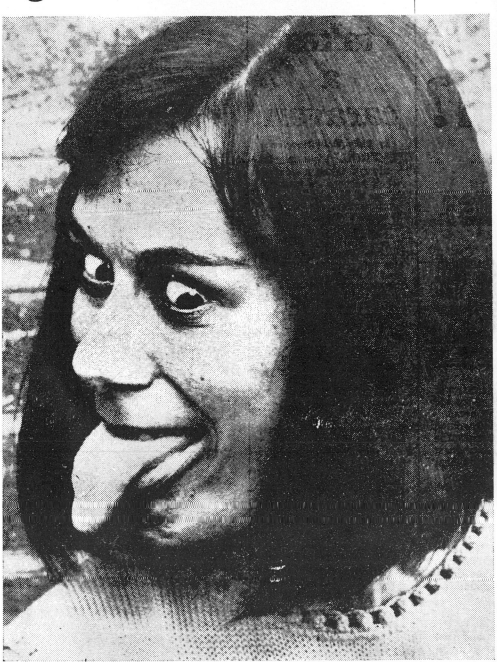

YVONNE RAINER IN UNTRADITIONAL POSE   Picture by WALTER BROWN

319

321

Epilogue

(for Merce Cunningham)

This is the story of a man who . . .

She pondered the problem of writing about him for a long time. She thought about it in several ways. What had she to say? If she were he, what would she like to read? She might find the whole enterprise somewhat unsettling. Milestones are nothing if not milestones. What would he like to hear about from her? What could be a gift of inspiration equivalent to what he had given her? She had been at the Graham School for a year knowing that she would end up at his place which had just opened up above the Living Theater on 14th St. and 6th Ave. She had heard funny stories about that Cage coterie, but she trusted that she would be no more taken in by all that than she had by all that Graham stuff. She would get what she needed and split. She can't remember her first class with him, but the first impressions he left with her remain: At a big loft party somewhere he was standing with Carolyn Brown. She went over to him and said she couldn't study with him yet because she was still busy with Graham, but it was only a matter of time — or something like that. This sly smile came over his face. If she knew that he had danced with Graham she certainly wasn't thinking about it then; in fact she didn't give that sly smile a second thought. *Now* of course, she can attribute all sorts of things to it — like "The old bag is still raking them in," or "racking them up," She now is remembering that her first classes with him were so quiet. He was so quiet and unemphatic. He just danced, and when he talked it was with a quiet earnestness that both soothed and exhilarated her. His physical presence — even when involved in the most elusive material — made everything seem possible. "It was truly the beginning of a Zeitgeist" she thinks: "You just do it, with the coordination of a pro and the non-definition of an amateur." Of course! It all comes flooding back to her: those early impressions of him dancing with that unassailable ease that made him look as though he was doing something totally ordinary. She knew that she would never dance like that. The ballet part of the shapes he chose she could only parody. But that ordinariness and pleasure were accessible to her. "No" she thinks, "she didn't know that then to articulate it like that but she knew about 'just doing it' because she remembers saying that to her friend Nancy Meehan and she knew there were specific things she could copy and other things she would absorb by watching and being around him." So she applied herself to learning the work part of his teaching: careful, sequential placing of different parts of the body on the floor in 4/4 time that carried the body from one side of the room to the other; sudden spurts of furious swift movement reversing direction on a dime; long long combinations with different parts — some slow, some fast — like the one from Aeon that ends with passé on half-toe and you stay there for awhile. And — as Judy Dunn later remarked on that one — "And everybody did it." Stayed there for awhile. Then there were the ones where one part of the body did one thing while another part did another, maybe even in a different rhythm. This in particular, as a way of multiplying movement detail, was later to characterize some of her own work. But mostly it was that mysterious ease of his — which he may even have tried to account for when he would say "down down down get your weight down" and now she is not really sure if he actually said that or if she *saw* it: him rooted in space, so to speak, even while in motion. She sees him in her mind's eye sailing and wheeling and dipping and realizes that it is always in the studio on 14th Street that she sees him rather than in more recent studios or in performance. That was where she saw him best.

2. The next day she takes another whack at it, and more memories surge in. He had to put up with a lot. They came and went and hung on his every word and paraded their callow opinions and innocence while he already had been doing it so much longer and knew all too clearly that the rewards would only be commensurate with the effort, that is — the reward of more work for work done. "You must love the daily work" he would say. She loved him for saying that, for that was one prospect that thrilled her about dancing — the daily involvement that filled up the body and mind with an exhaustion and completion that left little room for anything else. Beside that exhaustion, opinion paled. And beside that sense of completion, ambition had to be especially tenacious. But while absorbing the spirit of his genius she fought its letter. Her fantasies of her Show of Shows incorporated frenzied Bacchanalias of Cunningham Technique performed by the rankest of amateurs. Or ten dwarves and one bearded lady did the exercises-on-six. Or a contortionist performed them backwards (body-wise). Etc. Sophomoric fantasies of vindication against the tyranny of his discipline, which — even as she was objecting in terms both moral and aesthetic — was moving her ever nearer to her own body-ease. Now it is almost impossible for her to separate the fused lines of his influence. She has given much thought to teaching, to the two modes of the teaching-learning process — the one that can be codified and articulated, and the

one that resists such efforts yet exerts perhaps an even more powerful influence and lies somewhere in a kind of reciprocal empathy, not to be confused with equality. "Oh Christ" she thinks. "Don't get into a discourse on education now. What you were actually talking about was the fusion of your need to make a polemic out of your physical inadequacies with his technique — the fusion of that with his deeper effect on you." Then she visualizes herself running some years back and remembers the exhilaration and freedom and knows that she came as close as she would ever come to what she imagined he must have felt as he wheeled and dipped and glided in the studio on 14th Street. And she gives him his due for the part he played in that running.

Now she doesn't see very much of him anymore, but when she does she feels very happy.

New York City
March, 1973

Appendix

Chronology of work and places of first performance:

1961
Three Satie Spoons, Living Theater, New York City, July 31.
The Bells, Living Theater, July 31.

1962
Satie for Two, Maidman Playhouse, New York City, March 5.
Three Seascapes, Maidman Playhouse, March 5.
Grass, Maidman Playhouse, March 5.
Dance for 3 People and 6 Arms, Master Theater, New York City, April.
Ordinary Dance, Judson Memorial Church, New York City, July 6.

1963
We Shall Run, Judson Church, January 29.
Word Words (with Steve Paxton), Judson Church, January 29.
Terrain, Judson Church, April 28.
Person Dance (from *Dance for Fat Man, Dancer, and Person*), Pocket Theater, New York City,
     June 10.
Room Service (with Charles Ross), Judson Church, November 20.
Shorter End of a Small Piece, Judson Church, November 19.

1964
At My Body's House, State University College, New Paltz, N.Y., January 30.
Dialogues, Surplus Dance Theater, **Stage 73, New York City, February 9.**
Some Thoughts on Improvisation, Once Festival, Ann Arbor, Michigan, February 27.
Part of a Sextet, Judson Church, June 20.
Incidents (with Larry Loonin), Cafe Cino, New York City, July.
Part of a Sextet no.2 (Rope Duet), Kunstakademie, Dusseldorf, October 24.

1965
Parts of Some Sextets, Wadsworth **Atheneum**, Hartford, Connecticut, March 6.
Partially Improvised New Untitled Solo with Pink T-Shirt, Blue Bloomers, Red Ball,
Bach's Toccata and Fugue in D Minor (later referred to as *Untitled Solo*), Wadsworth
     Atheneum, March 6.

1966
The Mind is a Muscle, Part I (later called *Trio A*), Judson Church, January 10.
The Mind is a Muscle (first version), Judson Church, May 22.
Carriage Discreteness, Nine Evenings: Theater and Engineering at 69th Regiment Armory,
     New York City, October 15.

1967
Convalescent Dance, Hunter College, New York City, February 2.

1968
Untitled Work for 40 People, New York University Dance Department, New York City, February.
The Mind is a Muscle (final version), Anderson Theater, New York City, April 11.
Performance Demonstration no.1, Library for the Performing Arts, New York City,
     September 16.
North East Passing, Goddard College, Plainfield, Vermont, December 6.

1969

Rose Fractions, Billy Rose Theater, New York City, February 6.

Performance Fractions for the West Coast, Vancouver Art Gallery, Vancouver, B.C., April 2.

Connecticut Composite, Connecticut College, New London, July 9.

1970

Continuous Project—Altered Daily, Whitney Museum of American Art, New York City, March 31.

WAR, Douglass College, New Brunswick, N.J., November 6.

1971

Grand Union Dreams, Emmanuel Midtown YM-YWHA, New York City, May 16.

Numerous Frames, Walker Art Center, Minneapolis, Minnesota, May 29.

1972

In the College, Oberlin College, Oberlin, Ohio, January 21.

Performance, Hofstra University, Long Island, New York, March 21.

Lives of Performers (16mm, 90 minutes, cinematographer — Babette Mangolte), first screened at New Forms in Film, Guggenheim Museum, N.Y.C., August 12, 1972.

1973

This is the story of a woman who . . . , Theater for the New City, New York City, March 16.

European performances:

1964

Program shared with Robert Morris: *Some Thoughts on Improvisation, Three Seascapes, Part of a Sextet, At My Body's House*; plus Morris' *Site* and *Check*, Festival at the Moderna Museet, Stockholm, including Cunningham, Cage, Tudor, Hay, Paxton, Rauschenberg, September 11.
Same as above minus *Check*, plus *Part of a Sextet no.2*, Kunstakademie, Dusseldorf, October 24.

1965

Solo Section from *Terrain, Untitled Solo, Three Seascapes, Part of a Sextet no.2, Site, Waterman Switch* (Program varied in each place), Moderna Museet, University of Lund, Sweden; Odd-Fellow Palaeet—Copenhagen; September.

Solo Concert, Commonwealth Institute, London, September 13.

1967

Adaptation of material from *The Mind is a Muscle* for two performers — Y.R. and William Davis, Festival of Two Worlds, Spoleto, Italy, July.

1969

Program of Y.R.'s films with Steve Paxton simultaneously performing *Trio A* for one hour, Festival of Music and Dance, Rome, June 17.

1972

Selection of material from *Performance* performed by Y.R. and Philip Glass plus screening of *Lives of Performers*, Festival of Music and Dance, Rome, June 14.
Early version of *This is the story of a woman who . . .* (Y.R. and John Erdman) and screening of *Lives of Performers*, Festival D'Automne a Paris, November.

As a performer in other work:

Simone Forti
See Saw, 1960
An Evening of Dance Constructions, 1961

James Waring
Dromenon, 1961
Dithyramb, 1962
At the Hallelujah Gardens, 1963
Bacchanale, 1963
Musical Moments, 1965

Steve Paxton
Proxy, 1962
English, 1963
Afternoon, 1963

Carolee Schneemann
Newspaper Event, 1963

Philip Corner
Certain Distilling Processes, 1963

Al Carmines — Lawrence Kornfeld
Gertrude Stein's *What Happened*, 1963

Judith Dunn
Motorcycle, 1963

Lucinda Childs
Minus Auditorium Equipment
   and Furnishings, 1964

Aileen Passloff
Bench Dance, 1964

Dick Higgins
Opera, 1964

Robert Morris
Check, 1964
Waterman Switch, 1965

Beverly Schmidt
program of dances at the 92nd St.
   YM-YWHA, 1965

The Grand Union, 1970 —

David Gordon
Sleepwalking, 1971

Important moments as a viewer:

1946
Jeanne D'Arc, Carl Dreyer

1950
Orphée, Jean Cocteau

1957
Monogram, Robert Rauschenberg
Here and Now With Watchers, Erick Hawkins

1958
Cave of the Heart, Martha Graham

1959
Agon, George Ballanchine

1960
Clytemnestra, Martha Graham
Car Crash, Jim Dine
Tea at the Palaz of Hoon, Aileen Passloff

1961
Antic Meet, Merce Cunningham
Aeon, Merce Cunningham
Poems for the Theater I and II, Stephen Tropp

1962
Transit, Steve Paxton

Awards and grants:

1967
Harper's Bazaar "Woman of Accomplishment"
   (glass egg)

1968
Ingram-Merrill Foundation ($2500)
Lena Robbins Foundation ($1000)

1969
John Simon Guggenheim Foundation ($9500)

1970
Foundation for Contemporary Performing Arts
   ($1500)

1971
Experiments in Art and Technology, for travel
   in India (travel expenses plus $50 a week
   for 5 weeks)
National Endowment on the Arts ($9750)
Ingram-Merrill Foundation ($1000)
Lena Robbins Foundation ($750)

1973
Creative Artist Public Service (CAPS) ($4650
   including $930 in fees for public service)

333

Dance study (other than classical ballet):

Edith Stephen	1957-58
Emile Faustin	1958
Allan Wayne	1958-59
Sevilla Fort	1958-59
Martha Graham School	1959-60
Ann Halprin	1960
James Waring	1961-63
Merce Cunningham	1960-67
Carolyn Brown	
Judith Dunn	
Viola Farber	

Composition study:

Ann Halprin	1960
Robert Dunn	1960-62

Ballet study: 1959-66

Lisan Kay
Lynn Golding
Nina Stroganova
William Griffith
Michael Lland
Mia Slavenska
Peter Saul
Peter Nelson
Richard Thomas
Barbara Fallis

Etymology of objects, configurations, and characters:

red ball
Terrain ("Play"), 1963
Untitled Solo, 1965
Grand Union Dreams, 1971
Lives of Performers (Valda's solo), 1972
This is the story of a woman who . . . , 1973

other round objects
Volleyball (film), 1967
Trio Film (large white balloon), 1968
Grand Union Dreams (medicine balls), 1971

gun
Terrain ("Sleep Solo"), 1963
This is the story of a woman who . . . , 1973

rope and string
Parts of Some Sextets, 1965
Grand Union Dreams, 1971

books
North East Passing, 1968
Grand Union Dreams, 1971
This is the story of a woman who . . . , 1973

stairs
The Mind is a Muscle, 1968
Performance Demonstration (slides), 1968
Grand Union Dreams, 1971

bubble wrap and rubber matting
The Mind is a Muscle ("Trio A" and "B"), 1968
Rose Fractions, 1969
Grand Union Dreams, 1971
Performance Fractions for the West Coast
   (rug), 1969

packages, gift
Rose Fractions, 1969
Lives of Performers (film), 1972
This is the story of a woman who . . . , 1973

8½x11 inch white paper
Parts of Some Sextets, 1965
Carriage Discreteness, 1966
Rose Fractions, 1969
Continuous Project–Altered Daily, 1970
This is the story of a woman who . . . , 1973

white screen
The Mind is a Muscle ("Film"), 1968
Continuous Project–Altered Daily, 1970
Grand Union Dreams, 1971

mattress and mat
Room Service, 1963
Parts of Some Sextets, 1965
The Mind is a Muscle ("Trio A" and "Mat"), 1968
Performance Demonstration, 1968
Continuous Project–Altered Daily, 1970
This is the story of a woman who . . . , 1973

food
Rose Fractions (aspic fish on a platter), 1969
Grand Union Dreams (pot of rice), 1971

wings
Continuous Project–Altered Daily, 1970
Grand Union Dreams, 1971

pillows
Terrain ("Sleep Solo"), 1963
Continuous Project–Altered Daily ("Chair-Pillow"), 1970
WAR, 1970

fake grass
WAR, 1970
Grand Union Dreams, 1971

large wooden box
Grand Union Dreams, 1971
Performance, 1972
Lives of Performers (film), 1972

suitcase
Grand Union Dreams, 1971
Performance, 1972
Lives of Performers (film), 1972
This is the story of a woman who . . . , 1973

letter
Performance, 1972
Lives of Performers, 1972
This is the story of a woman who . . . , 1973

"people walls"
We Shall Run, 1963
Parts of Some Sextets, 1965
North East Passing, 1968
Rose Fractions, 1969
Performance Fractions for the West Coast, 1969
Connecticut Composite, 1969
Grand Union Dreams, 1971

"herds"
We Shall Run, 1963
Terrain ("Diagonal"), 1963
The Mind is a Muscle ("Film", "Horses"), 1968
North East Passing ("Tracks"), 1968
In the College, 1972

American flag
WAR, 1970
Judson Flag Show ("Trio A"), 1970

Walk, She Said
Grand Union Dreams, 1971
In the College, 1972
Performance, 1972
Lives of Performers (film), 1972
This is the story of a woman who . . . , 1973

narrator
WAR, 1970
This is the story of a woman who . . . , 1973

eye shade
Performance ("Inner Appearances"), 1972
Lives of Performers (film), 1972
This is the story of a woman who . . . , 1973

Valda's solo
Grand Union Dreams, 1971
Performance, 1972
Lives of Performers (film), 1972

Story (trio)
In the College, 1972
Performance, 1972
Lives of Performers (film), 1972

Lulu
In the College, 1972
Performance, 1972
Lives of Performers (film), 1972

Epp and James Duet
Grand Union Dreams, 1971
Performance, 1972

Grand Union Dreams — photos and script
Performance, 1972
Lives of Performers (film), 1972

"sun"
Grand Union Dreams, 1971
Performance (only at Hofstra), 1972

Shirley's dream
Performance, 1972
Lives of Performers (film), 1972

"Drama"
Performance (first version at Hofstra), 1972
This is the story of a woman who . . . , 1973

black overcoat
Three Seascapes, 1962
Part of a Sextet, 1964
WAR, 1970

M(etropolis)-Walk
The Mind is a Muscle, 1966
WAR, 1970

"V" formation (forward lean)
WAR, 1970
Grand Union Dreams, 1971

Trio A
The Mind is a Muscle, 1966
Convalescent Dance, 1967
Performance Demonstration, 1968
Rose Fractions, 1969
Performance Fractions for the West Coast, 1969
Connecticut Composite, 1969
Judson Flag Show, 1970
This is the story of a woman who . . . , 1973

Inner Appearances
Performance, 1972
This is the story of a woman who . . . , 1973

Selected bibliography

Anderson, Jack
"Yvonne Rainer: The Puritan as Hedonist", *Ballet Review*, Vol.2, No.5, (1969), pp. 31-37.

Borden, Lizzie
"Trisha Brown and Yvonne Rainer", *Artforum*, (June, 1973).

Castle, Frederick
"To Go To Show Them", *Art News*, (Summer, 1968).

Goodman, Saul
"Brief Biography; Yvonne Rainer", *Dance Magazine*, (December, 1965).

Johnston, Jill
"The New American Dance", *New American Arts*,
edited by Richard Kostalanetz, Collier Books, N.Y. (1965), pp. 186-189.
"Judson 1964: End of an Era", *Ballet Review*, Vol.1, No.6, (1967).
"Rainer's Muscle", *Marmalade Me*, E.P. Dutton, N.Y., (1971).

King, Kenneth
"Toward a Trans-Literal and Trans-Technical Dance Theater", *The New Art, A Critical Anthology,* edited by Gregory Battcock, E.P. Dutton, N.Y., (1966), pp. 247-248.

Koch, Stephen
"Performance: A Conversation", *Artforum*, (December, 1972).

McDonagh, Don
"Yvonne Rainer/Why Does It Have To Be That Way?", *The Rise and Fall and Rise of Modern Dance,* Outerbridge and Dienstfrey, N.Y., (1970), pp. 136-146.

Michelson, Annette
"Yvonne Rainer, Part One: the Dancer and the Dance", *Artforum*, (January, 1974).
"Yvonne Rainer, Part Two: Lives of Performers", *Artforum*, (February, 1974).

Rainer, Yvonne
"Some retrospective notes on a dance for 10 people and 12 mattresses called 'Parts of Some Sextets' . . . ", *Tulane Drama Review*, Vol.10, No.2, (Winter, 1965).
"The Dwarf Syndrome", *The Dance Has Many Faces*, edited by Walter Sorell, Columbia University Press, N.Y., (1966), pp. 244, 245.
"Notes on Deborah Hay", *Ikon* magazine, (February, 1967).
"Don't Give the Game Away", *Arts* magazine, (April, 1967).
"A Quasi Survey of Some 'Minimalist' Tendencies in the Quantitatively Minimal Dance Activity Midst the Plethora, or an Analysis of Trio A", *Minimal Art, a Critical Anthology*, edited by Gregory Battcock, E.P. Dutton, N.Y., (1968), pp. 263-273.
"Responses to India", *The Drama Review*, (Spring, 1971).
"The Performer as a Persona: An Interview with Yvonne Rainer", *Avalanche* magazine, (Summer, 1972), pp. 46-59.

Siegel, Marcia
At the Vanishing Point. A Critic Looks at Dance, Saturday Review Press, N.Y., (1972).

Photo credits

Cover illustrations
Peter Moore: Transitional moment during the first version of *The Mind is a Muscle* at Judson Memorial Church, N.Y.C., May 24, 1966
Babette Mangolte: Moment of rest during the shooting of *Lives of Performers*, April, 1972

Endpapers: David Vivian

Chapter II
Al Giese: 1, 2, 3, 4, 5, 6, 7, 8, 9, 10, 12, 13, 14, 15
Peter Moore: 11
V. Sladon: 5

Chapter III
Peter Moore: 16, 17, 18
Phil MacMullan: 19

Chapter IV
Peter Moore: 20, 21, 22, 23, 24, 25, 30, 32, 33, 34, 35, 36, 37
Julie Abels: 26, 27, 28, 29, 31

Chapter V
Peter Moore: 38, 39, 40, 41, 42, 44, 45, 47, 48, 49, 50, 54, 55, 58, 59, 60
Susan Horwitz: 51, 53, 56, 57
Barry Goldensohn: 46

Chapter VI
Susan Horwitz: 65, 66, 67, 68, 69, 70
Peter Moore: 61, 62, 63, 64

Chapter VII
Peter Moore: 72, 83, 90
Babette Mangolte: 89, 91
Gianfranco Gorgoni: 88

Chapter VIII
Babette Mangolte: 94, 98, 99, 100, 102, 103
Peter Moore: 92
Lorraine Senna: 104

Chapter IX
Peter Moore: pages 290, 294, 295, 296, 298, 302, 304, 307
Warner Jepson: pages 281, 289
Al Giese: page 286
Henry Genn: page 293 below
Robert McElroy: page 293 above

Chapter X
Peter Moore: pages 311 above, 311 below, 312 below left, 316, 321 left
Susan Horwitz: page 312 below right
James Klosty: page 321 below